THE SECRET OF STALINGRAD

Books by Walter Kerr:

THE SECRET OF STALINGRAD

THE RUSSIAN ARMY

THE SECRET OF STALINGRAD

Walter Kerr

DOUBLEDAY & COMPANY, INC.
Garden City, New York
1978

ISBN: 0-385-13459-2
Library of Congress Cataloging in Publication Data

Kerr, Walter Boardman, 1911–
The secret of Stalingrad.

Bibliography
Includes index.
1. Stalingrad, Battle of, 1942–1943. 2. Russia—
History—German occupation, 1941–1944. I. Title.
D764.3.S7K47   940.54'21
Library of Congress Catalog Card Number 77-83936

Copyright © 1978 by WALTER B. KERR, JR.
All Rights Reserved
Printed in the United States of America

First Edition

*To Vivianne above all and to Philip and Cynthia—
for everything.*

FOREWORD

This is the story of an unknown chapter in the history of the European war. It is about Stalingrad and how it was fought and why at that turning point in the struggle on the eastern front the United States and Great Britain invaded North Africa instead of the coast of France as almost everyone in those days expected. It is about locked Russian archives and destroyed or missing German documents and a tangled web of forces and circumstances which, though it influenced the lives of us all, has been concealed for a generation.

The reader will recall that in the summer of 1942 the Germans opened the second year of their invasion of the Soviet Union with an offensive that took them to Stalingrad and the Caucasus and that just as they faltered there in massive defeat the Western allies went for North Africa out of fear of Russian collapse and the eventual transfer of German divisions and air power from east to west. He will also be aware of the consequences. We did not land in France until 1944 when the Russians were less than a year away from Berlin, Prague, and Vienna, and the war ended in political controversy fanned by the same mistrust and concern that characterize East-West relations to this day. There was talk in

Moscow of our having shied away from France to "bleed" Russia "white." Did they really believe *that*? There was indignation in London and Washington at Russia's control of eastern Europe. But when and how it all began no one seemed to know. Some said at Teheran and Yalta; others thought Potsdam.

But as I have tried to show in these pages it began in 1942 under obscure circumstances that are discernible but not readily apparent in the published record. I came across them in the course of a study I undertook in 1967 in an effort to find out what I had not known in 1942 when I was in Russia for the New York *Herald Tribune* and did not hear about in 1945 when I was in the army in Berlin with access to the recollections of German generals. For secrecy did not end with the war. It never does. Political considerations take over. In this instance, Russians and Germans alike, in an astonishing coincidence of self-interest, were vague, enigmatic, cryptic, equivocal. How had the Russians won at Stalingrad? They answered by extolling their system and calling attention to incidents of battle. Why did the Germans lose? The generals said because Hitler refused to heed their advice, which he often or sometimes did, not always at the right time and perhaps not frequently enough. In short, something—something vital—was missing from both accounts—missing evidently because it suited the Russians who survived the war at a terrible price, some 20 million military and civilian dead, and the Germans who disintegrated for reasons they could not bring themselves to discuss. But what was it? What happened to Adolf Hitler and the German High Command? Why were President Roosevelt and Winston Churchill so taken by surprise? To find out, I went back to Russia five times from 1967 to 1972. I went through scores of books and magazine articles in Moscow and Stalingrad. I cross-examined Russian officers and checked every promising clue and version of events against the more widely known German version and the lesser known German files that survived intentional destruction by the Nazis after the war; and in time a pattern emerged. There were answers, and they told a story that is, I think, of more than historical interest both for what it says about the Russians in our time and for what it says about us. It is a story of a secretive Kremlin in secretive action and of intelligence failure everywhere in an uncertain world.

THE SECRET OF STALINGRAD

PART ONE

1

Moscow a generation ago was a secretive city in a secretive state waging a secretive war. It is still secretive in an odd Russian way and has been perhaps since the beginning of Russian time, which was long, long ago. A stranger soon understands. A man with a loaf of bread or a few onions in a brief case carries it as if it contained the most sensitive papers of state. A woman at a cashier's desk refuses innocent questions as if to respond may compromise her. Nobody explains anything. A visitor is on his own, cut off from those about him by what appears to be an indisposition in the town to familiar intercourse. It closes in on him like the mist in Red Square on a winter morning. In the late spring of 1942, however, Moscow secretiveness was of a different order. It was blinding, almost tangible, like the fog that blankets the sea off the Siberian coast, and one can understand why. There were about 6 million German and satellite troops on Russian soil, and an enemy offensive was expected any day.

Security was grimly tight. The line of the front was unclear in the public mind. With few exceptions the names of Russian field commanders, including those defending Leningrad in the north and Sevastopol in the south, were unknown. The designations and dispositions of armies, corps, divisions, and brigades were concealed. Almost no one outside of the Kremlin and the upper reaches of the armed forces had more than an instinctive appreciation of Russian capabilities and intentions. Almost no one beyond this limited circle realized that Stalin was Supreme High Commander or that he operated through a headquarters called Stavka, which was above the General Staff, or that Aleksandr M. Vasilievsky was taking over as Chief of the General Staff or, for that matter, who Vasilievsky was.[1] And this goes for the American ambassador, Adm. William H. Standley, a former Chief of Naval Operations, the British ambassador, Sir Archibald Clark-Kerr, and their staffs and military missions. Information was so scarce that Col. Joseph A. Michela, the American military attaché, and Capt. John Duncan, the American naval attaché, failed repeatedly in their efforts to learn not what the Russians had or were doing—no chance of that—but what Russian intelligence knew of German strategy, tactics, forces, and equipment. The only door open to allied observers led indirectly to the aid section of the General Staff in Kirov Street that handled the planes, tanks, guns, and munitions that were coming by convoy from the United States and Great Britain.

For all that, it was possible through the logic of events and personal observation for an outsider in Moscow to have a feeling for the war and how it was going. Nazi Germany had invaded the Soviet Union the summer before. Its armies approached the city in October and November. In December and January they were driven back. In December the United States came into the war. In April, May, and early June there was open talk in London and Washington of an early allied invasion of western Europe, and no one I knew thought Germany could survive a war on two fronts.

In the town, too, there were encouraging signs, and at the Metropole Hotel where I was staying with other members of the foreign press corps the talk turned to fresh evidence of Soviet

[1] Stalin became Supreme High Commander on August 6, 1941, but did not announce it to the public until January 25, 1943. Marshal Boris M. Shaposhnikov, the Chief of the General Staff, was replaced by Vasilievsky, his chief of operations, on June 26, 1942, but Churchill and Sir Alan Brooke, the Chief of the Imperial General Staff, were unaware of the change when Brooke conferred with Shaposhnikov in August of that year.

strength and confidence. In May the Russians took down the iron, stone, and earth barricades they had erected across the streets when the enemy was approaching. They would not have done that, we thought, unless there were new and stronger fortifications farther out. In the same month they reopened the Gorki Park of Culture and Rest. Three military bands played there every afternoon. A Ferris wheel was running. Small boys climbed in and out of captured German planes on display.

Moscow was changing. In the fall when the Germans were closing in and during the winter when they were driven back, a Moscow face was a haggard face. While children, bundled against the cold, played in the snow, the men and the women, the boys and the girls, had pushed themselves and been pushed to the limits of human endurance. Some 2 million out of a population of 4½ million left for the army or for the Urals and beyond as factories and shops were transferred to safe areas. Ambulances brought the wounded straight from the front to the city's hospitals and clinics. Civilians who died accidentally or of malnutrition or disease were taken through the streets on sleds to the crematorium. Women ran the trolleys. They shoveled the snow and swept the boulevards with brooms and brushes. Like the men they marched to the public baths, each with a clean towel under her arm.

Every day brought its moving, poignant sights. Young soldiers on leave and in the capital for the first time looked in astonishment at wonders one only dreams of on a collective farm or in a provincial village. There was Lenin's tomb in Red Square. They stared at that, usually not knowing his embalmed body had been sent elsewhere for safekeeping. There was the deep subway with its steep escalators. Peasant women with white kerchiefs on their heads observed them warily before daring to step on. There was Dzerzhinsky Square, up the street from the Metropole, with the frowning stone façade of police headquarters, the NKVD. The timid passed by heads down, pretending not to be inquisitive about what was inside or to know that at the back was the Lubianka, one of the city's central prisons. There was that small box in the Kremlin wall where plaintive letters inquiring about arrested relatives were left for Stalin, the out-of-sight, never-out-of-mind dictator who exercised absolute power, visible and invisible, over one sixth of the land mass of the globe. Were they alive? What were they accused of? Where were they confined? Would Stalin intercede on their behalf? It was rumored, and the credulous or despairing believed, he read them all.

But with the coming of spring there was new life in the town. Men went about in shirt sleeves. Girls put on bright-colored dresses. A warm sun nourished hopes that were born in December when the sound of gunfire faded off to the west. In the event, secretive warfare was no burden to the people of Moscow who had a grapevine that told them more than the Kremlin wanted them to know and their own modern version of an old Russian proverb: "Nothing is above Moscow but the Kremlin, and nothing is above the Kremlin but heaven." Not the Kremlin of the czars but the Kremlin of Joseph Stalin, a short man with a hard face and cold eyes who was more simple than complex, more predictable than not. Neither genius nor especially gifted, he was, however, an intelligent man with a feel for the instruments of power and the will to exploit them totally, harshly, to which talents, if that is what they are, he brought a capacity for hard work it would be difficult to surpass. So far as I know, in all the time I was in Russia, from 1941 to 1943, he never took a day off or went to the front or visited the wounded in a hospital or made a public appearance. He worked like a one-man band eighteen hours a day, running everything from the war to the executive, legislative, and judicial branches of government, the industrial, commercial, and agricultural life of the nation, and every other conceivable activity including the Communist party. His jobs were:

General Secretary of the Communist party
Chairman of its Politburo
Chairman of the State Defense Committee
Chairman of the Council of People's Commissars
People's Commissar of Defense
Supreme High Commander

As Supreme High Commander he was no figurehead. Every night there was a decision-making meeting in his office of Stavka or the headquarters of the Supreme High Command, whose members were:

Stalin, Supreme High Commander

Vyacheslav M. Molotov, Foreign Minister, also a member of the Politburo and State Defense Committee

Klimenti E. Voroshilov, a Marshal of the Soviet Union, also a member of the Politburo and State Defense Committee

Boris M. Shaposhnikov, a Marshal of the Soviet Union, Chief of the General Staff

Semeon K. Timoshenko, a Marshal of the Soviet Union and field commander, former People's Commissar of Defense

Semeon M. Budenny, a Marshal of the Soviet Union and field commander

Georgi K. Zhukov, Colonel General and field commander, former Chief of the General Staff

In practice, however, Stavka was Stalin with a small staff of his own or more specifically Stalin meeting each night with the leading men of the General Staff and any other senior officers or members of the Politburo he wished to be present. Shaposhnikov was always there. So was Vasilievsky when he was in town. Stavka was serious business with a routine of its own:

9:00 P.M. The Kremlin telephone rang in the offices of the General Staff in Kirov Street. Col. Aleksandr N. Poskrebyshev, Stalin's aide and personal secretary, was on the line: "Stavka meets at ten o'clock."

9:45 P.M. The generals, riding in chauffeured cars with curtained windows, left for the Kremlin at high speed. They raced through streets that were nearly deserted not only because in all Moscow there was only one restaurant open at any time (the Aragvi) or because movies, theaters, and concert halls closed early but because there was a curfew and anyone caught out after hours without a pass was rounded up by an armed patrol and taken to a police station for the night. The cars crossed a land bridge to the Kremlin's Borovitskaya Gate, the only one used during the war. Here guards examined the identity papers of the officers and checked their names against a list. There was a second look at the entrance to the "corner," the building where Stalin had his office, a third outside Poskrebyshev's office, and a fourth and final look in Stalin's antechamber or reception room. The last was by the personal bodyguard of the Supreme, as Stalin was called behind his back by his top commanders.

9:55 P.M. The stage was set for the evening's chilling performance. It was a large rectangular room with a large rectangular conference table in the foreground. Stalin, who read without glasses despite his sixty-two years, would be working at his desk beyond. On one wall were pictures of Lenin, Marx, and Engels, on the facing wall portraits of Aleksandr Suvorov and Mikhail Kutuzov, old-time czarist generals whose memories and reputations Stalin glorified during the war to rouse patriotic fervor.

Four or five members of the Politburo, all in civilian clothes except Voroshilov, took their places on the left side of the table viewed from the entrance. The generals, in uniform, laid down their maps and brief cases and sat on the right side. They had a 1:200,000-scale map of every sector of the front. There was another on the scale of 1:2,500,000 for the entire front. In a red brief case were the most important operational documents. They would be gone through without fail. A blue one held papers of lesser significance. Whether they would be taken up depended upon the business at hand and Stalin's will. A green brief case held recommendations of the General Staff concerning promotions, transfers, retirements, decorations, and punishments.

The politicians spoke in hushed tones. The generals braced themselves for what was to come.

10:00 P.M. The Supreme stood up. Silence. With a curved pipe in his mouth he strolled up and down on the generals' side of the table as if to separate himself from the politicians and emphasize his role as *polkovodets,* or Great Captain. He wore a loose tunic of his own design. The pants were stuffed into highly polished black boots.

"The General Staff will report."

The voice was low, measured, controlled. If it was the voice of god, it was of a vindictive god with the accent of a Georgian from deep in the Caucasus. His associates were alert, apprehensive.[2]

[2] "Not everyone stood the tension," Gen. S. M. Shtemenko wrote later on. "Some of my comrades suffered from nervous exhaustion and heart disease for a long time. Many left immediately after the war although they had not reached the age of retirement." (Shtemenko, pp. 118–19.)

The General Staff began, and the Supreme listened attentively. He was prepared. Between ten and eleven o'clock every morning he called Kirov Street. *"Shto novovo?"*—What's new?—he asked Vasilievsky, and Vasilievsky, holding a telephone with a long extension cord, walked from map to map summarizing developments of the night before. In the afternoon between four and five o'clock he called again. Occasionally he gave an order to be sent immediately to the front. Usually he waited for the night meeting.

As the General Staff reported, Stalin went on pacing, once in a while returning to his desk to fill his pipe with Zolotoye Runo (Golden Fleece) pipe tobacco, at times breaking the filters of two Herzogovina Flower cigarettes and maneuvering their tobacco into the bowl.

He bore down. Each sector was examined. He insisted on knowing not only what had happened but why, what would happen, and what could. Plans were studied, amended, rejected, or approved. Performance was analyzed, criticism leveled. Bottlenecks were probed, security leaks explored. The session went on and on. A fresh estimate of the situation was prepared. Midnight came—one o'clock, two o'clock, three o'clock, not infrequently three-thirty or four. The pressure was intense. It oozed from Stalin's office. It permeated the Kremlin. It reached out in widening circles to field generals who were nervously aware that Stavka decisions would be based on information and perceptions unknown to them that were supplied by visiting "representatives" of Stavka who reported only to Stalin and by a Corps of Officers that had one or two "eyes" at every senior command post and reported only to the General Staff. Indeed, there were matters so sensitive they would not be discussed by Stavka but by the State Defense Committee and by Stalin dealing personally with the Chief of the General Staff and a small classified section of the General Staff.

Stalin ran the war with his own measure of brutality, prudent boldness, and cautious circumspection.

2

In those days the front lay like an exposed nerve on the scarred Russian land from west of Murmansk in the arctic north to the Black Sea in the deep south. With the coming of spring and *rasputitsa,* or the season of bad roads, the slaughter of men who spoke one language by the men who spoke another abated. It flared when Russians or Germans stepped over the 3,000-mile line, but elsewhere the rival armies lay paralyzed in anxious expectation, waiting for a change in the weather. In the interval, Stalin and Stavka turned to planning for the second year of the war. They went about it, as I have learned over the years, in a manner designed to deceive friend and foe alike.

"All warfare," wrote Sun Tsu in the oldest known treatise on strategy and tactics (500 B.C.), "is based on deception. Hence when we are able to attack, we must seem unable. When we are maneuvering our forces, we must seem to be inactive. When we are near, we must make the enemy believe we are far away; and when we are far away, the enemy must believe we are near."

Sound enough advice, but to Stalin, who may have seen himself as something of a modern Sun Tsu, the "enemy" was or might be anywhere and everywhere—in the Kremlin, on the General Staff, at the front, on a collective farm, in a factory, at a foreign embassy. Almost everyone was suspect, a potential security risk, and he so viewed both President Roosevelt and Winston Churchill. Perhaps in supplying him with more military aid than they could afford they led him to think they were trying to avoid combat themselves, or perhaps in that suspicious mind of his he feared a leak from Washington or London to Berlin. It is not that he sought actively to "deceive" them in Sun Tsu's terms. He simply told them nothing, and coalition warfare, which is difficult under the best of circumstances, is impossible without some measure of mutual confidence. This did not bother Stalin. In the Soviet Union's hour of trial and peril he played his cards close to his chest.

For Great Britain and the United States, to be sure, it was also a time of trial and peril, although it would not have seemed so to the Kremlin. England was in trouble. In the Far East, Malaya had fallen. Singapore with its garrison of 60,000 men had been surrendered without a struggle. Rangoon was gone, and the Japanese were moving into Burma. In the Western Desert of North Africa, Gen. Erwin Rommel's Afrika Korps, aided by Italian troops, had retaken Benghazi and was about to advance on Tobruk. Battleships had been sunk in the Mediterranean and Indian Ocean. Merchantmen were going down in the Atlantic at an unprecedented rate. London was asking questions. Was the army sound? Would the troops fight? Churchill's conduct of the war was challenged.

There was a different mood in the United States which was new to the war, angry about Pearl Harbor and sure of itself with the faith of the untested, but the army was small, the air force young, the surface navy crippled in the Pacific, and the defense of the Philippines about to end with the surrender of Gen. Jonathan Wainwright on Bataan. Even so, the President and his top advisers worried about Russia. Fearing it might collapse despite Russian victory in the Battle of Moscow, they planned an allied invasion of western Europe, as Roosevelt informed Churchill on April 1. Three days later he sent his friend and aide, Harry Hopkins, and Gen. George C. Marshall, the Chief of Staff, to London. There they won agreement in principle to a preliminary strike at the coast of occupied France in the summer or fall and full-scale invasion in 1943, prospects that so excited the President he rushed off a personal message to Stalin.[1]

"I have in mind," he wrote in part, "a very important military proposal involving the utilization of our armed forces in a manner to relieve your critical western front. This objective carries great weight with me.

"Therefore, I wish you would consider sending Mr. Molotov and a General upon whom you rely to Washington in the immediate future. Time is of the essence if we are to help in an important way. We will furnish them with a good transport plane so that they should be able to make the round trip in two weeks."

One can almost see and hear Stalin, Molotov, and perhaps Voroshilov and other members of the Politburo or State Defense Committee going over the White House message word by word. A second front? Yes. Stalin had been trying to get one since the summer before. But what else were the Americans suggesting? Why Molotov? Did Roosevelt have in mind some kind of treaty or executive agreement? A quid pro quo? What did he want in return? The independence of the Baltic states that Russia had absorbed in 1940? The restoration to Poland of its eastern frontier? Baku?

[1] In a variety of "personal diplomacy" that has become so common in recent years it is now almost a tradition in the conduct of American foreign relations, the President did not inform the American Embassy in Moscow of the contents of this message, nor did he later on inform Ambassador Standley of the nature or substance of his talks with Molotov. American presidents like to think they have a "personal relationship" with whoever is head of the Soviet government. As a consequence, important matters are handled by the President, his Secretary of State, or some other "representative" directly with the Kremlin or through the Soviet Embassy in Washington, an arrangement that suits the Kremlin as much as it handicaps the Department of State. This brand of diplomacy can take strange and astonishing forms as I found out when I was in Moscow in September 1972. I was at the Embassy residence one evening at a time when Henry Kissinger, who was then President Nixon's national security adviser, was there trying to arrange a cease-fire in Vietnam. Just before dinner Kissinger left the residence on foot. Where is he going? I asked. "We don't know," I was told. "We never know, and we never see the reports he sends back to Washington." What about an interpreter? I asked. Someone to sit in on any talks he may have with the Russians for both his own protection and that of the country? My friend shrugged his shoulders. "We never know," he repeated, "and there is nothing we can do about it."

Vladivostok? Why a general? Why an American plane? Better check it out.

On the fourteenth Maxim Litvinov, the Soviet ambassador in Washington, sought clarification of American intentions. Days passed. Stalin accepted on the twentieth. Weeks went by. On May 4 Roosevelt sent another message to Stalin:

"I look forward to a meeting with Molotov. We shall make preparations to provide immediate transportation for him the moment we know the route he is to follow. I had hoped that he can stay with me at the White House during his visit to Washington but we can make available to him a private house nearby if that is preferable."

Still no final arrangements. No date fixed. On a matter of such importance to the Russians as a second front on the continent of Europe? Evidently the Kremlin had a problem. It had to think this one out. Finally, on the fourteenth a message from Stalin reached the White House:

"The journey of Mr. Molotov to the U.S.A. and England must be put off for a few days owing to uncertain weather conditions. It appears that this journey can be made on a Soviet airplane both to England and to the U.S.A."

Stalin's mind was made up. Molotov's instructions would have been agreed to:

First, he would say nothing to Churchill or Roosevelt or anyone else about Russia's capabilities and intentions. This above all.

Second, he would warn of the dangerous consequences that could flow from a German offensive against Moscow or Rostov or the Caucasus and Russian oil far to the southeast.

Third, operating under these two restrictions, he would seek a firm commitment from the President and the Prime Minister to a landing in France that summer or in the early fall at the latest.

Molotov would know how to handle the assignment. He was about five feet seven, perhaps an inch taller than Stalin, with a graying mustache and pince-nez glasses that gave him the look of a middle-aged clerk in an old-fashioned law office. The appearance was deceptive. Molotov was diamond-hard, an able administrator, and a skillful negotiator with all the pertinacity of a born bureaucrat and veteran revolutionary. It was Molotov who negotiated the nonaggression pact with Nazi Germany in 1939 and Molotov ironically who received Germany's declaration of war on the night Hitler invaded the Soviet Union in the summer of 1941. Now he would fly to London on May 20, a long thirty-eight days after the receipt of Roosevelt's invitation. Possibly by then he would have some useful news from the front, which had erupted on the eighth with a German attack in the Crimea and on the twelfth with a strong Russian offensive in the Kharkov direction south of Moscow. We have to look briefly at both actions, for in the weeks to come they would strengthen the expectations of Russia's enemies and deepen the concerns of its allies.

The Crimea was a humiliating disaster. In late December three Soviet armies from the Caucasus attacked across the Kerch Strait on the eastern side of the peninsula with the intention of breaking through to the besieged garrison at Sevastopol on the western side. Bogged down during the winter, they planned a spring assault, but Gen. Erich von Manstein's 11th Army struck first and destroyed them all in an operation that cost the commander of the Russian front, Gen. Dmitri T. Kozlov, and the "representative" of Stavka on the spot, Lev Mekhlis, their jobs.

Kharkov started out differently. Timoshenko attacked on the twelfth with his 6th, 9th, and 57th Armies and half of his 38th and three days later was advancing rapidly with every hope of outflanking the city on the south and west and taking it frontally. Then he ran into a tank offensive the Germans had planned for weeks. They hit him on the seventeenth and eighteenth and kept it up. As some divisions struggled back to their starting line and others tried to break out of encirclement, Timoshenko with all the prestige of a Marshal of the Soviet Union and former People's Commissar of Defense called for help. Nikita Khrushchev, who was a member of his military council along with Ivan Bagramian, his Chief of Staff, joined in the appeal.

Stalin turned them down. On the eve of Molotov's departure for London and Washington he growled out this reply over the BODO, a teletype with a scrambler attachment, from the communications room behind his office:

STAVKA HAS NO DIVISIONS READY FOR COMBAT.
OUR RESOURCES IN EQUIPMENT ARE LIMITED.
YOU KNOW THERE ARE OTHER FRONTS TO THINK

OF BESIDES YOURS. TO FIGHT IT TAKES BRAINS NOT NUMBERS. IF YOU HAVE NOT LEARNED HOW TO LEAD YOUR TROOPS BETTER, ALL EQUIPMENT IN ENTIRE COUNTRY WILL NOT BE ENOUGH FOR YOU. KNOW THIS IF YOU WANT TO DEFEAT ENEMY SOME DAY.[2]

It was not true. He had reserves, but of them more later. For the present it is sufficient to note he had no more intention of disclosing their existence to one of his field commanders than he did to Roosevelt and Churchill or to Roosevelt and Churchill any more than to Adolf Hitler.

[2] Shtemenko, p. 52.

3

Adolf Hitler was a killer but neither a lone wolf nor alone at fault, as the generals he raised to high command later portrayed him. He ran with a pack, fought with a pack, and lived by the pack, and it was only when he was falling or down that the pack turned massively against him. Then those who had run with him all over Europe said the credit was theirs for the successful raids, the responsibility his for the failures, and they made out a case which is persuasive if one ignores the stunning fact they first destroyed much of the evidence, including significant parts of their war diary (*Kriegstagebuch*) and situation reports (*Lageberichte*). There is, however, a surviving record which shows, I think, they were all in it together in the spring of 1942 as they pored over their plans in the lake country of East Prussia at the headquarters of the Oberkommando des Heeres (OKH), or Army High Command, on the Mauersee and of the Oberkommando der Wehrmacht (OKW), or Armed Forces High Command, at the Wolf's Lair near Rastenburg a half hour away. Hopes were high after a disastrous November, December, and January during which they were stopped at Leningrad, pushed back from Moscow, and thrown out of Rostov. Germany needed oil. There was oil in the Caucasus, and the opportunity to seize it was thought to be at hand because, as the Fuehrer explained in an April 5 directive for the summer campaign: "The enemy has suffered heavy losses in men and equipment. Trying to take advantage of imagined initial successes, he used up this winter a great part of the reserves destined for future operations." Halder thought so, too, and Halder was Chief of the General Staff. So apparently did a slightly built man with a receding hairline and wide ears, Lt. Col. Reinhard Gehlen, head of Foreign Armies East, the army's intelligence branch for the eastern front. He is the Gehlen who put his organization at the disposal of the American army after the war and ran it for the Central Intelligence Agency until it was taken over by the Federal Republic of Germany in 1955.

What did Gehlen think?

"Late in May," he wrote years later, "I presented my own conclusion on the Russian reserves position to General [Franz] Halder, and by the following month we had enough information to make a reliable estimate of the size of the reserve."[1]

Or so he would have us believe, just as he would have us think that he and his organization achieved their results not by "black magic" but by "application, thoroughness, expert knowledge, and speed."[2] What did he tell Halder on that spring day in 1942?

Well, as he recalls it, he first estimated the Russian population in 1939 at 170 million, and since there is a rule of thumb which says that a country can mobilize 10 per cent of its people at most, he put the number in the service or called up since 1939 at 17 million. From questioning prisoners and studying captured documents and following another line of reasoning, he arrived at the same figure. So far so good—no "black magic" there. But wartime losses had to be subtracted. Gehlen took away 430,000 casualties for the 1939–40 winter war with Finland and another 7,530,000 dead, disabled, and taken prisoner in nine months of the German war on the Russian front. That left 9½ million, and of this number he thought 6 million were in the army, 1½ million in the air force, and 300,000 in the navy.

And so?

[1] Gehlen, p. 50.
[2] Ibid., p. 47.

"On paper, therefore, the Russians had a manpower reserve of 1,700,000 able-bodied men, but for various reasons they could only be made available gradually to the combat units, and several thousand men had to be tied down in the supply, training, clothing and logistics echelons."[3]

He went further:

"There were ways in an emergency in which Russia could theoretically find the manpower to raise new divisions, and we would no doubt learn more as the year progressed. But we had to bear in mind that with Russia we were dealing not with a central European country, but with half of Asia, a territory thirty-two times the size of Germany, covering about one-sixth of the earth's surface. We could safely assume that it would not prove possible for Moscow to tap more than a fraction of these manpower reserves."

In short, Gehlen's assessment, as he recalls it, agreed with Halder's and Hitler's, which would have made for a comfortable working relationship between Gehlen and Halder at OKH and between Halder and Hitler when Halder went over to the OKW situation conferences that were held at the Wolf's Lair about noon each day. During these sessions the Fuehrer sat down while his generals stood before him, unlike Stalin, who stood while his associates were seated, but I am not suggesting there was any significance to this difference in form. Both dictators were allergic to dissent. Both surrounded themselves with men who found it more advantageous to be wrong with their Commander in Chief than right against him, and the candid or foolhardy who carried opposition too far were punished in one way or another, which may have been the fate of Gehlen's predecessor, Col. Eberhard Kinzel. Gehlen, who was Halder's former adjutant and an officer out of the operations department with no experience in intelligence, replaced Kinzel on April 1, four days before Hitler issued his campaign plan with its premise that the Russians had "used up" a great part of their reserves "destined for future operations." Kinzel was shipped off to the front as Chief of Staff of the 29th Army Corps.

Why? Did he, as Gehlen says, find it difficult to "get along" with Halder? For what reason? Had he, as Gehlen explains,

[3] Ibid., p. 51.

"failed" to keep pace "with the rapid war of movement that characterized the early months of the campaign"?[4] If so, why was he not fired long before?

Or was it because Kinzel disagreed with Halder and Hitler? Because he thought the Russians had a larger manpower pool and more divisions in the armed reserve? There is some evidence to this effect, although it is not conclusive and Halder's diary is not of much help:

March 31
"Replacement of Chief Section *Foreign Armies East,* who does not live up to my expectations."
End of entry. Halder does not explain.

There is, however, a clue to be found in the history of the German 6th Army whose fate was linked inextricably to the High Command's appreciation of Russian power and whose trail will be followed so closely in these pages. Col. Wilhelm Adam, who was adjutant to Gen. Friedrich Paulus, the commander of that army, says that on Kinzel's arrival at 6th Army to take over his post at 29th Army Corps Paulus asked whether Kinzel shared the view, which Paulus did not, that the Russians were about finished and that Kinzel replied he had never held that opinion, that on the contrary his judgment was they were forming "many new armies" and that in his reports he had made this clear "on many occasions."[5]

Another clue is a document that surfaced after the war. Dated May 1, 1942, and signed by Gehlen, who does not refer to it in his memoirs, it called attention to previous reports, which must have been issued by Kinzel, to the effect the Russians might be holding out some sixty divisions as an operational reserve. There was now, Gehlen went on, a Swedish source that put the figure at thirty-five. He himself thought the correct figure was somewhere in between, though he wished to point out in this connection that the Russians, as they had in the previous year, could and would throw in improvised formations from the labor force when it suited them.[6] From

---

[4] Ibid., p. 29.
[5] Adam, pp. 31–32.
[6] *Kriegstagebuch des Oberkommandos der Wehrmacht 1940–1945,* Vol. II, pp. 1273–75. In his introduction to this volume, Andreas Hillgruber quotes a Gehlen report dated June 28, 1942 (*Gedanken über die vermutliche*

which we may believe Gehlen discounted Kinzel's estimate and even questioned the combat worthiness of some of the divisions he would concede.

Even Gehlen agrees that Kinzel gave a lot of thought to the matter:

"One vital question mark hung over the first half of 1942: how many new divisions could the Russians still create from their reserves? My predecessor had assembled a file of unmistakable indications that the flow of reinforcements to the front was drying up, and he tried to determine whether this was because the Russians had no fresh manpower reserves available or whether this indicated they were secretly creating fresh units somewhere to hold in reserve for the summer operations."[7]

But, says Gehlen looking back over the years, in March Kinzel "somewhat optimistically" concluded that Soviet reserves were "virtually exhausted." If so, then everyone around Halder at OKH and Hitler at the Wolf's Lair was in agreement. If not, they were after Kinzel's departure. The Russians, according to Hitler and the High Command, were about through. Still, it was thought advisable to confuse them into thinking that Moscow and not the Caucasus was the principal target. Then perhaps they would weaken the southern front to strengthen their forces in the center. Accordingly, the Fuehrer turned to his Propaganda Minister, Paul Joseph Goebbels.

"For certain reasons," Goebbels wrote in his diary on May 15, "we launched an unauthorized article in the *Frankfurter Zeitung* which disclosed the economic and operational possibilities of the attack on Moscow. With this article we are trying to divert the attention of the enemy from a different sector from the one which we actually intend to attack."[8]

There was a longer entry for May 20, which read in part:

"Things have advanced to the point where I can send the jour-

---

Kampfkraft der sowjetrussischen Armee bei Winterbeginn 1942), which indicates that at that time Foreign Armies East thought the Russians could introduce forty reserve divisions at most during the summer and fall. Later, on August 2, Gehlen told Halder the estimate was sixty from early May *"bis zur Schlammperiode"* (the fall rainy season).

[7] Gehlen, p. 49.

[8] *The Goebbels Diaries,* p. 214.

nalist Dr. [Otto] Kriegk, now that he has made a trip to the Eastern front, to commit several indiscretions on orders from me. He is to get tipsy and, with his own impressions as a background, is to spread the assertion that the German attack is planned not for the south, but for the center. I hope it will be possible in that way to launch this canard as a rumor in the world organs of publicity."[9]

So confident was the Fuehrer he had the Russians where he wanted them that a bogus German order was leaked intentionally to Russian intelligence in early June. Dated May 29 and broadcast over the signature of General Field Marshal Guenther von Kluge of Army Group Center, it described German intentions as follows: "To defeat enemy forces west and to the south of the enemy's capital, to seize firmly the territory close to Moscow, to encircle the city and to deprive the enemy of the possibility of making operational use of this region."[10]

It was an astonishing idea. If German intelligence had been as good as it thought it was and the High Command's appreciation of the situation as accurate as it believed, why not lure the Russians to the south and destroy them there? If held in the Moscow region, would they not live to fight another day?

There is no evidence in the surviving record or in the recollections of German generals that the questions were debated or raised.

[9] Ibid., pp. 221–22. Kriegk was sent to neutral Lisbon, a hangout for allied intelligence agents and Western correspondents.
[10] *Kriegstagebuch des Oberkommandos der Wehrmacht,* Vol. II, p. 1276.

4

For all the pretentious talk that was heard in the lake country of East Prussia, almost everyone from Hitler down had some misgivings about the war on the Russian front in the spring of 1942. They were suppressed, however, by the limited scope of the campaign Hitler announced on April 5 in Fuehrer Directive No. 41. Operation Siegfried, renamed Blau I, II, and III and still later Braunschweig, did not call for attack everywhere along the line like Barbarossa the year before or even against the Russian capital. "I see no possibility," Halder told his diary at the time, "that a German offensive against Moscow in 1942 can be successful." The 1942 target was only the Caucasus, and for that it was believed Germany had the strength. In reaching out for the Caucasus, the army would expose its left flank to Russian counterattack but the plan foresaw that, and so Stalingrad on the Volga came into the picture, not as an objective of value in itself but as the distant anchor of a defensive line to protect the thrust to the southeast. The line would run to Voronezh, then south and southeast along the Don, then from the Don to the Volga at Stalingrad. But Germany did not have the reserve manpower, tanks, guns, and planes it had the year before. Who would man the line? German troops up to Voronezh and from the Don to Stalingrad with Hungarians and Italians in between. But the satellite armies were poorly equipped. No need to worry, said the Fuehrer, so the planning began as it always had in the Nazi past with careful attention to German operations and little serious consideration for what the Russians could or might do. This was the way of National Socialism and National Socialist generals. Like Hitler they were contemptuous of the Russians. Like Hitler they viewed concern for Russian capabilities and intentions as a sign of weakness which, however understandable in a front-line soldier, was unworthy of professional planners of the master race. They talked, acted, and tried to look like generals who were teaching a new kind of sleeves-rolled-up warfare—*plunge on, forget about your flanks and rear, disorganize the enemy, disrupt his communications, then destroy him*—and for a while they were so successful that much of the world came to believe they were revolutionizing strategy and tactics. They were not. Successes in Poland, Denmark, Norway, the Netherlands, Belgium, France, and the Balkans concealed their weaknesses, among them the most deadly of all, their unawareness they had any except in manpower and economic resources.

The weakness that interests us here was a belief that an enemy of the Third Reich could have no intentions of his own, that he could only react to German initiative. Accordingly, it was thought unnecessary for Foreign Armies East to issue written appreciation reports in the early months of the Russian war. What was there to say about Russian capabilities if the Russians were not capable of much? What was there to say about Russian intentions if all the Russians could do was respond to German operations? Not enough to bother Halder, who was satisfied with oral reports and daily digests until in the snow around Moscow, Rostov, and Tikhvin he was hit with unexpected reserves. Then he wanted a daily "Report on Enemy Trends" in which, Gehlen says, "some attempt" was made to go into an appreciation of the enemy's probable intentions.[1] *Some attempt*—no more—and this was the attitude when spring came around and it was time to cut the orders for Siegfried-Blau-Braunschweig. Siegfried-Blau-Braunschweig was not supposed to end the war. In his over-all directive Hitler

[1] Gehlen, pp. 35–36.

did not even mention this as a possibility, from which fact we may believe he did not expect quick success in the east that would enable him to turn everything against a second front in the west. It is more likely he was trying to get set for a long war in which he would need all the oil and food he could get. The Caucasus had both and more. It accounted for 70 per cent of Russia's oil production and 65 per cent of its natural gas. It had electric power and mineral ore including the world's largest manganese deposits at Chiaturi. It was rich in cotton, wheat, corn, sunflower seeds, sugar beets, grapes, citrus fruit. It had cattle, sheep, horses, pigs. There were other advantages in a thrust to the Caucasus. Russian forces in the open steppe country of southern Russia would be smashed. Bringing Stalingrad under German shellfire would cut lines of supply and communication between the southern and northern parts of the country.

In the surviving documents of the day there is no indication of discontent with the plan at OKW or OKH or at Reichsmarschall Hermann Goering's Luftwaffe headquarters not far away. Halder wanted more troops for the war on the eastern front, but in his diary notes to himself he never expressed opposition to or anxiety about the summer campaign. That would come later with a rough awakening.

5

During the third week in June tension was building on the German and Russian sides of the line. Hitler was at his Bavarian retreat on the Obersalzberg near Berchtesgaden, resting before the assault he had fixed for June 26. Stalin was in the Kremlin, quite sure he knew about when and where the Germans would strike and quite confident he could stop them despite the unpromising outcome of Molotov's mission to London and Washington from which he had returned with half a loaf. This is the way of war. High commanders are spurred to optimism by a tendency to overrate their own forces, about which they know much, and underestimate their enemy's, of which they know little. Stalin, however, was in a fairly solid position. He was stronger than was generally believed, and sending Molotov west had not been his idea but Roosevelt's. He could, then, live with the results which were summarized in two inconclusive documents, one public, the other secret, that followed hard upon his decision not to take Roosevelt and Churchill into his confidence but to meet the enemy alone with what he had if it should come to that.

It had come to that although it did not appear so to an uninformed world. There was a communiqué, drafted by Molotov, that

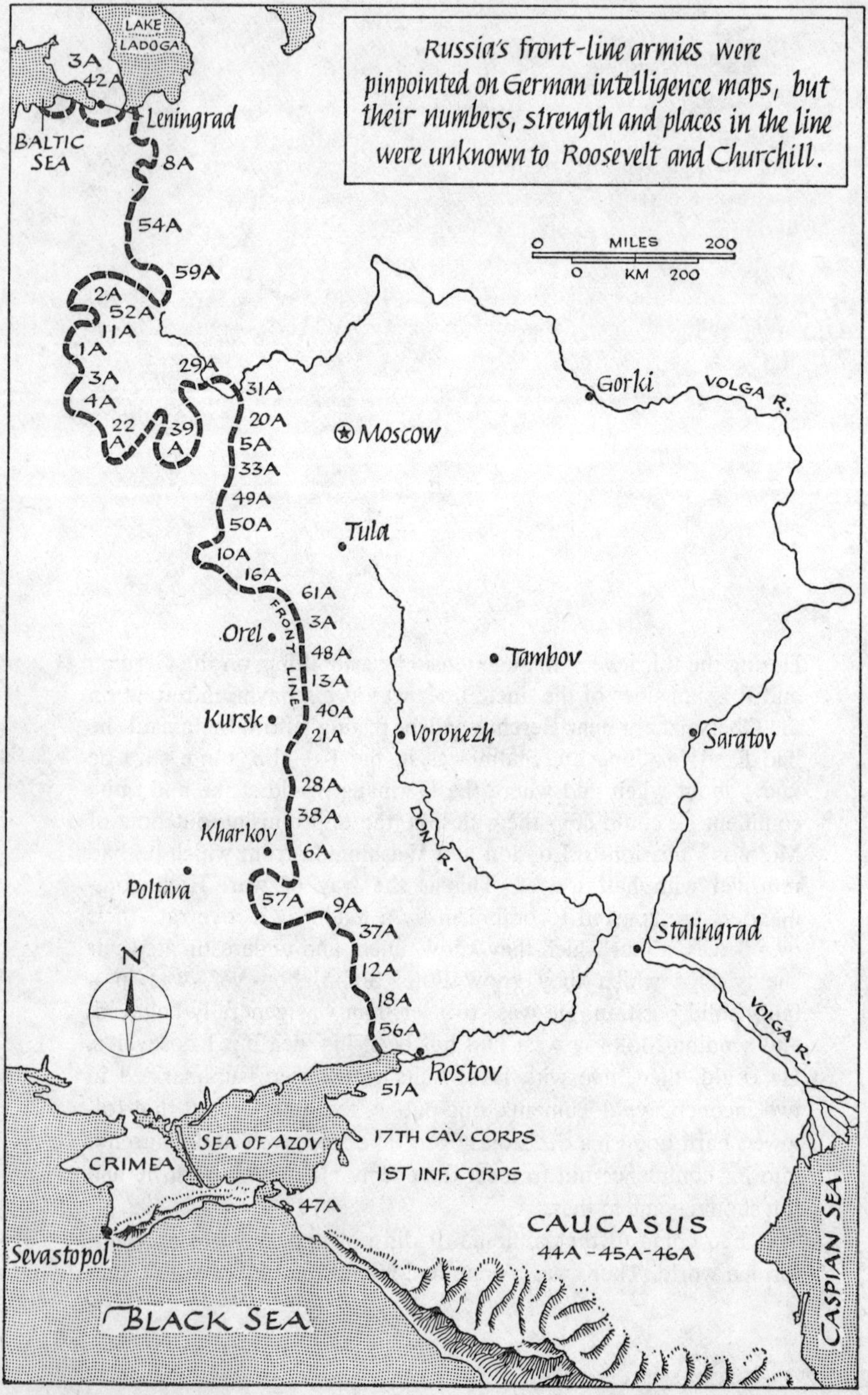
Russia's front-line armies were pinpointed on German intelligence maps, but their numbers, strength and places in the line were unknown to Roosevelt and Churchill.
LAKE LADOGA
3A
42A
Leningrad
BALTIC SEA
8A
54A
59A
2A
52A
11A
1A
3A
4A
22 A
39 A
29A
31A
20A
5A
33A
49A
50A
10A
16A
61A
3A
48A
13A
40A
21A
28A
38A
6A
57A
9A
37A
12A
18A
56A
51A
FRONT LINE
Moscow
Tula
Orel
Kursk
Kharkov
Poltava
Tambov
Voronezh
DON R.
Gorki
VOLGA R.
Saratov
Stalingrad
VOLGA R.
Rostov
0 MILES 200
0 KM 200
N
SEA OF AZOV
CRIMEA
17TH CAV. CORPS
1ST INF. CORPS
47A
Sevastopol
BLACK SEA
CAUCASUS
44A-45A-46A
CASPIAN SEA

included the sentence: "In the course of the conversations full understanding was reached with regard to the urgent tasks of creating a Second Front in Europe in 1942." To outsiders this sounded like a commitment. It sounded like a commitment to me and other correspondents in Moscow and to Ambassador Standley, who was "astonished" to hear the news on a BBC radio broadcast on the twelfth of the month.[1] But Stalin knew better. The communiqué meant no more than it said. One can agree on the "urgent tasks" involved in doing something without agreeing to do it, and this was the most Molotov got. Indeed, he got less, for in London on his way back to Moscow the Prime Minister handed him an aide-mémoire saying "there could be no promise in the matter."

Stalin took it standing up. He did not protest to Churchill or Roosevelt or take any other step at the time to turn the loose, negative wording into a commitment. Instead, he turned the half loaf into a small full loaf by summoning the Supreme Soviet to the Kremlin from all over Russia and causing the public statement with its misleading implications to be read out on the night of the eighteenth. I was present that evening. The assembled legislators cheered and cheered. An early second front looked like a certainty. They would have cheered louder, however, if they had known what Stalin knew—that Russian hopes rested not on allied intentions but on great strategic reserves that lay concealed in the vast Russian countryside. There were some 1½ million of them, more than all the American, British, and French forces General Eisenhower would have on the Rhine in early 1945, and they were organized in ten field armies and two tank armies that were the largest armored formations in the Russian military establishment. Never mentioned by Molotov to Roosevelt and Churchill, they were not to be used or spoken of outside of Stavka and a small section of the General Staff until Hitler and Halder showed their hand. Even then—as to this day—their role would be concealed by the Russians for reasons of military security or political necessity and by the few Germans who learned of them, perhaps because in war there are blunders it is more convenient to forget.

How extraordinary that the Germans—for all their interrogation of prisoners of war, their seizure of Russian documents, their in-

[1] Standley, pp. 203–4.

terception of Russian radio calls, and other sources of intelligence —knew so little about them! How extraordinary that at a critical hour in the life of the Third Reich they did not allow for the possibility of their existence or greatly underestimated them![2] How still more extraordinary they did not speak of them later on after they had met the reserves in battle! But there is not one reference to their numbers or dispositions in the surviving OKH situation reports of 1942, in Gehlen's memoirs, or in any German history of the war I am familiar with; and Halder's diary mentions them only once (July 10)—vaguely, uncertainly—after the offensive was under way. The Russians kept their secret well. If there was a leak at the time, it was to an ally which did no harm and might have done some good if it had been taken into consideration by the United States and Great Britain. See this entry in the diary of Harold Nicolson, a Member of Parliament and a shrewd observer of the London scene, for March 13 of that year:

"Go to see [Ivan] Maisky.[3] He seems pleased with the military situation and says the Russians have new armies for the spring offensive."[4]

Nicolson does not say whether he took this remark seriously and passed it on for what it was worth to his friend Winston Churchill or someone else. Presumably he did not or, if he did, it was rejected as unworthy of trust.

In my case, it was not until 1969 that I had reason to believe in the existence of a strong Russian reserve before the German offensive of 1942. In 1967 and 1968 I had thought it possible—no more —for three reasons. First, the Russians had not disclosed how they won at Stalingrad; therefore, something was being obscured. Second, the use of a strategic reserve after the force of an enemy's offensive has spent itself was a principle of Soviet military doc-

[2] Because a Russian rifle division numbered some 7,000 men at this stage of the war, the strategic reserve of 1½ million men was about five times the size of the force estimated by Gehlen in his report to Halder on May 1. See p. 19.

[3] The Soviet ambassador. The late Vincent Sheean once asked Maisky why he, a Menshevik or member of the minority of the old Russian Social Democratic Labor party, had become a Bolshevik, one of the majority wing. "Vell," said Maisky, "I look around and I see there are more Bolsheviks than Mensheviks. So I become Bolshevik."

[4] Nicolson, p. 216.

trine, originally emphasized by Mikhail Frunze, the Deputy Commissar for War who succeeded Trotsky in 1925 and died soon after. And third, the Russians had won the Battle of Moscow in precisely this way—by introducing reserve armies as the Germans faltered in the snow at the gates of the capital.

Then, one day in the summer of 1969 I found a clue at the Central Museum of the Armed Forces in Moscow. It was a map prepared by the Soviet Ministry of Defense showing the use at or near Stalingrad of five armies I already knew about. They were the 1st, 3rd, 5th, 6th, and 7th Reserves. But the map also showed without explanation the whereabouts of five other armies, the 2nd, 4th, 8th, 9th, and 10th Reserves, and two tank armies, the 3rd and 5th. There were arrows showing where the known five had gone to battle but none for the others. What about them? Had they, too, fought at Stalingrad? When were they organized? When were they activated? Under what names? The answers would not be easy to get. It had been hard enough to track down the known five, and there was a substantial amount of published evidence, both negative and positive, that few reserves existed at all until later on. No Russian history listed the ten armies or discussed their role in the struggle.[5] No German history mentioned them.[6] Liddell Hart, the British military historian, wrote in *Strategy* that Timoshenko's May offensive in the Kharkov direction "used up the Russian reserves." In his *History of the Second World War* he said "few reserves were in hand to meet the Germans when they launched their own main stroke in June."[7] Still, I thought, the map might be right. It was easier to believe the Ministry of Defense had been careless in sending an accurate if incomplete map to the museum than to think it had deliberately prepared and sent over a false one, especially because no attempt whatsoever was made to call

---

[5] Russian reticence about the reserves may be gathered from three sources. Marshal Chuikov, writing in his book *Nachalo Puti* about the 64th and 62nd Armies he commanded at Stalingrad, did not identify them as having been the 1st and 7th Reserves. Later on, the historian Samsonov used only a footnote on page 82 of *Stalingradskaya Bitva* to say the 64th, 62nd, and 65th were the 1st, 7th, and 5th Reserves. Marshal Zhukov revealed parenthetically on page 399 of his memoirs (1st ed.) that the 60th and 6th were formerly reserve armies.

[6] Gehlen's memoirs ignore them.

[7] Liddell Hart, p. 249.

attention to its significance. In fact, it was displayed so casually and unobtrusively among thousands of other maps, orders, flags, messages, uniforms, weapons, and the usual booty of war that I must have looked at it a dozen or more times on previous visits without actually "seeing" it. Besides, I already knew that the tale of Russian weakness and German power Molotov told in London and Washington was partially untrue and totally misleading. This was the flaw in his instructions which were based on a Kremlin belief (assumed, not proven) that the Western allies were more likely to land on the continent if they thought Russia would be knocked out of the war unless they did. As things turned out, Molotov's words had the opposite effect, for Churchill, who was a stronger personality than Roosevelt, believed the time to strike in the west was when the Germans—not the Russians—were in trouble in the east.

So began the search which was essentially an effort to identify the divisions that had fought at Stalingrad, to determine the active armies they were attached to, and to link the active armies with the reserve armies that were in being before the German offensive. It called for many trips to Moscow and Stalingrad, a more thorough reading of Russian history than I had undertaken before, and intensive questioning of Russian officers who had been in the battle, but in the end I had much of what I was looking for, subject to confirmation, and in 1972 and 1973, in response to lists of written questions, Russian officials in writing made a few corrections in the findings and filled in the blanks. Here, then, are the strategic reserves (excluding the independent rifle and cavalry divisions and tank brigades Gehlen was aware of) as they existed in the spring of 1942—unknown to the German High Command, unknown to Churchill and Roosevelt, unknown to each other so far as I can determine, and, what is still more astonishing, unknown to some members of the Stavka staff.[8]

Ten field ("all-arms") armies scattered behind the upper Don and along or near the middle and upper Volga. In each army there

---

[8] When Gen. Stepan A. Kalinin, the head of the Saratov Military Region where the 8th Reserve Army was deployed, telephoned Stavka on August 23 to discuss the first German breakthrough to the northern outskirts of Stalingrad, the Stavka man he talked to asked what troops were stationed in the area. (Kalinin, p. 211.)

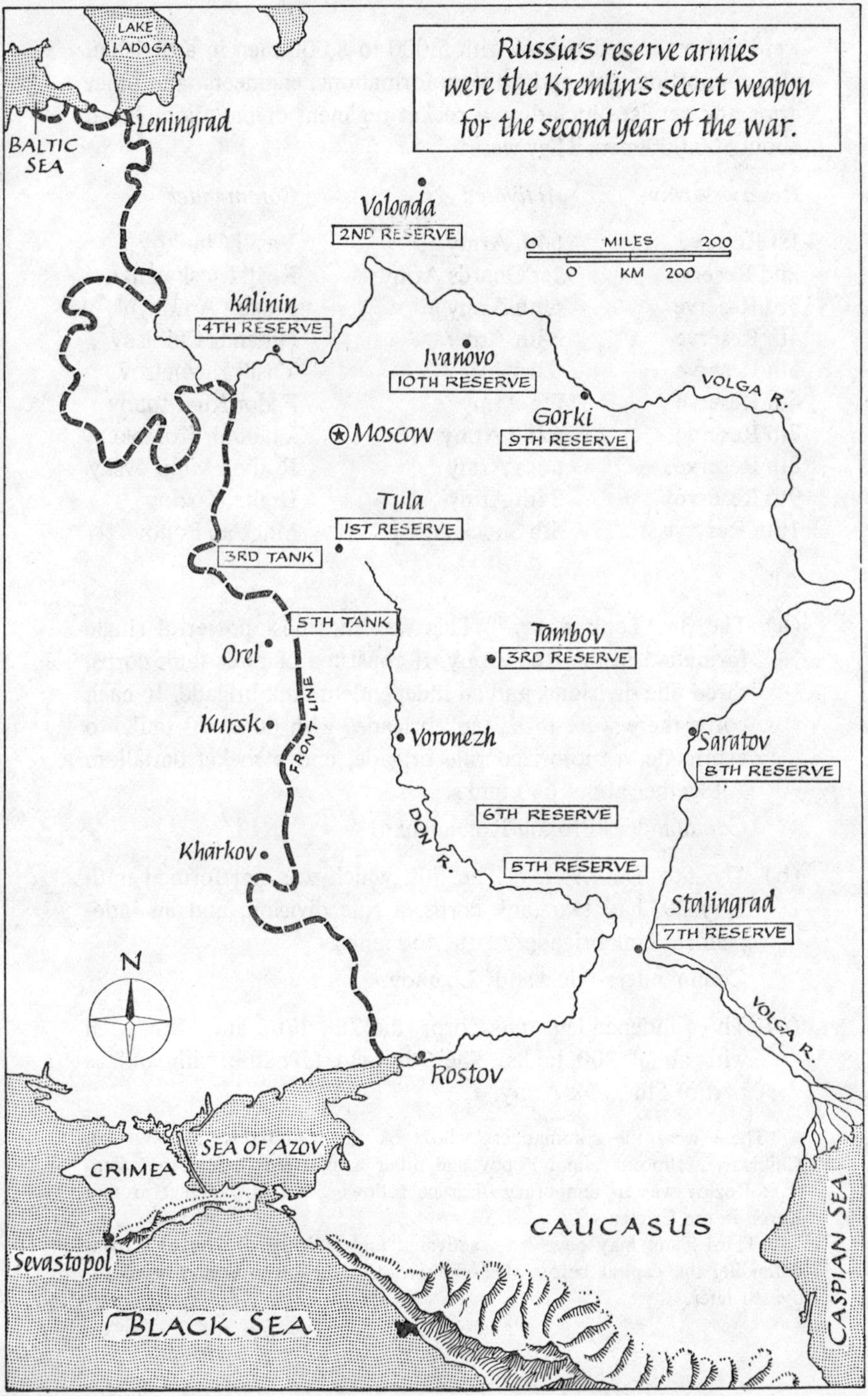
Russia's reserve armies were the Kremlin's secret weapon for the second year of the war.
LAKE LADOGA
Leningrad
BALTIC SEA
Vologda
2ND RESERVE
MILES 200
0
KM 200
Kalinin
4TH RESERVE
Ivanovo
10TH RESERVE
VOLGA R.
Gorki
9TH RESERVE
Moscow
Tula
1ST RESERVE
3RD TANK
5TH TANK
Tambov
3RD RESERVE
Orel
FRONT LINE
Kursk
Voronezh
Saratov
8TH RESERVE
DON R.
6TH RESERVE
Kharkov
5TH RESERVE
Stalingrad
7TH RESERVE
N
VOLGA R.
Rostov
SEA OF AZOV
CRIMEA
CAUCASUS
CASPIAN SEA
Sevastopol
BLACK SEA

were six to seven divisions with 5,000 to 8,000 men in a division, plus supporting tank and artillery formations, engineers, and other arms and services including a rocket regiment or battalion. In all about 800,000 men. They were:

Reserve Army	Activated As	Commander[9]
1st Reserve	64th Army	Vasili Chuikov
2nd Reserve	1st Guards Army	Kirill Moskalenko
3rd Reserve	60th Army	Maxim Antonyuk
4th Reserve	38th Army	Nikandr Chibisov
5th Reserve	63rd Army	Vasili Kuznetsov
6th Reserve	6th Army	Fedor Kharitonov
7th Reserve	62nd Army	Vladimir Kolpakchi
8th Reserve	66th Army	Rodion Malinovsky
9th Reserve	24th Army	Dmitri Kozlov
10th Reserve	5th Shock Army	Markian Popov

Also:

(a) The 3rd Tank Army.[10] This was the most powerful single formation in the Red Army. It consisted of three tank corps, three rifle divisions, and an independent tank brigade. In each corps there were three tank brigades with 60 to 70 tanks to a brigade, a motorized rifle brigade, and a rocket battalion. Altogether about 640 tanks.

Commander: Prokofi Romanenko.

(b) The 5th Tank Army. The 5th, which was not formed until May 29, had two tank corps, a rifle division, and an independent tank brigade. About 460 tanks.

Commander: Aleksandr Lizukov.

(c) Three independent tank corps, the 7th, 17th, and 18th, each with about 200 tanks. The 7th went to battle with and as part of 5th Tank Army.

[9] These were the commanders who took them to battle. Moskalenko, Chibisov, Malinovsky, and Popov had other assignments before the offensive. Kozlov was in temporary disgrace following his May defeat around Kerch in the Crimea.

[10] Third Tank may have been activated and assigned to Zhukov's front defending the capital before the offensive. All the other armies were activated later.

(d) Two Guards rifle corps. The word *Guards* in the Red Army did not mean a professional unit as in the British army but a veteran formation that had earned the title and the higher pay that went with it.

(e) One cavalry corps. A corps consisted of two or three divisions or three or four brigades. Cavalry was more widely used on the Russian front than in any other theater of war, in part because the Russians had more horses than trucks, in part because of the nature of the terrain, the requirements of winter warfare, and tradition.

(f) Fifteen independent rifle brigades. A brigade of 2,000 to 4,000 men was larger than a regiment and smaller than a division.

(g) Two brigades of marines. Unlike the Americans who used marines primarily to seize and hold enemy-held beachheads, the Russians used them to defend coastal positions.

(h) Four brigades of engineers.

(i) Nine independent tank brigades with another 600 tanks.

(j) An undetermined number of independent regiments and battalions of all arms and services—rockets, mortars, tank destroyers, antiaircraft, sappers, and so on.

Altogether, a secret reserve that was almost half as strong in numbers as all German forces on the front line in the spring of 1942 (excluding Germans in rear areas and satellite troops)—a reserve that was three times larger than the entire American military establishment in the summer of 1939, counting Regular Army, Army Reserves, National Guard, Regular Navy, Navy Reserves, and Marine Corps.

Collectively it was known as the *Reserve Army* as opposed to the *Active Army* or more specifically the Reserve of the Supreme High Command or Reserve of the High Command, which is often referred to in Russian history with intriguingly few details. I say "known" but I mean of course "known" to a select few, of whom Molotov was one, a fact that compels us to take a fresh and closer look at his May trip to Washington, which I judge to be one of the missed opportunities of the war. At the time it appeared to be the occasion for a frank exchange of views. In retrospect, however, it will be seen as a revelation of Stalin in political action and of the United States dealing with the Kremlin in Stalin's time, for although Molotov was less than candid throughout, at no time, according to the American record, did anyone put to him the hard questions that, it would seem, called for answers before a second front could be opened. How strong were the Russians? How many divisions did they have? How strong were the Germans? How many divisions in the east? Which ones? How many in the judgment of Soviet intelligence did they have in the west? Which ones? In reading Sherwood's report one has the uneasy impression there was a feeling in the White House that to inquire about such matters was thought to be indiscreet or embarrassing to the visitor or otherwise inappropriate. Why? In the real world there is no such thing as an indiscreet question. There are only indiscreet answers. And this was a vital matter. Two hundred years before, Frederick the Great had written: "Above all things, the one who is to draw up a plan of operation must possess a minute knowledge of the power of his adversary and of the help the latter may expect from his allies. He must compare the forces of the enemy with his own numbers *and those of his allies,* so that he can judge what kind of war he is able to lead or to undertake."[11] Instead, at his second meeting with Molotov on Saturday, May 30, the President merely stated it as fact that the Germans had enough superiority in aircraft and mechanized equipment on the Russian front to "make the situation precarious." He then asked Molotov to "treat the subject in such detail as suited his convenience."[12]

No detail suited Molotov's "convenience." The Russians, he said, "might" hold on and fight through 1942, but it was only right to look at the darker side of the picture. Hitler might throw in such reinforcements that the Red Army "might not be able to hold out." Then he would have (for use on a western front) not only more troops but also the foodstuffs and raw materials of the Ukraine and the oil fields of the Caucasus. He urged the Western powers to land in France and draw off forty divisions from the eastern front.

[11] Vagts, p. 373.
[12] Sherwood, p. 562.

Molotov was on solid ground, for the President was already worrying about Russia's staying power, and Harry Hopkins, Secretary of War Henry L. Stimson, and Gens. Marshall and Dwight D. Eisenhower agreed with their constitutional Commander in Chief.

Hitler, Molotov continued, was slightly stronger than the Russians in men, planes, and mechanized equipment, a statement contradicted after the war by General Zhukov, who said they had 4,959 tanks to 3,250 for the enemy (counting self-propelled guns).[13] But the real "danger," according to Molotov, lay in the "probability" the Germans would try to deal the Soviet Union a "mighty crushing blow," in which case, if there were no second front, the Americans and British eventually would have to bear the brunt of the war.

Roosevelt was impressed. The Molotov visit, he wired Churchill the next day, was a "real success." He and Molotov were "on a personal footing of candor." The Russian position was "precarious"; therefore, he was more than ever anxious that Bolero, the code name for the cross-Channel invasion build-up, "proceed to definite action in 1942."[14]

Churchill, however, thought otherwise and was already planning a trip of his own to Washington to change the American mind. He arrived on June 18, by coincidence the day the Supreme Soviet gathered in the Kremlin to cheer the tripartite communiqué with its talk of "full understanding" having been reached on the "urgent tasks" of opening a second front that year. And he brought with him a tough memorandum, which said in part:

"No responsible British military authority has so far been able to make a plan for September 1942, which has any chance of success unless the Germans become utterly demoralized, of which there is no likelihood. Have the American staffs a plan? At what points would they strike? What landing-craft and shipping are available? Who is the officer prepared to command the enterprise? What British forces and assistance are required?"[15]

Not knowing the answers, still poorly briefed on the substance of the operation he had pushed for almost three months, the Presi-

---

[13] Zhukov, pp. 392–93. Actually the Russians had far more than 4,959, which was the number of tanks in the Active, not the Reserve, Army.

[14] *Roosevelt and Churchill,* pp. 217–18.

[15] Churchill, *The Hinge of Fate,* pp. 381–82.

dent got off a message from Hyde Park, New York, where he was meeting with Churchill, to General Marshall and Adm. Ernest J. King, the Chief of Naval Operations, in Washington. Where could American and British forces execute an attack on the Germans prior to September 15, he wanted to know, that could compel a withdrawal of German forces from the Russian front?[16]

A month later, despite the objections of his advisers, Roosevelt gave way to Churchill. But how different the decision might have been if the President and Prime Minister had known what Molotov knew and did not tell them.

[16] Sherwood, p. 588.

6

On June 19, just one week before Hitler's D day, there occurred a development that sent shock waves through the rival armies and may have caused a postponement of the offensive for two days.[1] It was a Friday and a time of bitter but local combat on four widely separated sectors of the front.

Southeast of besieged Leningrad, Gen. Kirill Meretskov, a former Chief of the General Staff, tried with tanks and infantry to break through to Andrei Vlasov's 2nd Shock Army that lay trapped in German encirclement. The 2nd, which was out of food, fuel, and medical supplies and short of ammunition, was unable to fight its way out of the peat bogs and marshes or defend itself. Meretskov made some progress toward evening but not enough. Southwest of Moscow, General Zhukov, commander of Russian forces defending the capital and also a former Chief of the General Staff, watched Lt. Gen. Konstantin Rokossovsky's 16th Army launch a limited attack toward Briansk so the air force could test its new rocket-firing planes under combat conditions. The test was a fizzle. Confused by erratic signals, pilots mistook their observa-

[1] Halder told his diary on June 26 the offensive was put off to June 28 because of rain.

tion post for a German strong point, and the two generals, who may have been the best the Russians had, narrowly escaped death by diving into a ditch. Farther down the line, in the Kharkov direction, the Germans continued to press Timoshenko to the Oskol River. And at Sevastopol in the Crimea a German offensive was in its thirteenth day and the end for the defending Russians was in sight. Germans and Romanians took everything but a coastal battery on the north side of the bay and brought the naval base on the south side under direct artillery fire.

Early that afternoon a German major stood alone in no man's land hundreds of miles south of Moscow and watched a dust cloud approaching.[2] Who were they? Germans? Russians? He fingered a map case in one hand, with a brief case clutched in the other. Behind him the burning wreckage of a light observation plane, a Fieseler Storch, sent a column of black smoke curling into the blue Ukrainian sky. The pilot was dead at the controls.

With a sleeve the officer wiped the blood that was pouring from a cut on his forehead. He could see it now. It was a truck hurtling toward him over the furrows of the plowed land, *and it was Russian*. He spun around and with a backhand motion flung the map case into the flames. It must not fall into enemy hands, nor the brief case. Against standing orders banning classified material from forward areas he had taken them with him on a flight over the lines to inspect the terrain his panzer and motorized regiments would cross and the field defenses they would storm in the opening phase of the summer campaign.

The truck stopped several hundred yards away, and a dozen men of the 76th Rifle Division piled out. Their faded uniforms—forage caps, blouselike shirts, and pants stuffed into dark boots—were the color of drying hay or the dirt of a country road. As they spread out and closed in, the major pulled a pistol, dropped to the ground, and fired. With his other hand he clawed at the brief case as if to open it, and when they rushed him seconds later, he threw this, too, into the flames and died in multiple bursts of submachine-gun fire.

[2] This incident is referred to rarely, fleetingly, and vaguely in Russian history of the war. The story related here was told to me by a Moscow source who was not present at the time but professed to be familiar with the details.

The immediate consequences were electrifying. Within an hour the charred documents were at division headquarters in a shallow ravine near Belianka, a small village northeast of Kharkov and Volchansk. They included:

—a map on which dates had been marked and pencil lines drawn. It remains classified in the files of the Soviet Ministry of Defense but is said to have been on the scale of 1:100,000.

—typed orders for a German division to attack and seize Volokonovka on the Oskol. They, too, are classified to this day.

—other information, how precise I do not know, including indications that this division turning north would meet another coming down from the northwest.

But who was this major and what was his division? The papers disclosed his identity, Maj. Joachim Reichel, and the German order of battle kept by Russian intelligence showed him to be the chief of operations of the 23rd Panzer Division. The news passed swiftly up the Russian chain of command—from division to 28th Army headquarters, from army to Timoshenko's command post in Voronezh, from Timoshenko to the General Staff in Moscow and on to the Kremlin and Stavka.

That evening Reichel's disappearance was reported to his division and corps commanders. Consternation! Was the plan for the offensive betrayed to the enemy? Forward artillery observers and infantry outposts were questioned. Any sign of a Fieseler Storch? Again the news passed swiftly, this time up the German chain of command—from 40th Panzer Corps in Kharkov to General Paulus of 6th Army, from Paulus to General Field Marshal Fedor von Bock of Army Group South at Poltava, from Poltava to Halder on the Mauersee in East Prussia, from Halder to the Wolf's Lair near Rastenburg and on to Hitler on the Obersalzberg.

The news shook the German High Command. Would the plan have to be changed or D day postponed?

Moscow asked other questions. Were the papers genuine or a plant? If genuine, as appeared certain, what did they indicate? What should be done about them? Only Stalin would decide, and that decision was passed on to Timoshenko the following day when Vasilievsky walked to the communications room behind Stalin's office and directed an operator to summon the marshal to the BODO at the other end of the line. A high-speed-transmission telephone, the VCH, called the vetch, might have been used. The vetch was quick, personal, difficult to tap successfully, and there was an instrument on Stalin's desk. But Stalin preferred the BODO. It was more secure.

Vasilievsky to Timoshenko

COMRADE STALIN IS COMING ON LINE. STAVKA ASKS YOU TO REPORT BRIEFLY ON SITUATION. YOUR ATTITUDE TOWARD SEIZED DOCUMENTS AND MEASURES YOU THINK SHOULD BE TAKEN RIGHT AWAY.

(It would appear Stalin was not interested in what Timoshenko thought but he usually observed the amenities of military intercourse.)

Timoshenko to Vasilievsky

(The marshal began by saying the authenticity of the Reichel papers was beyond question. He described the circumstances of their capture and told of Reichel's death, which Stalin and Vasilievsky already knew.)

IN OUR JUDGMENT . . .

(He meant his own, Khrushchev's and General Bagramian's.)

. . . INTENTION OF ENEMY BOILS DOWN TO FOLLOWING—ENEMY SEEKS TO DEFEAT OUR FLANK ARMIES AND THEN THREATEN OUR ARMIES ON VALUIKI-KUPIANSK FRONT.

(Stalin, disagreeing, stepped up beside the operator.)

Stalin to Timoshenko

FIRST, TRY TO KEEP SECRET FACT WE HAVE SEIZED DOCUMENTS.

SECOND, IT MAY BE SEIZED DOCUMENTS DISCLOSE ONLY ONE PART OF ENEMY'S OPERATIONAL PLAN. IT IS POSSIBLE TO CONSIDER THERE ARE SIMILAR PLANS FOR OTHER FRONTS.

(i.e., something else may turn up)

WE THINK GERMANS ARE TRYING TO SPRING SOMETHING FOR ANNIVERSARY OF WAR AND PLANNING OPERATION FOR THAT DAY.

(June 22, two days off)

TIME OF ENEMY OFFENSIVE WAS GIVEN WITH COUNTDOWN OF SIX DAYS, BUT BASIC INTENTION OF HITLERITES REMAINS UNKNOWN TO SOVIET COMMAND.[3]

In short, nothing would be done about the Reichel papers. The Russians would sit tight.

[3] Samsonov, pp. 72–73.

7

If Adolf Hitler, resting at the Berghof near Berchtesgaden, blazed to fury when he heard of the Reichel papers, his anger was tempered by a conviction that in the main after a terrible winter and an uneasy spring he was doing well enough. He insisted upon or approved the dismissal of Reichel's division commander, General von Boineburg-Lengsfeld, and the dismissal and court martial of his corps commander, Gen. Georg Stumme, and Stumme's Chief of Staff, Lieutenant Colonel Franz, but as he viewed the war from a mountain retreat that was far from the muck and pain of battle the immediate outlook was bright. Having heard the talk of an allied landing in France, he considered it for the present no more than that. Later on, in moments of doubt and indecision, he would move a division from east to west or west to east and back again. For now, however, he was unconcerned. The British 8th Army in Egypt was on the run while on the Russian front he was strangling Vlasov's army near Leningrad, crushing Sevastopol in the Crimea, and with the approaching offensive reaching out for the initiative that had been torn from him in December.

At such times the Fuehrer swelled with confidence. Unlike Stalin, who was a cold political professional with an instinct for management, Hitler was a hot amateur, intuitive, with an impulse to risk. He would not change the plan. It being the judgment of the High Command that if the Russians had the missing documents—and it was assumed they did—there was not much they could do about them in so short a time, arrows on German maps stayed pointed toward Stalingrad and the Caucasus. At that late date none of his military advisers cared or dared to raise the linchpin questions if they gave much thought to them. Was the plan sound? Was it based on a reasonably accurate estimate of Russian capabilities? Did Germany and its Italian, Hungarian, and Romanian allies have the strength to carry it out?

Meanwhile, there was feverish activity in the Russian camp. It began the day after Reichel's death when Vasilievsky issued precautionary instructions to the four field commanders on the line from just west of Moscow to the southern coast. Because of a prewar purge that had killed off most of their superiors, the four were relatively young men, about ten years younger on the average than the German generals they faced. They were:

1. General Zhukov, peasant-born, a cavalryman, whose western front with eight armies defended the capital from direct assault. Zhukov was forty-five years old.

2. Gen. Filipp I. Golikov, a native son of the Urals, whose Briansk front with five armies blocked attack out of Orel and Kursk. Golikov was forty-two.

3. Marshal Timoshenko, another cavalryman, whose four armies of the southwest front covered the area east of Bielgorod and Kharkov. As commander of the southwest direction, a control arrangement that was about to be liquidated, Timoshenko also had oversight over Golikov to his right and Malinovsky to his left. Timoshenko was forty-seven.

4. Gen. Rodion Malinovsky, who had been a noncommissioned officer in the Russian brigade that fought in France on the allied side in World War I. Malinovsky's south front had six armies but three had been crippled in recent fighting below Kharkov. He was forty-three.

The long-anticipated enemy offensive, Vasilievsky told them, might come within the next twenty-four to forty-eight hours. All units were to be alerted, all leaves canceled. Ground and air reconnaissance were to be intensified and any fresh concentration of enemy armor reported promptly to the High Command. In addition, as security against surprise attack senior command posts were to be moved before dawn the next day, Sunday, June 21, the first day of summer. But no orders went to the ten field armies and two tank armies of the strategic reserve which by definition consisted of all combat forces not at the front that were at the sole disposal of general headquarters. According to Russian doctrine, a strategic reserve was released in whole or in part as a last resort or when it was thought it might turn the tide.[1] Stalin used his sparingly like a miser.

What did he expect at the time? An offensive against Moscow as the Germans hoped or against the southern part of the line as the Reichel papers suggested and other information reaching Gen. Leonid V. Onyanov's intelligence section of the General Staff had indicated for weeks?[2] We cannot be sure, for the documentary evidence has not been published, and the entire subject is so sensitive in the Soviet Union it has not been explored for public consumption. It would appear, however, that Stavka thought there might be offensive action in either one or both directions but looked on a combination of the two—attack out of the near south aimed at getting in behind Moscow—as potentially the most dangerous. Accordingly, its two tank armies were in the Orel region southwest and south of Moscow—the powerful 3rd at Kozelsk, behind but not assigned to Zhukov's front, and the 5th at Yefremov, behind but not assigned to Golikov's front. If the Germans struck from Orel toward Moscow, the 3rd and 5th would hit their left and right flanks respectively, and the 1st Reserve Army under Chuikov would come up to assist them from Stalinogorsk near Tula. If, on the other hand, the Germans moved not northeast but east toward

[1] The war on the western front was fought quite differently. See this entry in the diary of Gen. George S. Patton, Jr., for February 23, 1945: ". . . SHAEF [Supreme Headquarters Allied Expeditionary Force] has a new toy called SHAEF reserve, and every time they let an army have a division, they want one in return." (*The Patton Papers*, p. 646.)

[2] It is, I think, indicative of their differing attitudes toward intelligence that a general headed this section of the Russian General Staff while Gehlen of Foreign Armies East was only a lieutenant colonel.

Voronezh, 5th Tank would hammer at their left flank and three other reserve armies would meet them along or near the upper reaches of the Don. They were the 3rd at Tambov, the 5th at Novo-Annenski, and the 6th at Novo-Khopersk. Other armies would be brought up as needed. The 7th under Kolpakchi was near Stalingrad. The 8th was at Saratov on the Volga to the north, the 9th at Gorki higher up the river, and the 10th at Ivanovo northeast of Moscow. Finally, or so I have been told, the 2nd Reserve was at Vologda on the rail line north of Moscow and the 4th at Kalinin off to the northwest just in case all expectations proved erroneous and Germany's Army Group Center under Von Kluge went straight for the capital.[3]

Was this a mistake—a blunder—that cost the Russians dearly in the early weeks of the campaign? Samsonov, the historian, and Zhukov, the commander, seem to think so in two of the rare and cryptic references to the reserves in Russian literature on the war. Samsonov's guarded allusion to the hidden armies is confined to three sentences on page 62 of *Stalingradskaya Bitva*. Without identifying them or pinpointing their whereabouts, he writes: "Expecting that the enemy would strike his main blow in the central direction [i.e., against Moscow], Stavka gathered its strategic reserves in the Tula, Voronezh, Stalingrad and Saratov regions. Depending upon the development of events, they could be used in the southwestern [Timoshenko] or western [Zhukov] directions. In view of the military situation, such a decision was a half measure." Also without identifying them or disclosing their whereabouts, Zhukov mentions them twice. He says in his memoirs on page 399: "If several of Stavka's reserve armies had been standing on the operational rear lines of the southwest direction [Timoshenko], then the troops of the southwest direction would not have suffered catastrophe in the summer of 1942." He returns to the

[3] I place the 2nd Reserve at Vologda and the 4th at Kalinin because these were the dispositions supplied to me by Soviet military sources in 1972 and 1973. I do so, however, with reservations, for the map in the Central Museum in Moscow shows the 2nd at Lublino, which is now within Moscow's city limits but was then on its southern outskirts, and the 4th at Borisoglebsk between Tambov (3rd Reserve) and Novo-Annenski (5th Reserve). If the map is accurate, Stavka had seven armies, not five, in the critical area between Moscow and Stalingrad: the 1st, 2nd, 3rd, 4th, 5th, 6th, and 7th Reserves.

fray on page 407: "If we [on the western front] had had at our disposal one or two [more] armies and had used them in conjunction with the Kalinin Front under General I. S. Koniev's command, we not only might have smashed the Rzhev group of German forces but the entire Rzhev-Vyazma group and significantly improved the operational situation in the entire western strategic direction. Unfortunately this real possibility was neglected by the Supreme High Command."

Be that as it may, Stavka's plan for dealing with the offensive may have been the safest possible in an uncertain situation, for the concealed armies, excluding the tank formations, were not mobile. If "several" of them had been sent south to stand with Timoshenko, they could not have been brought back if the Germans rushed the capital. If "one or two" had attacked near Rzhev, they would not have been available when they were needed later on. Still, the decision to withhold them all caused problems for front commanders who had to get along with insufficient troops and equipment. For them June 21 like many others was a day of anguish.

Near Leningrad that Sunday Meretskov opened a corridor three hundred to four hundred yards wide for Vlasov's army, but the Germans quickly closed it off and only a part of the trapped force got out. Near Kharkov, Timoshenko tried to consolidate his line with indifferent results, for the replacements he got instead of trained and equipped reserves were recruits who scarcely knew the rudiments of warfare. They were peasants, office workers, shopkeepers, and schoolboys, none of whom had been taught to fire the new 25-mm antitank rifle that was being issued for the first time. In the panic of battle they sometimes turned it on German infantry. Others looked in terror at the new light mortars, fearing their hands would be blown off when they dropped bombs into the tube. It happened. Then, there was Sevastopol, Russia's last bastion in the Crimea. In seven months two German and Romanian assaults had been beaten back. The third in June could not be contained. Balaclava and Inkerman fell. Malakhov Kurgan was threatened, and over German loudspeakers to the defending troops came sneering reports of the British surrender of Tobruk in North Africa. Young Russians turned to their officers:

"Is it true?"

"No. It is wrong and a lie."[4]

The harbor was a stink hole of half-sunken ships, burning oil, and the decomposing corpses of horses and human beings. Food, drinking water, ammunition, and medical supplies were running out. In two weeks it would be all over.

But the center of high attention that day was the ominously quiet sector south of Moscow. Vasilievsky, who would become Chief of the Russian General Staff on Friday, two days before the German offensive, had his eye on Orel 200 miles below the capital and on his reserves that were being tested for competence by commissions sent out from the General Staff. Vasilievsky was forty-five years old, stocky, of medium height. He had been an infantry officer in the czar's army in World War I. Halder, the Chief of the German General Staff, had his eye on the broad line from Kursk, a hundred miles farther to the south, down to the coast. Halder was fifty-eight, an artilleryman and the first Bavarian and first Catholic ever to hold that post. Halder had been an officer in the Kaiser's army in World War I. He would drive eastward in the direction of a summer wind that blows across southern Russia.

The wind blows away the morning mists. It sears the mown hay that has been soaked by rains of the night before. It hardens the ruts in the dirt roads and stirs the dust of steppe and ravine until at times the sun shines orange-red out of a brownish-blue sky. As it comes out of the Ukraine, it crosses the Chir River into the land of the Don Cossacks, and from there blows steadily eastward to the quiet Don and from the Don over a narrow neck of land to the Volga, the longest, the widest, and the most Russian of all European rivers.

In the summer of 1942, Stalingrad (the City of Stalin) was strung along the Volga's high west bank. Stalingrad was rough, dusty, and booming. It was a river port, a communications center, and a factory town on the frontier of Asia. It is not there any more. Volgograd (the City of the Volga) has taken its place.[5]

This is disturbing country. It is peaceful enough but as you travel from the Chir to the Don and the Don to the Volga something strangely mysterious awakens the imagination and perplexes

---

[4] Voyetekhov, p. 219.
[5] The city became Volgograd after Stalin's death, but the battle is still called the Battle of Stalingrad.

the spirit. A pervasive stillness gives to the lonely land the air of a cultivated wilderness. Great fields of grain stretch for miles unbroken by fence or farmhouse. Solitary horsemen, cowboy fashion, stand motionless guard over herds of grazing cattle. In the scattered villages, perhaps because of the heat, the houses are shuttered, the people out of sight.

The stillness recalls the tumultuous past. Walk along the narrow Chir and you think you hear the ring of Cossack sabers. Stand by the Don and there comes to mind a royal barge on which long ago the czars floated the swinging bodies of rebellious serfs who were hanged as a warning to grumbling boatmen. Or look out from the high Volga bank and you will know that hordes of raiding Tartars once came riding out of the east. But the most shattering violence occurred in our time, for by accident or by that lethal process whereby one mistaken decision leads irresistibly to another a fearsome struggle was waged on this fateful ground.

Look about you—look anywhere—and the living past comes through the stillness like the sound of echoing "Taps." Here a furious battle of furious movement left behind it more unknown soldiers than any other in modern times. Here at a terrible price a strategic reserve that was hidden in the Russian countryside destroyed what may have been the best army Germany ever put in the field.

But any such thought was far from Halder's mind as he readied the offensive he would launch on Sunday, June 28. First prize, according to the plan, was not Stalingrad but the Caucasus, which had much of what Hitler needed to carry on the war. So confident was the Fuehrer the Caucasus would be his that an order was issued to a printing plant in Leipzig for maps and language guides for Iran beyond the mountain crest.[6]

[6] Speer, p. 238. This was more than a frivolous move by the home front. On August 9, according to the German edition of his diary, Halder discussed with his top operations officers the possibilities of action through Iran (*"Operationsmöglichkeiten im Irak durch Iran"*).

PART TWO

1

Except for the rail line on its southern outskirts, Nizhnye Olshanets looks like any sleepy village in an old Russian print. A dirt road, approaching from the west, moves out of tall fields of rye, passes between two rows of frame houses with gable roofs and fretwork at the windows, and disappears into an oak forest in the distance. Usually not much goes on here. A man leads a cow through the village street. Women with weathered faces wait for the government food store to open. Two boys throw stones at a magpie that has stopped by for a look around, and every once in a while a battered truck roars by, raising clouds of yellow-gray dust that settle languidly on the man, the cow, the women, the boys, and the magpie. It has been like this for a long time and might have been forever if early that Sunday, the first day of summer, the breath of history had not brushed against Nizhnye Olshanets and lifted it from the obscurity of the countryside two hundred miles south of Moscow to the exhilarating if brief renown of a settlement that merited a red flag on the maps of Stavka and the General Staff. Overnight it became the headquarters of the Briansk front whose five armies with some 250,000 men and 950 tanks held a hundred miles of the line between Zhukov's forces to the right and Timoshenko's to the left. Suddenly it teemed with troops, trucks, motorcycles, men stringing telephone wire, and boys and girls hauling water from the wells. Antiaircraft guns and batteries of field and antitank artillery went to the fields and the edge of the forest as soon as they pulled in. Tanks were parked on the west side of the houses to get from the morning shade a measure of protection from enemy air observation; in the afternoon they would be moved to the east side. Everywhere there was a rushing about to get ready for the next day, the first anniversary of the German invasion and the day Stalin and Vasilievsky thought the Germans might "spring something."

Monday, June 22

All quiet on the Briansk front.

Despite the absence of natural obstacles—a river of tactical importance or heights of unusual size—Golikov's position was sound enough and his men well rested. On his left, which he considered the least likely point of attack, lay M. A. Parsegov's 40th Army. The 40th screened the road and railway coming in from Kursk toward Voronezh. To the right of the 40th and in increasing density were the 13th, 48th, and 3rd, with the 61st on the far side of the Orel-Moscow highway. Behind the strong right wing were two tank corps, the 1st and 16th, both about three times the size of any armored units the Russians had used the previous winter, and two cavalry corps, the 7th and 8th. Behind them, although under Stavka's, not his, control, lay 5th Tank Army—the secret 5th.

Golikov watched the Moscow road. He was an experienced officer and one of the few Soviet generals known abroad. A short man with a shaved head, he was chief of military intelligence in the months before the German invasion, then head of an aid mission to London and Washington. After commanding one army and later another in the Battle of Moscow, he took over the Briansk front in April.

Tuesday, June 23

Still quiet on the Briansk front.

Wednesday, June 24

There were intelligence reports of enemy armor gathering in staging areas between Orel and Kursk to the south.

Thursday, June 25
Nothing.

Friday, June 26
All quiet.

Saturday, June 27
Still quiet.

Sunday, June 28
And the long-awaited storm broke over the land with a mighty thrust out of the Kursk region led by Hermann Hoth's 4th Panzer Army heading for Voronezh. Hoth bore down on the weak Russian left between Parsegov's 40th and the 13th Army to its right, and the campaign was on with the Russians taking a terrible pounding from the air. Offensives begin this way. The attacking force strikes at a time and place of its choosing and soon controls the skies. The defenders do not understand. "Where are our planes?" There is the distant hum of engines. A few black specks appear over the horizon. "Ours," someone shouts. Then wary veterans dive for cover, for at this stage of combat planes are usually "theirs" not "ours." By nightfall, which comes late in the hot summer months, Hoth had advanced seven to eight miles along and on both sides of the Kursk-Voronezh rail line.

Stavka, it would appear, reacted coolly to that first day's action. It touched neither one of its tank armies and none of the ten field armies in reserve but released seven air regiments[1] and an independent tank corps, the 17th,[2] and ordered up two more, the 4th and 24th, from Timoshenko's unengaged front. Now Golikov would have his own 1st and 16th Corps driving on Hoth from the right, the 17th moving up from Voronezh behind him and the 4th and 24th coming in from his left, and in these five formations, all recently organized and all, I believe, as yet unidentified by German intelligence, there were about a thousand tanks, twice as many as the Germans were sending to battle.[3] But what Stalin gave with

[1] About 170 planes.
[2] About 200 tanks.
[3] Both sides reorganized their armor in the spring of 1942. Because of severe winter losses, the Germans now had one tank regiment with 130 to 150 tanks and two motorized regiments in each panzer division instead of one motorized and two tank regiments as before. The Russians on the other

one hand he took away with the other. He sent Yakov N. Fedorenko, the chief of the Red Army's tank and mechanized directorate, to co-ordinate the armor, thus limiting Golikov's control of his front. Fedorenko flew to Kastornoye at the junction of the Kursk-Voronezh line along which Hoth was attacking and the Moscow-Rostov railroad, the Russians' main line of lateral communications.

At dawn on the second day it was raining hard in the area of the offensive although warm and sunny in Moscow and hot and clear in the Crimea, where Germans and Romanians were breaking into Sevastopol's last defenses. Muddy roads and fields slowed Hoth's assault and gave the Russians some respite from air attack, but the weather began to improve about eleven o'clock and by one o'clock the offensive was resumed, this time on a somewhat wider front with 24th Panzer Division fresh from France still in the lead, the motorized Grossdeutschland to its left, 16th Motorized to its right.

Soon there were heavy losses on both sides. The Russian 1st Tank Corps under Mikhail Katukov went into action not as a unit, as planned, but by battalions because of the risk involved in concentrating the corps in the absence of adequate air cover. So did M. I. Pavelkin's 16th.

German armor, operating in close co-operation with artillery and air, hammered the Russian line, disorganized it, and drove it back. Enemy tanks rushing the village of Buikovo overran Parsegov's command post and almost took him prisoner.

There was alarm in the Kremlin. It was not that something was going wrong. Everything was going wrong. Because of an astonishing shortage of tank and aviation fuel, the 17th Tank Corps from the strategic reserve did not arrive from Voronezh or the 4th and 24th from the south, and only four of the seven air regiments reported in. Fearing the enemy driving along the railway toward Kastornoye and Voronezh would turn north and cut off 13th Army or south and envelop the 40th, a worried Stalin called Golikov on the vetch some time after midnight.

---

hand strengthened their formations. They formed corps of 200 tanks, twenty in all, by putting together three tank brigades and adding to them a brigade of motorized infantry. It is noteworthy that brigades only were listed by Gehlen on the intelligence maps he prepared on June 1 "for Hitler's personal use." See the end papers in the American edition of his memoirs.

"Do you consider both dangers real?" he asked. "And how do you propose to deal with them?"[4] When things were going according to plan, the Supreme was inclined to throw his weight about. In doubtful situations he asked first and acted later.

Golikov was not concerned about the 13th; he had enough strength in that direction. But communications were breaking down on his left. Could he withdraw the 40th to a new line? Stalin would let him know, and several hours later a rough answer reached Nizhnye Olshanets on the BODO. No, he could not withdraw the 40th. Pulling back to unprepared positions was a dangerous maneuver that could precipitate a rout. What was the matter with his communications? If he were not careful, he would soon have contact with no one and his command would turn into a disorganized mob. Still later that night another message arrived from Stavka, this one transmitted through Fedorenko at Kastornoye:

BEAR IN MIND YOU HAVE MORE THAN 1,000 TANKS ON YOUR FRONT, ENEMY NOT EVEN 500. THIS, FIRST OF ALL.

SECOND, IN AREA WHERE ENEMY HAS THREE TANK DIVISIONS YOU HAVE MORE THAN 500 TANKS, ENEMY 300 TO 400 AT MOST.

EVERYTHING NOW DEPENDS ON YOUR ABILITY TO MAKE GOOD USE OF THESE FORCES AND GET MOST OUT OF THEM.[5]

Golikov needed air support and armor. What he got was responsibility for a situation he could not control, as became evident on the third day when the German High Command launched a second offensive, this one farther to the south, by 6th Army against Timoshenko.

That Tuesday was hot, messy, and dangerous as hell for everyone on the line. Black smoke poured from burning tanks. Enemy planes caught Russian infantry on the dirt roads, and Russian artillery hit enemy personnel carriers. While trembling peasants hid in nearby woods and in the shallow dugouts beneath their wood

[4] Kazakov, pp. 115–16.
[5] Ibid., p. 118.

huts, or *isbas,* fields of ripening wheat soaked up the blood of young men from the Volga and the Rhineland.

"God help you, little sons," a Moscow reporter heard a bearded old man call out to Russian soldiers moving up to the line or the confusion that passed for a line.[6]

They all needed God's help—the defending Russians and attacking Germans—but nothing could protect a frail body from the searing heat of a flame thrower or the wrenching blast of an exploding shell. That evening, while the dead lay unburied and the wounded waited for death, a cooling wind sprang up. It dried the sweat on the bodies of exhausted men and bent the grain that circled the bomb craters in the soft earth.

Stavka was in trouble. The 4th and 24th Tank Corps were stalled somewhere between Timoshenko's and Golikov's forces and of no help to anyone. Something had to be done, and at three o'clock on the morning of the fourth day, July 1, the BODO at Nizhnye Olshanets clattered out another coded message from the Kremlin:

PERMISSION TO WITHDRAW 40TH ARMY GRANTED AS REQUESTED.

It was too late. Parsegov of the 40th was moving his command post for the second time and Golikov did not know where he was. What was left of the Russian line began to crumble.

July 2

On the north side of the German thrust Hoth's panzers broke through to Kastornoye and Gorshechnoye below it. On the south side 6th Army with the late Major Reichel's 23rd Panzer Division in the lead reached Stary and Novy Oskol on the Oskol River.

And that night the Kremlin turned massively for the first time to its secret reserve. It ordered the 3rd, 5th, and 6th Reserve Armies, each with about 80,000 men, and its 18th Independent Tank Corps up to the Don from the rear—the 3rd to the north of Voronezh, the 6th to the south of the town, and the 5th to the south and southeast of the 6th. At the same time in alerted the 5th Tank Army, the most powerful single formation in the vicinity, and the

[6] Yuri Zhukov, p. 183.

7th Independent Tank Corps which was concentrated in the Kalinin sector northwest of Moscow. They would move down from the north on the German left wing.

Be it noted, however, that an outsider—very much an outsider—saw Stalin this day and learned nothing of either decision or of the circumstances that made them possible. At his request Admiral Standley went to the Kremlin to speak of American aid, and in the conversation there was a brief reference to a second front in 1942. "Wanting" one and "having" one were two different things, Stalin said, which led American observers to conclude after the war he quite understood there was no allied pledge in the matter.[7] It is also possible to conclude he did not expect one, despite his later assertion to Churchill, which was picked up and emphasized by Marshal Andrei A. Grechko, a Soviet Minister of Defense, that Stavka had counted on allied action in the west in formulating its strategy for the summer campaign.[8] A third possibility is that Stalin was intentionally vague because he could tell from his conversation with Standley that Standley knew nothing about the Roosevelt-Molotov or Churchill-Molotov talks, which indeed was the case.[9]

July 3

Things were getting wild.

In Golikov's sector on the Russian right, Hoth's 4th Panzer broke out of Kastornoye and headed for Voronezh through thinly defended country. By evening it had covered forty-five miles and

[7] Feis, p. 71.
[8] Grechko, p. 40.
[9] Admiral Standley did not know what had happened during Molotov's trip to London and Washington but it appeared to him as a former Chief of Naval Operations that a landing in France in 1942 was a fantastic notion. For this reason he became concerned at the extent to which the hopes of the Russian people were raised upon Molotov's return to Moscow, so much so that toward the end of June he sent the following message to the State Department: "For the President. Russian people becoming convinced that you intend a landing and a real Second Front in Europe in 1942. If this construction on Molotov communique June 12 is a false one, strongly advise steps be taken immediately to correct this impression, otherwise our relations with Russian people will be seriously damaged when real intent becomes known." To this warning the ambassador received no acknowledgment or reply from the White House. (Standley, pp. 203–4.)

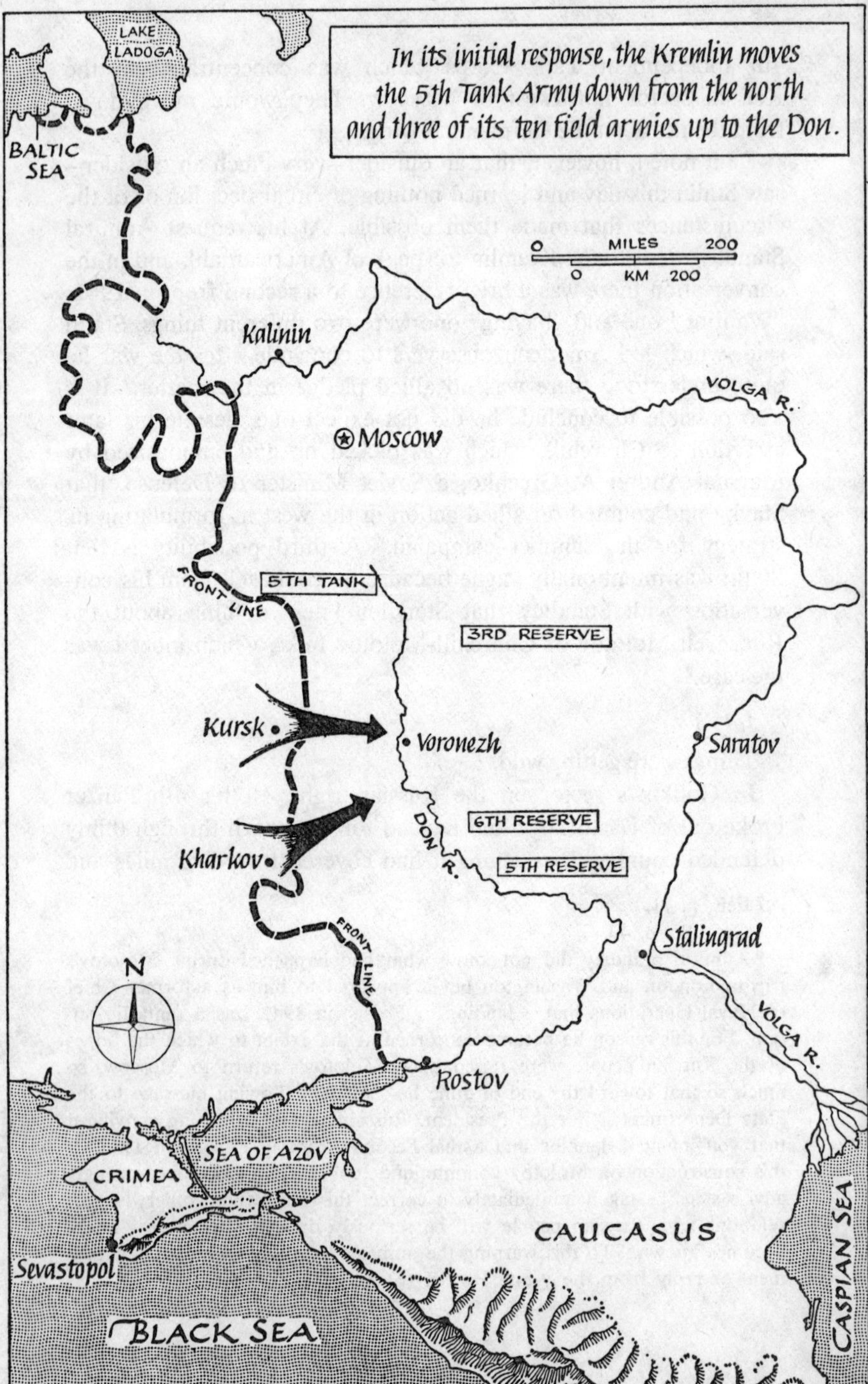
In its initial response, the Kremlin moves the 5th Tank Army down from the north and three of its ten field armies up to the Don.
LAKE LADOGA
BALTIC SEA
MILES 0 200
KM 0 200
Kalinin
VOLGA R.
Moscow
FRONT LINE
5TH TANK
3RD RESERVE
Kursk
Voronezh
Saratov
DON R.
6TH RESERVE
Kharkov
5TH RESERVE
Stalingrad
FRONT LINE
N
VOLGA R.
Rostov
SEA OF AZOV
CRIMEA
CAUCASUS
CASPIAN SEA
Sevastopol
BLACK SEA

was standing on the west bank of the Don only five miles from the town beyond.

In Timoshenko's sector on the Russian left, the German 6th under General Paulus hammered at V. N. Gordov's 21st Army and D. I. Ryabishev's 28th. Moskalenko's 38th held its breath.

This called for a word from the Supreme, and he turned to the BODO with an order that would seem as unnecessary as it was impossible to execute:

Stalin to Timoshenko
ON YOUR FRONT ENEMY HAS CROSSED OSKOL RIVER AND IS CONCENTRATING FORCES ON EASTERN BANK IN REAR OF SOUTHWEST FRONT. THIS CREATES MORTAL DANGER FOR SOUTHWEST FRONT AS WELL AS FOR BRIANSK FRONT.

I ASK YOU TO TAKE WHATEVER STEPS ARE NECESSARY TO LIQUIDATE THIS BREAKTHROUGH. I AWAIT YOUR REPORT ON MEASURES YOU ARE TAKING.[10]

Timoshenko was powerless. Paulus smashed his main line of resistance and striking out with 6th Army to the east and southeast reached the west bank of the Don below Hoth's panzers.

There was another Russian problem. Through a mix-up that has not been explained to this day, the 5th Tank Army was still around Yefremov instead of on its way south to hit Hoth's flank. It is said an order to move did not reach its commander, Gen. Aleksandr Lizukov, apparently because Stavka thought Golikov had sent it, Golikov thought his deputy Chibisov had sent it, and Chibisov thought Stavka had sent it.

July 4
This was the seventh day of the offensive and, being American Independence Day, the first day of American action on the continent of Europe. General Eisenhower, who had just arrived in London to take over the European Theater of Operations, observed it by sending out six American bombers with a large British formation. Two of the six did not come back.

[10] Samsonov, p. 74.

The day also marked the beginning of a Russian nightmare that would never end for tens of thousands of men. There had been a cold rain the night before. Roads were slippery, the fields muddy, Russian forces reeling, but Stavka had an aggressive plan to roll up the German left wing and stop the offensive in its tracks. On Kremlin maps, where everything was neat and clean and nothing smelled like death, the High Command visualized an armored strike out of the north with 1,100 tanks and strong infantry support, and to assure that all went well Vasilievsky flew from Moscow to Yefremov and personally handed Lizukov his orders. The 5th would assemble at Zemliansk and driving south would cut across the rear of Hoth's army standing on the Don before Voronezh. Its 2nd and 11th Corps, reinforced by the 7th coming down from Kalinin, would be aided by Golikov's 1st and 16th. No such armored power had been concentrated by the Russians since the early days of the war.

Nor could it be concentrated now because for a reason that has never been explained Lizukov was short of fuel.

Pavel A. Rotmistrov's 7th Tank Corps reached the field first and went to battle unaided on the sixth.

Lizukov, arriving late although he had a much shorter distance to travel, attacked with his 11th Corps the next day, but unprotected by fighter or attack planes he was bombed in open fields and got no place. His 2nd Corps, moving by rail instead of by road, arrived too late.

Stalin exploded. His great 5th Tank Army was literally going up in smoke. Blaming it all on Lizukov, he disbanded the army and demoted Lizukov to command of his 2nd Corps. But things went from bad to worse. Three days later the High Command ordered the 2nd and Katukov's 1st Corps to attack out of the oak forest along the west bank of the Don. This could do it; this could isolate Hoth's spearhead. Another disaster. As the two corps moved into the open, they were hit by antitank fire, then by field guns, then from the air. The Russians were stopped. One of Lizukov's brigades was cut off, the other two forced back.

At that moment Chibisov, Golikov's deputy, arrived on the scene and ordered Lizukov in to bring out his trapped brigade. Lizukov objected.

"Protect us from the air," he said, "and we will do whatever is necessary."[11]

Whereupon in the presence of Lizukov's men Chibisov accused him of cowardice. Lizukov took it. In tight-lipped anger he climbed into his heavy KV tank and ordered it forward. He never got out.

Aftermath:

Lizukov, a veteran of the Battle of Moscow, was buried in the village cemetery at Vereiyka, a few miles from the field where an armor-piercing shell exploded inside his tank, though Stalin would not believe it. Lizukov, he insisted, was not dead; he had turned traitor.

A premonition? Within a week General Vlasov, commander of the now-destroyed 2nd Shock Army near Leningrad, was taken prisoner. He later went over to the enemy.[12]

And so ended the first phase of the summer offensive. In nine days Hitler's forces had advanced a hundred miles to the east. They had hit the Russians in an unexpected direction, beaten back an armored counteroffensive, and about taken Voronezh.

And yet, except for the broken 5th Tank Army, Russia's secret reserve was intact and undetected.[13]

The 3rd, 5th, and 6th Reserves were moving up to the east bank of the Don.

The 1st, 2nd, 4th, 7th, 8th, 9th, and 10th Reserves and 3rd Tank were lying low.

[11] Yuri Zhukov, pp. 232–33.

[12] In the spring of 1945 Vlasov was captured by allied troops, turned over to the Russians, and hanged as a traitor.

[13] On July 6 General Halder confided to his diary: "The actual picture of the enemy situation is not yet clear to me. There are two possibilities: Either we have overestimated the enemy's strength and the offensive has completely smashed him, or the enemy is conducting a planned disengagement or at least is trying to do so in order to forestall being irretrievably beaten in 1942."

2

Without knowing what Stalin thought of the first nine days of the German offensive, we may believe that, though concerned, he had a strategic eye for both sides of the balance sheet and that his assets as he saw them at this stage of the campaign were considerable. The enemy had not attacked at the decisive point, which in the judgment of Stavka and the General Staff was closer to Moscow. He had not come to grips with the main forces of the Red Army. He had suffered losses in men and equipment, and replacing them would put a punishing strain on long lines of supply that ran all the way back to Berlin and the far corners of occupied Europe. Nevertheless, at noon on the tenth day, July 7, Stalin put in a call for Golikov, who was now in the Voronezh area. Stalin used the vetch.

"Can you guarantee Voronezh will be held?"[1]

Golikov could not. For one thing, most of it was already gone. For another, the 3rd, 5th, and 6th Reserves (activated as the 60th, 63rd, and 6th Armies) had not arrived and he had little to fight with. Besides, a man's life could depend upon fulfillment of a personal guaranty to the Supreme.

[1] Kazakov, p. 131.

Not satisfied, Stalin spoke to Nikolai F. Vatutin, the Deputy Chief of the General Staff who was at Golikov's headquarters as the eyes, ears, and voice of the High Command. What did Vatutin think? Vatutin professed to be more optimistic.

Better check it out—an instinctive Kremlin reaction to uncertainty—so another line was opened to the chief of (police) security in the Voronezh region. The chief of security maintained order, guarded important installations, rounded up deserters, and directed SMERSH, the counterespionage organization. What did he think? The chief of security implied the army had bugged out and that he and his two police regiments were holding on alone.

This was enough for Stalin. Still believing the Germans intended to swing north to get in behind Moscow and, therefore, that Voronezh was the key to the developing campaign, he wanted a strong man at the pivotal point. Without waiting for the night session of Stavka, he ordered Vatutin to take over the Voronezh front and Golikov to stay on as his deputy.

But the order coincided with a startling move. Suddenly and to the astonishment of Golikov, Vatutin, and the Kremlin, the German High Command, acting on phase two of its over-all plan, took a bewildering step that was linked to the code name "Clausewitz." It was bewildering because it was so unexpected by the Soviet High Command. It was ironic because it violated a major principle that had been laid down more than a hundred years before by Gen. Karl von Clausewitz, a director of the General Academy of War in Berlin and later Chief of Staff to General Field Marshal Count August Neithardt von Gneisenau. Clausewitz had explained his thinking in a famous treatise on the art of war that for generations was studied in the Western world.[2]

"Destruction of the enemy's force is the principal object of war," he had written, and *". . . an attack directed to the destruction of the enemy which does not have the boldness to shoot like the point of an arrow to the heart of the enemy's power can never hit the mark."*

Operation Clausewitz, together with its companion action in the north, was something else again. Instead of going for the main

---

[2] *On War* (London: Kegan Paul, Trench, Truebner & Co., Ltd.; New York: E. P. Dutton & Co., 1918).

forces of the Red Army, it called for a violent thrust to the east out of the deep south by 1st Panzer and 17th Armies. At the same time 4th Panzer and 6th Armies turned away from the Moscow direction to join them in open country where all the Russians had outside of the Caucasus were the weakened armies of Timoshenko and Malinovsky and one reserve army, the 7th, near Stalingrad. Hoth's panzer army left Voronezh and plunged south into the steppe along the west bank of the Don and, in so doing, overlooked the three reserve armies approaching the east bank. The German 6th also swerved south to hit the remnants of the Russian 28th and the flank of the 38th. The offensive was in full swing. Hitler and Halder had two panzer and two field armies driving into the great bend of the Don. But Clausewitz had written:

"It is not by conquering one of the enemy's provinces, with little trouble and superior numbers, and by preferring the secure possession of this unimportant conquest to great results, but by seeking out constantly the heart of the hostile power and staking everything to gain all, that we can effectually strike the enemy to the ground."

He had explained why in a haunting passage that survivors of the German High Command may well have thought about after the war:

"If the enemy's principal force"—he was always concerned about the principal force—*"is not on our road, and our interests otherwise prevent our going in quest of him, we may be sure we shall meet with him hereafter, for he will not fail to place himself in our way."*

And so it happened. So happened Stalingrad, the decisive battle that was neither sought by the Germans nor anticipated by the Russians who were so sure in the beginning the Germans would turn north out of Voronezh that for two days they did nothing about the change of direction to the south. On the first day and the second, on July 7 and 8, Stavka went on doing what it had been doing before. It pushed 5th Tank Army into the disaster that would overcome it. It strengthened the Voronezh front to prevent a breakout toward Moscow. And it tried by exhortation to stiffen Timoshenko's crumbling forces that were in a desperate situation at the western entrance to the Don bend. But not for long.

Early on, I wrote that Moscow was a secretive city in a secretive

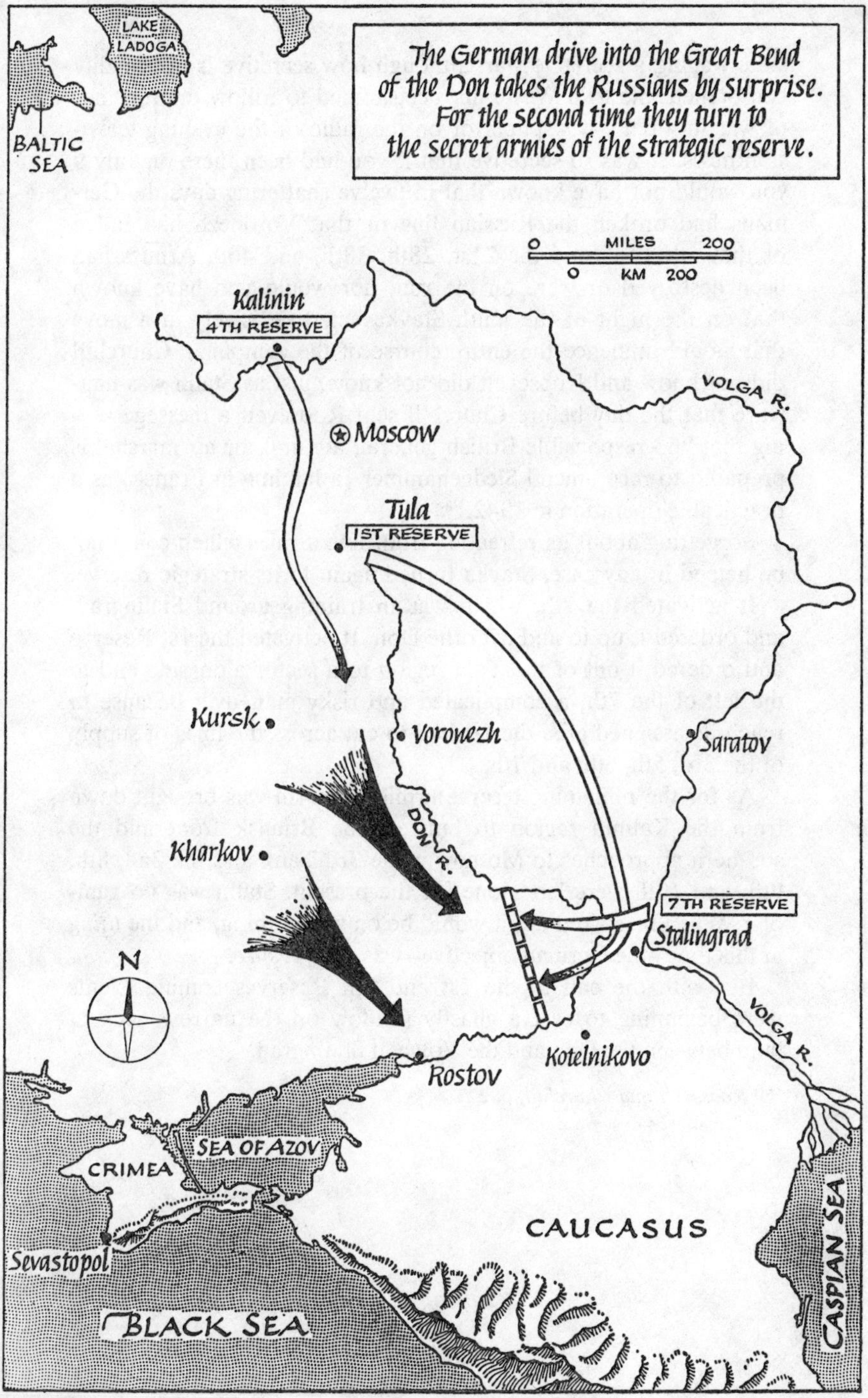

The German drive into the Great Bend of the Don takes the Russians by surprise. For the second time they turn to the secret armies of the strategic reserve.
LAKE LADOGA
BALTIC SEA
0 MILES 200
0 KM 200
Kalinin
4TH RESERVE
Moscow
VOLGA R.
Tula
1ST RESERVE
Kursk
Voronezh
Saratov
DON R.
Kharkov
7TH RESERVE
Stalingrad
N
VOLGA R.
Kotelnikovo
Rostov
SEA OF AZOV
CRIMEA
CAUCASUS
Sevastopol
BLACK SEA
CASPIAN SEA

state waging a secretive war, although how secretive is not readily comprehensible to a Westerner accustomed to follow the fortunes of war in a daily newspaper or on the radio or the evening television news. It was so secretive that if you had been there on July 9 you would not have known that in twelve shattering days the Germans had broken the Russian line or that Voronezh had fallen or that 5th Tank and the 21st, 28th, 38th, and 40th Armies had been destroyed or were on the run, nor would you have known that on the night of the ninth Stavka acted decisively in a move that would influence the entire course of the campaign. Churchill did not know and Roosevelt did not know, just as Stalin was unaware that the day before Churchill sent Roosevelt a message saying that "no responsible British general, admiral, or air marshal is prepared to recommend Sledgehammer [a landing in France] as a practicable operation in 1942."[3]

Forgetting about its retreating front-line armies which could not be helped in any case, Stavka turned again to its strategic reserve.

It activated the 7th, which was in training around Stalingrad, and ordered it up to and over the Don. It activated the 1st Reserve and ordered it out of the Tula region to a sector alongside and to the left of the 7th, a complicated and risky maneuver because to reach its assigned area the 1st had to cut across the lines of supply of the 3rd, 5th, 6th, and 7th.

As for the remaining reserve armies, the 4th was brought down from the Kalinin region to buttress the Briansk front and the southern approaches to Moscow while 3rd Tank and the 2nd, 8th, 9th, and 10th were left alone for the present. Stalin was no gambler. When he staked all, it would be on a sure thing, and the *thing* at this time—the German objective—was not yet *sure*.

But with the call to the 1st and 7th Reserves coming events were beginning to cast a ghastly shadow on the narrow neck of land between the Don and the Volga at Stalingrad.

[3] *Roosevelt and Churchill,* p. 222.

3

It was long after midnight, close to dawn on Friday, July 10, and a fresh breeze blowing through open windows cooled the schoolhouse at Arsenyevo, a very Russian village near Stalinogorsk in the Tula region south of Moscow. In one of the classrooms General Chuikov, until recently Russian military attaché in China, now acting commander of the 1st Reserve Army, was analyzing the performance in training of two of his six rifle divisions. Others had spoken before him, among them Col. T. M. Sidorin, the army's chief of operations, Colonel Burilov, its chief of engineers, and Gen. Ya. I. Broud, chief of artillery, all of whom would be killed at a Don crossing sixteen days later. Now it was Chuikov's turn, and Chuikov was an impressive-looking man. He was forty-two years old, more than six feet tall, strongly built, with curly black hair and bold eyes.

Suddenly the door opened and a duty officer, entering quietly, handed a paper to Konstantin K. Abramov, commissar of the army, who passed it on to Chuikov. Chuikov looked at it briefly and then at the officers before him.[1]

[1] Biryukov, pp. 36–37.

"You will excuse me," he said, interrupting his critique. "No one is to leave the room."

He walked out presumably to the message center or vetch telephone or BODO teletype. When he returned:

"Comrades, it is good we have finished our training successfully. . . . But the analysis must be postponed. A directive has come from Stavka of the Supreme High Command according to which our army, from now on the 64th, is to move to a new region."

Renamed the 64th? That would be in the Active Army, and the Active Army meant the front. A new region? Which one? Chuikov did not say. It was Stalingrad but few men in the Red Army had the *need to know* a matter of such significance or the reasons for it. Chuikov concluded:

"We prepare to move out as of ten o'clock this morning."

The scene shifts to the Stalingrad area and the headquarters of General Kolpakchi, commander of the 7th Reserve. Kolpakchi, also forty-two, was an aggressive officer who had taken part in the recapture of Rostov in November. Even so, he would have been somewhat startled by the Kremlin orders that reached his desk that day. They said German forces of undetermined strength were in the Don bend and might be headed his way whereas he had thought they were 150 miles or so farther to the west. There had been reports of enemy offensive action and tank battles—"in the Kursk and Kharkov directions," according to High Command communiqués—but no news had come to him of a breakthrough and nothing had appeared in the press about the fall of Voronezh. Kolpakchi was told to take his army, henceforth the 62nd, across the Don and stop the enemy in the bend if he came that way. This was fair enough, but in the bend he was to man a line a hundred miles wide from Serafimovich, a Cossack ranch town on the Don to his right, down to Suvorovski, a Don fishing village to his left, and a hundred miles in open country was a lot of front for a young army of six divisions, few of whose officers and men except those recovering from wounds had been in combat. The only veteran division he had was the 33rd Guards, and the 33rd was a former parachute corps with little heavy equipment. Still, the outlook was not altogether bleak. The army had been through a rough course of day and night marches combined with tactical problems during which it was exposed to live shellfire and friendly tank assault. Besides, Stalingrad, on which Kolpakchi could fall back, was more suitable for defense than the enemy realized. Stalingrad had three partially built defense lines that turned in concentric semicircles before it from the Volga northeast of town to the Volga on the southeast. Furthermore, in addition to three known railways coming in from the northwest, west, and southwest, Stalingrad was connected to the rest of the country by three secret rail lines that were built during the war.

The outer or "O" line of the defensive system was three hundred miles long. It reached out to and took in the east bank of the Don above and below Kalach. The center or "K" line followed the narrow and shallow Rossoshka and Chervlennaya rivers and was a hundred miles long. The inner or "S" line ran for fifty miles from the village of Rinok on the north side of Stalingrad to Kuporosnoye and Krasnoarmeisk to the south. True, the winter snow and spring rains had spoiled some of the antitank ditches and firing points but in June and July men and women were out again repairing the damage and constructing a fourth or "G" line closer in.

Of equal or greater significance were the secret railways, two of which were completed after the Battle of Stalingrad began. One was a hundred miles long and went from Ilovaya northwest of the city to Kamishin on the Volga to the northeast. In late summer it would be extended from Kamishin up to Saratov. The other, which was two hundred miles long, was laid from Astrakhan in the south along the west side of the Caspian Sea to a rail network at Kizlyar. Paralleling Caspian shipping lanes, it would speed the flow of oil, minerals, and food from the Caucasus and of any American and British military supplies that might be coming through the Persian Gulf and Iran.[2] The third line ran for a hundred miles from the far side of the river at Stalingrad. At Nizhnye Baskunchak to the east it linked up with the north–south railroad that joined the Saratov–Tashkent trunk line in the north to Astrakhan at the mouth of the Volga to the south. Thus, contrary to Hitler's expectations, Russian lines of supply to the city and between the Caucasus and

[2] In its only reference to this line Halder's headquarters announced in its situation report (*Lagebericht*) for August 20 that it was completed on the seventh of the month.

the rest of Russia would remain open even if the Germans dominated the river at Stalingrad.

Kolpakchi of the 62nd (7th Reserve) rushed his battalions from the wide Volga to the deep Don in the west. Soon 80,000 men were on the move, some by train, others in trucks and wagons, most of them *peshkom,* as the Russians say, on foot. But the eyes of Russia were not upon them. Although they were marching toward what would turn into the greatest battle in history, tight security concealed from the world their existence and whereabouts as effectively as the thick dust swirling about them obscured their vision.

Front-line armies of the southwest front, now liquidated, were retreating or fleeing before the Germans in the Don bend, but on Sunday, July 12, Timoshenko opened a new Stalingrad front headquarters near Gumrak airport just outside of Stalingrad city. Soon he would have forming behind them the 63rd Army (5th Reserve) on his right, the 62nd (7th Reserve) in the center, and the 64th (1st Reserve) on his left.

The fight for the approaches to Stalingrad was about to start.

4

The Don is a big, lazy, country river that falls a mere 632 feet in its 1,222-mile course from the Russian upland below Moscow to Rostov and the Sea of Azov in the deep Russian south. In a wide loop to the east where it comes to within thirty-seven miles of Stalingrad and the Volga, it drops only a foot every two miles, which is why it takes so long for a stick of wood or an old cardboard box to float by a farmhouse and why the Cossacks called it Tikhi Don, the Quiet Don. It is the loop to the east that forms the Great Bend, and it was here within it that a new and more crushing phase of the German offensive was in the making on the fifteenth day of July. By dawn that Wednesday most of Kolpakchi's young army was up from the Stalingrad region, over the Don, and digging in. Approaching him from the west but still out of sight was the far more powerful German 6th, whose commander, General Paulus, was a man of intimidating appearance, even later on as a Russian prisoner of war, which he was when I saw him on the outskirts of Stalingrad in early February. Paulus was fifty-two years old and six feet four. His movements were deliberate, the eyes cool, steady, challenging. A thin mouth drooped at the corners as if he never smiled, and the right side of his face twitched from a nervous affliction.

Paulus inched his way forward like a mouse feeling for cheese in a suspected trap. In each of three columns, reconnaissance battalions were in the lead followed by motorized infantry, tanks, and marching men who suffered from the hot, dry taste of dust in their mouths:

On his strong left
One panzer, two motorized, and five infantry divisions.

In his weak center
One panzer and two infantry divisions.

On his strong right
One panzer, two motorized, and four infantry divisions.

Altogether about 225,000 men, more than 7,000 guns and mortars, and 500 tanks. Motorcyclists and light aircraft reported nothing ahead but peasants harvesting the grain and Russian troops they took to be the remnants of escaping front-line armies.

Some, however, were Kolpakchi's men of the untested 62nd. Knowing he could not hold a line a hundred miles wide, which Stavka had assigned him, Kolpakchi occupied only half of it, leaving his left bare and concentrating four of his six divisions in the center on both sides of the rail line coming in from Kamensk, Morozovsk, and Surovikino. Reasoning that if the Germans came his way they would follow the tracks, he put his 196th Division on the south side, the 147th to its right, then the 181st and 33rd Guards. Two regiments of the 192nd covered an equal distance from the Guards up to the wide waters of the Don, which meant a weak Russian right against a strong German left. In reserve were the 184th, the third regiment of the 192nd, his only tank brigade (up to seventy tanks), his one rocket regiment, four regiments of officer cadets he would use as fire-brigade infantry, and ten regiments of heavy artillery recently released from the strategic reserve.

At nine o'clock that night the following report was entered in the war diary of the 62nd:

"With the exception of the 184th Rifle Division, the 62nd Army is constructing defensive positions on the line it has occupied. Reconnaissance detachments are out. No contact with the enemy."[1]

[1] Samsonov, p. 96.

At about the time Kolpakchi was reporting "no contact with the enemy" in the Don bend, a drama of a different nature was unfolding thousands of miles away near the banks of the Potomac. Returning that day with Hopkins from Hyde Park, President Roosevelt found waiting for him in Washington another uncompromising message from Churchill, the second of its kind within a week. He also found the American Chiefs of Staff, who disagreed with Churchill, in a grim mood, and there followed "a very tense day in the White House."[2]

"I am most anxious for you to know where I stand at the present time," the Prime Minister wrote. "I have found no one who regards Sledgehammer [France in 1942] as possible. I should like to see you do Gymnast [North Africa in 1942] as soon as possible, and that we in concert with the Russians should try for Jupiter [a landing in Norway]. Meanwhile all preparations for Roundup [the full invasion of France] in 1943 should proceed at full blast, thus holding the maximum enemy forces opposite England. All this seems to me as clear as noonday."[3]

It was not "clear as noonday" to General Marshall, Admiral King, Lt. Gen. H. H. Arnold, General Eisenhower, or Stimson, the Secretary of War. Marshall thought a move to North Africa in 1942 would make it impossible to invade France in 1943, and they all viewed the North African proposal as a dangerous dispersion of combat resources that should be concentrated in the United Kingdom for a cross-Channel assault. Marshall and King, who argued with Roosevelt in the White House that Wednesday, were tired of Churchill's opposition to Sledgehammer. They thought so much time had been wasted talking about it that the United States might better forget about Europe for the present and plan for major operations against Japan in the southwest Pacific.[4]

Not Roosevelt. In his judgment it had to be Germany before Japan, and in this instance as on several other occasions if he had to choose between Churchill and his military advisers, he would go

[2] Sherwood, p. 600.
[3] *Roosevelt and Churchill*, p. 224.
[4] Sherwood, p. 600.

with Churchill. If he could not have Sledgehammer and had to decide between North Africa and the Southwest Pacific, he would take North Africa. Under these circumstances, his overt decision was to send Marshall, King, and Hopkins to London the next day to see if they could change Churchill's thinking. His private decision, which he communicated to Hopkins after dinner that evening, was that if they failed in this effort "we must take the second best—and that is not the Pacific."[5]

Thus, the President's own early hopes for a second front in Europe that year were crumbling just at the outset of the Battle of Stalingrad.

*

On Thursday, July 16, as Marshall, King, and Hopkins were taking off for London, Adolf Hitler, to be in on the kill, moved OKW and OKH from East Prussia to an advance headquarters near Vinnitsa in the Ukraine, and on that same day Kolpakchi made contact with the German 6th Army in the Don bend. At nine o'clock that night the Russian 62nd reported to Timoshenko:

"1. Units of the army continue to improve their defensive line and to carry out reconnaissance.

"2. a) At 2000 Hours 16.7.42 a reconnaissance battalion clashed with the enemy at Morozovsk [on the railroad out ahead]. Three enemy antitank guns were put out of action after which our detachment withdrew to the vicinity of Verkhnye Gnutov.

"b) A prisoner was taken in the Chernishevskaya area [on the narrow River Chir about midway between Morozovsk and Serafimovich on the middle Don to the north].

"3. Ground reconnaissance confirms information with regard to presence of enemy motorized and tank forces at Chernishevskaya and at the state bird farm 25 kilometers [15 miles] northwest of Chernishevskaya.

"4. Army intelligence units are carrying out reconnaissance along the [north to south] line Serafimovich, Pronin, Malakhov,

[5] Ibid., p. 602.

Chernishkovski [on the railroad east of Morozovsk], Tormosin [south of the tracks].

"5. Ground reconnaissance has not established enemy's presence on other sectors of the front."[6]

That evening word reached the Kremlin of the 62nd's first contact with the enemy and of the escape over the Don of the frontline 38th under Moskalenko, but Stalin made no reference to either development in a teletype directive he fired off to Timoshenko in Stalingrad. The message, which indicates how little he knew of what was going on in the Don bend, read:

STAVKA AND SUPREME HIGH COMMAND DIRECT THERE BE ORGANIZED IMMEDIATELY AND UNDER YOUR PERSONAL RESPONSIBILITY STRONG FORWARD DETACHMENTS AND THAT THEY BE SENT TO LINE ALONG RIVER TSIMLA FROM CHERNISHEVSKAYA [he meant Chernishkovski] TO ITS MOUTH, ESPECIALLY THAT THEY FIRMLY SEIZE TSIMLIANSKAYA AND THERE ESTABLISH COMMUNICATIONS WITH TROOPS OF NORTH CAUCASUS FRONT.[7]

The order could not be carried out or even attempted for the present. The Tsimla flows from Chernishkovski on the railroad along which Paulus was advancing to Tsimlianskaya on the lower Don to the south, but the new 64th Army (1st Reserve), which was to occupy this sector to the left of the 62nd (7th Reserve), had not arrived, its acting commander Chuikov had only reached Stalingrad that day, and the only division the 62nd had south of the tracks, the 196th, had its hands full on the rail line.

Stavka, however, did recognize the need for early reinforcements. That night or the following day it called up from Siberia seven independent rifle divisions. They were the 126th, 204th, 205th, 208th, 321st, 399th, and 422nd.

[6] Samsonov, p. 96.
[7] Ibid., p. 95.

5

By July 18 and the close of the third week of the German offensive, the pressure was overwhelming in the narrowing no man's land between the German 6th and Russian 62nd Armies in the Great Bend of the Don and in the inner recesses of the Kremlin where Stalin, sternly at work, was beginning to feel the strain of defeat in the field. He had lost or was losing the better part of ten armies.[1] He did not know whether the enemy, moving toward Stalingrad, planned a wide end run to get in behind Moscow or whether the objectives were Stalingrad and the Caucasus or one or the other, and until he knew he dared not commit more forces inside the bend than the 62nd and the 64th that would take its place to the left of the 62nd when it pulled in from Tula.

This, then, was the situation that Saturday when a striking message addressed to "my comrade and friend"[2] arrived from Churchill in London. Churchill wrote that PQ 18, a large convoy that was to have sailed for Russia's arctic ports with military and other supplies, had been canceled because of heavy losses suffered by

[1] The 5th Tank of the strategic reserve, the 40th of the Briansk front (Golikov), the 21st, 28th, and 38th of the old southwest front (Timoshenko), and the 9th, 12th, 18th, 37th, and 56th of the south front (Malinovsky).
[2] Sherwood, p. 600.

PQ 17 due to enemy action. This is what the message said, and this evidently is why President Roosevelt considered it a "good one."[3]

The Kremlin, however, read something else into and between the Churchillian lines. It read, correctly as it turned out, an indication there would be no second front in Europe in 1942, a matter that had not been decided officially because Hopkins, Marshall, and King only reached London to argue the point on the day Stalin studied Churchill's message.

How did he take the news? We cannot be sure, for he waited five days before answering, and then his response was one of icy but restrained anger. We do know that Churchill lost his temper that Saturday because Hopkins, Marshall, and King did not stop at Chequers where Churchill was passing the weekend but went on to London against Churchill's will.[4] And we know that two days later Stalin's studied composure broke. Whether Churchill's note had anything to do with it we cannot say. Perhaps not. In any event early on Monday morning he struck out in a wild frenzy that cost Timoshenko his command at the perilous onset of the battle because without his permission or knowledge V. F. Gerasimenko and his staff of the Stalingrad Military Region had been transferred out of the city to Astrakhan at the mouth of the Volga. One would think the move was of no great importance because the military region was an administrative headquarters concerned with the mobilization and training of replacements and had nothing to do with the command of troops. The Supreme, however, saw things differently. To his suspicious mind it looked like an indication the army would not defend Stalingrad to the death if it should come to that. The story comes from Aleksei Chuyanov, the secretary of the Communist party organization in the Stalingrad area and a member of Timoshenko's military council along with Khrushchev and P. I. Bodin, who had taken Bagramian's place as Chief of Staff.

Soon after dawn that Monday the telephone rang in Chuyanov's office. He picked up the receiver.

OPERATOR: Comrade Stalin will speak to you.

---

[3] *Roosevelt and Churchill*, p. 224.
[4] Sherwood, p. 607.

Pause.

STALIN (*angrily*): Have you decided to surrender the city to the enemy? Why have you transferred the Military Region to Astrakhan? Who authorized you to do that? Answer me.

Chuyanov said he had received a signed order from the Deputy People's Commissar of Defense (Timoshenko).[5]

STALIN: We are meeting here and will punish the guilty. But I charge you, Comrade Chuyanov, to locate the commander of the Military Region and tell him that if his staff is not back in Stalingrad tomorrow he will be punished severely. Do you understand me?

CHUYANOV: Yes, I understand. Your order will be transmitted immediately.

Stalin asked several questions about the city and the output of its arms factories. Then:

STALIN (*still angry*): I direct you to wage as merciless a fight against panic-mongers and cowards as you would against those who undermine the defense of the country. Rouse the spirit of the people. Get still more out of the factories. Tell all that Stalingrad will not be surrendered.

This was the Supreme speaking, the man with the power of life and death over everyone in the country, and now it was clear to Chuyanov how in this crisis he would exercise that power, for Chuyanov understood the meaning of code words like "merciless fight," "panic-mongers," and "cowards." They meant anyone would be shot who disobeyed an order or flinched in the defense of Stalingrad or was thought to have done so. Shades of the *chistka* —the cleanup, the combing out, the prewar purge!

Chuyanov laid down the receiver, picked it up again, and told Gerasimenko to get back. Gerasimenko got back.[6]

[5] In what he called his wartime "diary" Chuyanov used the words Deputy Supreme High Commander but my Russian sources say this was a mistake, that Timoshenko never held that post, which was created for Zhukov on August 26, 1942.
[6] Ironically Stalin himself on September 10 sent Gerasimenko to Astrakhan to take command of a new 28th Army.

Then, Stalin struck swiftly. Consider the timing:

Monday, July 20
Stalin called Chuyanov.

Tuesday, July 21
Stalin summoned to the Kremlin General Gordov, former commander of the destroyed 21st Army, whom he had put in command of the young 64th only two days before.

Wednesday, July 22
Stalin fired Timoshenko, who had been People's Commissar of Defense and Chairman of Stavka before Stalin took over both positions in the summer of 1941. He put Gordov in command of the Stalingrad front.

Now, Gordov's appointment could not have come at a worse time nor been more coolly received by his fellow officers.

Chuikov, acting commander of the 64th before and after Gordov, recalled after the war Gordov's assumption of command:

"This was the first time I had an opportunity to meet V. N. Gordov," he wrote. "He was a grizzled general"—gray hair was an oddity in the Red Army after the prewar purge—"with tired, unseeing, gray eyes that seemed to say: 'Do not tell me about the situation. I know everything but there is nothing I can do about it.'"[7]

Moskalenko, former commander of the destroyed 38th, got the word when on the day Timoshenko was dropped he reported in at front headquarters to receive a new assignment.

"The substitution did not seem to me to be worth it," he recalled in his memoirs. "Gordov did not have it, and we still thought Timoshenko was capable of running the Stalingrad front."

Nikita Khrushchev, who would have to work with Gordov, scarcely knew him.

Gordov, it was said, had a way of shouting at subordinates that did not go down well with other commanders. Rokossovsky did not like him. Eremenko, who succeeded Gordov a few weeks later, thought he had neither the stomach nor the ability to lead large

[7] Chuikov, p. 15.

forces in difficult conditions. Zhukov, according to Rokossovsky, could not stand him.

Be that as it may, the timing of Timoshenko's dismissal was strikingly inept. The day before, 4th Panzer stormed out of the lower Don bend and crossed the river at Tsimlianskaya. The day after, the German 6th crashed into the weak right of Kolpakchi's 62nd. And the more troublesome the situation became, the angrier Stalin grew until on the following Thursday, July 28, he issued one of the most terrifying directives of the war. This was Order No. 227 of the People's Commissar of Defense (Stalin), and it spelled out the meaning behind the code words he had used in his talk with Chuyanov on the morning of the twentieth. Without a word of it being breathed to the public (until September 11 when its contents and importance were disclosed by all Moscow newspapers), the order went to every unit in the armed forces in the Stalingrad and Caucasus directions, and it was read and read again to the troops until many of them knew it by heart. The vital paragraph:

"Panic-mongers and cowards must be destroyed where they stand. From now on, iron law of discipline must be imposed on every commander, every Red Army man, every political worker— *not a step back without order from higher command.*"

The Supreme was not fooling. Blaming his reverses on treason and treachery, he defined the words in his own way. Fear was treason or treachery. Surrender was treason or treachery even if it were followed by escape from a German prison camp. As a consequence, in the coming weeks hundreds of men would be shot without court-martial, and after the war thousands taken prisoner would be sent to Siberian labor camps for ten years' penal servitude if they lived that long. But that was later on. For the present, Stalin, now up to his neck in battle in the Don bend, faced two questions of challenging proportions. What was Hitler's true objective? Had Churchill and Roosevelt really given up any thought of a second front in 1942? By coincidence, the answers, though they would not come his way until August, were arrived at on July 23, the day after Timoshenko was removed and the day the Germans plowed into the weak Russian right on the north side of the bend and drove the Russian left into the streets of Rostov on the south side.

On that Thursday, a fateful day of the war, Adolf Hitler from his advance headquarters near Vinnitsa issued Fuehrer Directive No. 45 which lifted Stalingrad from the status of a secondary objective to one of equal priority with the Caucasus.[8] In a decision from which there would be no turning back he ordered his northern force (Army Group B) to take Stalingrad and move on down the Volga to Astrakhan and the Caspian Sea (Operation Heron) while his southern force (Army Group A) turned its might from the lower Don toward the Caucasus (Operation Edelweis).

On the same day Roosevelt, giving in to Churchill over the opposition of his military advisers, abandoned Sledgehammer and agreed to a strategy that called for North Africa instead of France.[9] To General Marshall this meant no France in 1943 as well, and Churchill knew it because Field Marshal Sir John G. Dill, his representative in Washington, had so informed him on the fifteenth of the month.[10]

Knowing nothing of either development, Stalin that Thursday replied to Churchill's message received the previous Saturday announcing the cancellation of convoy PQ 18. He sent what the Prime Minister later referred to as a "rough and surly" answer.[11] His "specialists," Stalin wrote, considered it "incomprehensible and inexplicable" that allied warships had abandoned en route the freighters in PQ 17. He could not "imagine" the British government would call off PQ 18. "As for the second question, namely the question of organizing a Second Front in Europe," he went on, "I am afraid it is beginning to take on a frivolous aspect. In view of the actual position on the Soviet-German front, I must declare most categorically that the Soviet Government cannot accept a postponement until 1943 of the organization of a Second Front in Europe."[12]

Stalin did not say he was being betrayed by the American and British governments, which he was not, nor did he accuse Churchill of breaking faith with an ally. The Prime Minister's aide-mémoire to Molotov on June 11 had taken care of that. But Stalin

[8] The directive formalized an order to the same effect dated July 17.
[9] Sherwood, p. 610.
[10] Churchill, *The Hinge of Fate*, p. 439.
[11] Ibid., pp. 270–71.
[12] Samsonov, p. 40.

was in a bind of his own making from which he could not hope to extricate himself without disclosing his reserve power, and this he would not do. He could refuse to "accept" the decision. He could protest. He could do no more. Perhaps if he had known it meant no invasion of France until 1944, he would have acted differently. We cannot say. He did not know.

In any event, he now had reason to believe—and may well have believed before—he would have to fight the European land war alone in 1942, and the situation at the front was growing more desperate by the hour. That evening he received this message from Kolpakchi after 62nd Army's first day of battle on the north side of the bend:

ARMY IS STUBBORNLY DEFENDING ITS PREPARED LINE. FORWARD UNITS, ATTACKED BY SUPERIOR FORCES, ARE WITHDRAWING.[13]

The second sentence was an understatement. Kolpakchi's weak right was hit so hard by Paulus's 6th Army of Army Group B that he had to throw in his only tank brigade, the 40th, and part of the one division he had in reserve, the 184th. He also had to pull the 196th Division from his shaky left where the 64th Army was gathering and move it around behind his army to bolster the flagging right.

This was the good news. The bad news came the next day, Friday, July 24, when Chuikov, following orders from Stalin and Gordov, sent elements of his assembling 64th thirty miles forward toward the Tsimla River where they were soon outflanked and forced into precipitous retreat. Stalin did not consider himself to blame:

Stalin to Gordov

IN SENDING TROOPS TO TSIMLA ENEMY DIVERTED OUR ATTENTION TO SOUTH WHILE SLYLY CONCENTRATING STRONG FORCES ON RIGHT FLANK OUR FRONT. THIS MILITARY CUNNING OF ENEMY SUCCEEDED OWING TO ABSENCE OF TRUSTWORTHY INTELLIGENCE. THIS SHOULD

[13] Ibid., p. 103.

BE TAKEN INTO ACCOUNT AND RIGHT FLANK OF FRONT STRENGTHENED IN EVERY POSSIBLE WAY.[14]

But any quick help for Kolpakchi and the 62nd was out of the question. The seven reserve divisions called up from Siberia were still on the trains, and another four or five days would pass before a dozen or so tank brigades and more antitank and artillery regiments reached the area. Kolpakchi's right collapsed. The German 60th Motorized Division, now joined by the 3rd, overran the headquarters of the 184th and 192nd Divisions near Verkhnye Buzinovka and came out on the Don in the Russian rear. A little to the south, 16th Panzer, supported by the 113th Light Infantry, broke through the 33rd Guards and took Kachalinskaya, Kolpakchi's forward command post.

Things were getting out of hand. Encirclement of the 62nd Army was in the making, and in an operational summary written at ten o'clock that night the 62nd reported it had been heavily bombed. Col. S. T. Koïda, head of the 184th Division, was missing in action (he showed up later). Col. A. S. Zakharchenko of the 192nd was killed, and Kolpakchi's operations chief, Col. K. A. Zhuravlev, was flown in to take over both units while staff officers tried to follow him by car over the steppe. The summary ended on this optimistic note:

GROUND AND AIR RECONNAISSANCE HAS NOT OBSERVED WITHDRAWAL OF INFANTRY. THERE IS REASON TO BELIEVE UNITS ARE CONTINUING TO HOLD LINE.[15]

Whatever the reason, it was wrong. There was no withdrawal because the troops, now without telephone or radio communications with headquarters, were almost surrounded. Indeed, by midnight the Germans had cut off all of the 184th and 192nd Divisions, two of the three regiments of the Guards, the only tank brigade, the 644th Tank Battalion, the four cadet regiments, and three of the army's ten artillery regiments.

[14] Ibid., pp. 103–4.
[15] Ibid., p. 104.

Some time after midnight Vasilievsky, who had flown in from Moscow, and Gordov, up from Stalingrad, met at Kalach on the east bank of the Don to speed the formation of two new tank armies, the 1st and 4th, which, it was hoped, could stand between the crumbling 62nd and Stalingrad city. A rescue operation was planned for dawn the next day or the day after that or whenever one could be organized.

Small wonder Adolf Hitler at his Werewolf headquarters near Vinnitsa was in a confident mood. Not yet suspecting what could hit him, he saw when all reports were in that on this one day, Friday, July 24, he had:

1. encircled half of one Russian army (the 62nd) and outflanked the other half;

2. broken into a second (the 64th) and in places pushed it back over the Don;

3. seized Rostov, the communications and commercial center near the mouth of the Don; and

4. forced Malinovsky's routed armies to the south bank of the river along with thousands of fleeing civilians who drove before them thousands of cattle, sheep, and horses.

Altogether it was an auspicious opening for Hitler's amended plan of campaign. But the Kremlin was not stampeded into ill-considered action. Counting for now on the rifle divisions coming in from Siberia and on the tank armies it was trying to form overnight on the not-so-quiet Don behind Kolpakchi, it continued to withhold 3rd Tank and the 2nd, 8th, 9th, and 10th Reserves.

1 As he had with Winston Churchill, Foreign Minister Molotov keeps silent about Russia's secret reserves in his talks with President Roosevelt. SOVFOTO.

2 Unknown to the Germans (or to Roosevelt and Churchill), Aleksandr Vasilievsky, shown here as a Marshal of the Soviet Union, became Chief of the General Staff a few days before the German summer offensive. SOVFOTO.

3 Lt. Col. Reinhard Gehlen, chief of German intelligence on the Russian front, whose reports to the high command seriously underestimated Russian capabilities. DEUTSCHE PRESSE-AGENTUR.

4 Unaware of Russian reserves massing before them, German troops roll eastward toward Stalingrad. DEUTSCHE PRESSE-AGENTUR.

5 German soldiers watch a battle for control of the skies over Stalingrad. BUNDESARCHIV, KOBLENZ.

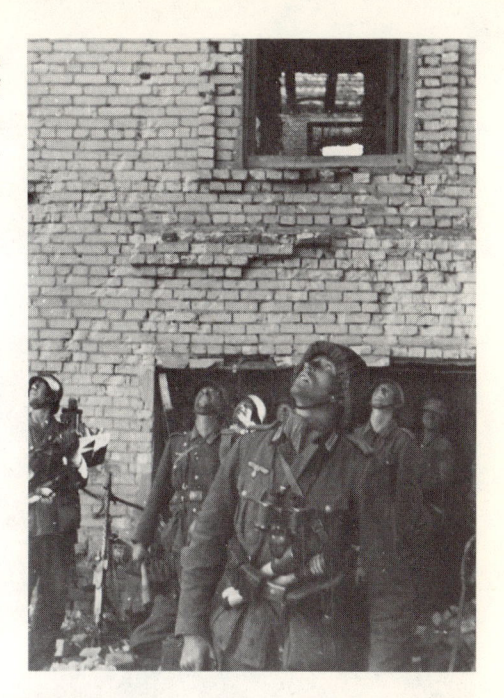

6 No man's land in the heart of the city. BUNDESARCHIV, KOBLENZ.

7 A pilot's view of Stalingrad, the Volga, and the flat country beyond. DEUTSCHE PRESSE-AGENTUR.

6

The range of the still-developing Battle of Stalingrad was now of such dimensions it could only have been followed at the headquarters of the rival high commands and then unevenly, in some respects uncomprehendingly, with the distant optic of commanders and staff officers to whom war at times is a bloodless duel of power and wits. In contrast to Waterloo (1815), where the field was a mile or two wide, or Gettysburg (1863), where it was never more than three, the struggle for the approaches to Stalingrad and the Caucasus was waged on a three-hundred-mile front. Here in slightly undulating, almost treeless country, weary, often hungry and thirsty men did what they had to do out of habit or anger or fear or submission. Moscow and Vinnitsa, however, had other problems. Stalin had German intentions to fathom and a concern not to throw in reserves too heavily too soon or in the wrong place. Hitler, although he appears not to have known it, had Russian capabilities to re-evaluate.[1]

---

[1] German history and memoirs are replete with generalized statements like that of Walter Warlimont, deputy chief of operations at OKW, in *Inside Hitler's Headquarters*, p. 244: "As regards enemy intelligence he [Hitler] only accepted what suited him and often refused even to listen to un-

Russian reinforcements in moderate strength were early on the way so that by the third week in July ten independent divisions, none of them part of the original reserve armies, were approaching Stalingrad from the north, three on the west side of the Volga and seven from Siberia on the east side.

The three on the west side ran into every conceivable difficulty: tracks torn by enemy bombs, food rations that went astray, long delays at railroad sidings, no maps of the countryside, guns unloaded at one station and their shells at another. If anything could go wrong, it did at one time or another. There were misdirected orders, dead telephone lines, radios that did not work, conflicting instructions, bridges out, dried-up streams. Still, they pushed on.

The Siberian seven faced a problem of a different kind, for there was something forbidding about the steppe on the far side of the river. The land was flat, dreary, uncultivated, uninhabited. Dry, shallow creek beds looked as if they had been dry since the beginning of time, and the few tracks in the sand were of wagons that had passed long before. It was not so much the desolation that troubled a traveler in these lonely parts. It was the stillness, the silence, the absence of movement—until on a stifling morning in July clouds of yellowish-brown dust filled the northeastern sky. Early on, they were no more than faint discolorations above the horizon, but as the hours wore on they billowed and drifted until they covered the noon sun like an approaching storm, shading but no longer concealing long lines of marching infantry, wagons with food and ammunition, water carts, trucks with steam hissing from their engines. The men walked easily, quietly, like country boys who had been in the army for a year or more, which many of them had been, and as if they knew where they were going, which most of them did not. They were headed for the front, although where that was they could not have said, perhaps a day's march away or maybe a hundred miles and more. They would know soon enough.

The dust hung thickly about them. They brushed it from their eyelids. They shook it from the handkerchiefs that covered their mouths and noses. They slapped it from their pants and their

---

palatable information." But Halder's diary, OKH situation reports, and OKW's war diary contain nothing "unpalatable" about Russian power in the long months from April to September.

loose-fitting shirts. And they, too, pushed on, speaking little to each other, never singing. As they neared the Stalingrad ferries over the Volga, four divisions turned off to the left toward Chuikov's 64th Army. The other three turned to the right to join the three coming down the west side of the river and to stand with or behind the embattled 62nd.

Reinforcements were gathering. Above the Don and the bend were the 60th, 63rd, and 6th Armies, formerly the 3rd, 5th, and 6th Reserves. Within the bend were the 64th and 62nd, once the 1st and 7th Reserves. Altogether more than half a million men.

Yet, strangely, little attention is paid to them in the murky German source material and memoirs of this period or in British and American history that has drawn so heavily on what German commanders and staff officers said after the war, from which fact we may draw one of three almost incredible conclusions. Either the German High Command did not know at this late date it had run into six reserve armies (including the now destroyed 5th Tank), or it thought they were not worth talking about then or later on, or it did know and kept quiet about them, in which case there has been a massive cover-up of one of the great intelligence failures of all time. If all three possibilities appear inconceivable, none can be rejected until the full record to the extent it exists has been exposed.

The story told after the war, the only one I am aware of that addresses itself to the question, is that "during the second half of July" Halder and his associates wondered not where all the Russians were coming from—there is no mention of that—but why not more were being taken prisoner. To find out, Halder sent to the front an operations officer, Major Count Kielmannsegg, instead of his intelligence chief, Lieutenant Colonel Gehlen. At this time, according to Kielmannsegg, Halder "had no definite knowledge of enemy strengths and intentions."

Kielmannsegg brought back an uncertain report.[2] After visiting the attacking armies, he was not sure what Germany was up against but suggested one of two possibilities, both of which were

[2] Schröter, pp. 18–24. In Schröter's book the account of Kielmannsegg's mission was written by Kielmannsegg himself, who strongly suggested he visited all the attacking armies of Army Groups B and A.

responsive to Halder's question but neither one to the realities of the situation.[3] He thought:

(a) There had been strong Russian forces in the south that had managed to escape destruction in the early weeks of the campaign, in which case they would have to be reckoned with at a future date, or

(b) There had never been strong Russian forces in the south, in which case "the Russians must have large quantities of troops standing by in the Moscow area" and "these would in due course appear on the southern battlefield."

In fact, as has been seen, Russian forces were no longer "standing by" in the Moscow area "during the second half of July"; they had already appeared "on the southern battlefield," and it is difficult to understand how they could have escaped the attention of Kielmannsegg or German intelligence. Gehlen suggests they did not escape his, but he is very vague about all this, does not refer to Kielmannsegg or his mission, and confines what he, Gehlen, thought at this time to two hazy sentences:

"In my view our forces would shortly succeed in overrunning the oil fields of the Caucasus and consolidating our position on the Volga before winter set in, although we had to expect strong resistance. As early as July 12 the Russian High Command had created the Stalingrad front under Marshal Timoshenko, and on the 15th I briefed General Halder on the new Russian forces appearing in the eastern front and on agents' reports that the enemy was preparing for the determined defense of Stalingrad."[4]

The words obscure more than they illuminate. He does not reveal what he said about these "new Russian forces"—whether they were large or small, strong or weak, where they came from, or when and where they first appeared. It would seem he did not think they amounted to much.

What about Halder? For one answer we turn to Shirer's *The*

---

[3] Halder's wartime notes or diary tell a somewhat different story for he wrote as if Kielmannsegg had a more limited mission—to Army Group A only: "Maj. Count Kielmannsegg: Report on his tour to AGp. A. Graphic portrayal of the demoralization of the enemy forces as well as our own difficulties due to vehicle and fuel shortages." The date of this entry is July 26.

[4] Gehlen, p. 55.

Rise and Fall of the Third Reich, where he is quoted as having said after the war:

"Once"—Halder is imprecise about the date—"when a quite objective report was read to him [Hitler] showing that still in 1942 Stalin would be able to muster from one to one-and-a-quarter million fresh troops in the region north of Stalingrad and west of the Volga, not to mention half a million men in the Caucasus, and which provided proof that Russian output of front-line tanks amounted to at least 1,200 a month, Hitler flew at the man who was reading with clenched fists and foam in the corners of his mouth and forbade him to read any more such idiotic twaddle."

And later:

"You didn't have to have the gift of a prophet to foresee what would happen when Stalin unleashed those million and a half troops against Stalingrad and the Don flank. I pointed this out to Hitler very clearly. The result was the dismissal of the Chief of the Army General Staff."[5]

Or so he recalled it. Yet Halder, who did not hear he was going to be fired until September 9, had been fighting Russian reserves since early July. On July 23, when Paulus first rushed the 62nd Army, there were sixteen Russian reserve divisions inside or defending the north and east sides of the Don bend. At the end of the month there were forty-four in the line, and by August 23 sixty with another thirteen on the way. Indeed, before Halder was actually replaced on September 24 the Kremlin had "unleashed" 75 per cent of the forces it would send to Stalingrad. Did Gehlen know? He does not say. Did Halder know? He does not say. Did OKH so report to OKW? Did OKW ask? The answers are not to be found in the German history of the war. Nor the questions.

For all that, there was still hell to pay out on the line which at the end of July roughly followed the Don from Voronezh down to Rostov. The Russian right, behind the Don, was safe enough for it covered a direction that was not included in German plans. But the fate of the center before Stalingrad city depended upon the timely arrival of reinforcements, and the left was doomed, for no help for Malinovsky was possible. Malinovsky's south front quickly fell apart. Army Group A, strengthened by part of Hoth's

[5] Shirer, p. 917.

4th Panzer Army from Army Group B, tore over the lower Don and put Malinovsky to flight. Having opened this road to the Caucasus, the German High Command now turned Hoth to his left toward Stalingrad.[6]

But Stavka foresaw the danger before it fully developed. It sent Gen. Mikhail S. Shumilov to take over the 64th Army, leaving Chuikov as his deputy. The 64th would defend the rail line along which Hoth was approaching from the southwest. Shumilov got the four Siberian divisions that had turned off to the left at the Stalingrad crossings. To protect his left flank a new 57th Army of two divisions that had just been formed north of Stalingrad was thrown in between the 64th and the Volga.

At the same time Stavka fired Kolpakchi and put Anton Lopatin, commander of the destroyed 9th of the front-line armies, at the head of the suffering 62nd.

This, occurring on Thursday, July 30, shows what was going on when Churchill that day drafted another personal message to Stalin. Knowing nothing of Hoth's threat to Stalingrad or of the predicament of the 64th and 62nd or of Moscow's efforts to help them both, Churchill feared the Germans would reach the Caucasus, go around or over the mountain crest, seize the oil fields of the Middle East, and come out behind the embattled British 8th Army in Egypt.

[6] The shifting of part of Hoth's force from Army Group B to Army Group A and back again in late July has long been viewed by German participants and British observers as a dangerous error for which Hitler was alone responsible. Whether he was solely responsible I do not know. Whether it was an error I cannot say. But as I have sought to show in the text the fatal error—underestimation of Russian capabilities—had already been committed, although Liddell Hart, the British historian and military expert, saw it differently. In his view Timoshenko's May offensive near Kharkov had "used up the Russian reserves" and German operations were "brilliantly successful" up to the time the High Command began tampering with Hoth's force: "So widespread was the Russians' collapse in the Don-Donetz corridor that Stalingrad and control of the Volga could have been gained with ease in July if the 4th Panzer Army, advancing in that direction (along with Paulus's 6th Army), had not been diverted southward to help the 1st Panzer Army in crossing the lower Don on its way to the Caucasus. That help was not needed, whereas by the time that the 4th Panzer Army turned northward again the Russian forces . . . had begun to rally." (*Strategy*, pp. 264–65.)

"I am willing," he wired Stalin, "if you invite me, to come myself to meet you in Astrakhan, the Caucasus, or similar convenient meeting-place. We could then survey the war together and take decisions hand-in-hand. I could then tell you plans we have made with President Roosevelt for offensive action in 1942. I would bring the Chief of the Imperial General Staff [Gen. Alan Brooke] with me."[7]

The message differed in tone from the one he had sent on July 17 when he strongly implied there would be no second front that summer. Now that the decision was final he was more outgoing. Stalin would have to be told of North Africa. It would not do to let a wound fester in the allied camp. Therefore, although no British Prime Minister had been there before him, he would go to the Soviet Union—to, as he later put it, "this sullen, sinister Bolshevik state I had once tried so hard to strangle at birth." Perhaps he could soothe Russian irritation. In any event he would tell Stalin about plans for an offensive by the 8th Army out of Egypt and for an Anglo-American invasion of North Africa in October (later put off to November). And maybe—just maybe—he could stiffen Stalin's will to hold the Caucasus.

Stalin answered the next day, and he, too, was more conciliatory than he had been in his answer to the earlier message. He agreed to the visit but suggested Churchill come to Moscow "as neither I nor the members of the government and the leading men of the General Staff could leave the capital at a moment of such intense struggle with the Germans." The enemy threat to Great Britain, the United States, and the Soviet Union, he said, has "reached a special degree of intensity."[8]

It had reached a "special degree of intensity," and Stavka reacted to the threat.

First, it activated the 2nd Reserve Army, renamed it the 1st Guards, and ordered it down from the Vologda region to Moscow where it would board the trains for Stalingrad. The new 1st was a strong force made up of a veteran rifle division and five former parachute or airborne corps.

[7] Churchill, *The Hinge of Fate,* pp. 453–54.
[8] Ibid., p. 454.

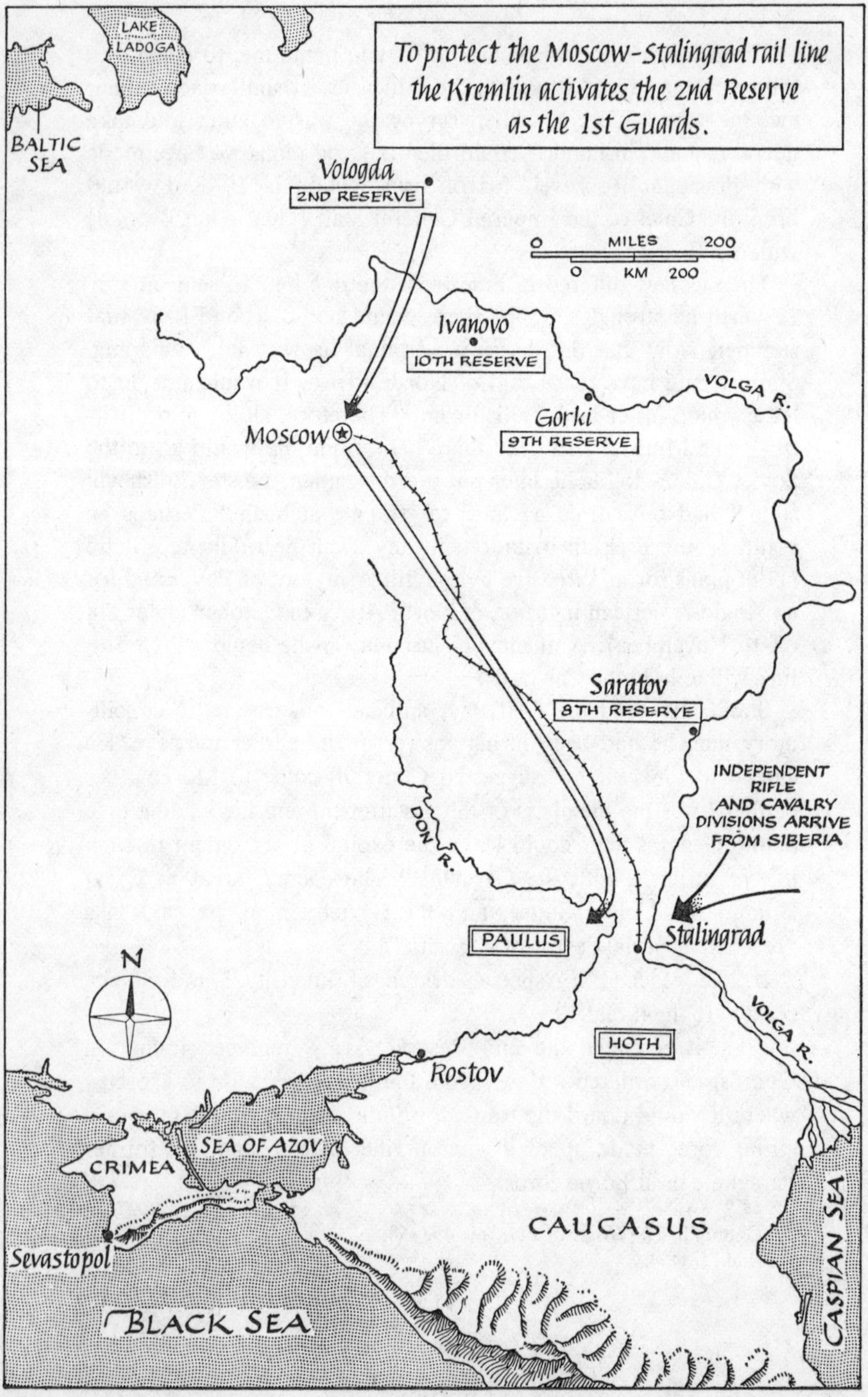

To protect the Moscow-Stalingrad rail line the Kremlin activates the 2nd Reserve as the 1st Guards.
LAKE LADOGA
BALTIC SEA
Vologda
2ND RESERVE
0 MILES 200
0 KM 200
Ivanovo
10TH RESERVE
VOLGA R.
Gorki
9TH RESERVE
Moscow
Saratov
8TH RESERVE
INDEPENDENT RIFLE AND CAVALRY DIVISIONS ARRIVE FROM SIBERIA
DON R.
Stalingrad
PAULUS
N
HOTH
VOLGA R.
Rostov
SEA OF AZOV
CRIMEA
CAUCASUS
Sevastopol
BLACK SEA
CASPIAN SEA

Then it turned some artillery and tank destroyer regiments over to Shumilov of the 64th.

Finally, to manage the 64th and the new 57th to its left, Stavka split the Stalingrad front and organized a southeast front to parry Hoth's thrust from the southwest.

First question: Who would command it?

Answer: Andrei Eremenko, who was in a Moscow hospital recovering from a severe thigh wound. Eremenko was forty-nine.

Second question: What would he do for a headquarters?

Answer: Give him Moskalenko and the staff of the young 1st Tank Army that never really got going and should be disbanded anyway.

Within a week the Russians stopped Hoth and drove him back in the first German defeat since the opening of the summer campaign. The situation was changing, slowly, but changing for all that. The closer the enemy got to Stalingrad, the less room he had for maneuver; and the farther he got from his base of supplies, the more he suffered from a shortage of fuel and ammunition.

PART THREE

1

As the reflective light of history reveals with disconcerting persistence, things are seldom what they appear to be in the present or the recent past. It is not surprising, then, that as the Battle of Stalingrad neared its climax in the second week of August they were not what they appeared to be to any one of the four towering figures of their day, each of whom caressed an illusion that would have a decisive impact on the course of the war and its aftermath. Hitler's was a conviction he was looked upon with fond favor by whatever occult forces guided the destiny of the German people. Somehow, he thought, he would overcome whatever unforeseeable difficulties lay ahead. He always had. Stalin's was a continuing belief that on his own terms, without disclosing his power to the United States and Great Britain, he could wring from his allies a landing in France, if not in 1942, then 1943. He could live with that. Churchill and Roosevelt, seeing none of the advantages and all the risks of joining what they took to be a weak Russia in a continental land war against Nazi Germany, looked mainly to North Africa. It was an extraordinary week characterized by vicious battle in the field and political drama of a high order in the allied camp.

On the ninth, a Sunday, the State Defense Committee and Stavka met exceptionally at Stalin's dacha outside of Moscow, perhaps because it had been a hot day and the Supreme was reluctant to return to the Kremlin. There was much to talk about. Churchill, then in Cairo, was arriving on Wednesday with his top military and personal advisers and W. Averell Harriman, the American Lend-Lease administrator in London. Then there were the day's battle reports to be gone over and decisions to be taken. Two sensitive areas were under scrutiny:

Stalingrad on the Russian right

Trouble. On Friday the remnants of the surrounded divisions of the 62nd Army had escaped from encirclement but on Saturday the remaining divisions were sealed off by panzers of the German 6th that met on the west side of the bridge over the Don at Kalach.

Stavka acted. To do battle with the 6th, it ordered its new 1st Guards Army, formerly the 2nd Reserve, off the trains from Moscow before it reached Stalingrad city. Then, in a reorganizing move that put Gordov's front under Eremenko's new southeast front "in an operational sense," it took command of the Guards from Golikov and gave it to Moskalenko, Eremenko's deputy. No one apparently understood what was meant by an "operational sense" but it sounded like a compromise between those officers of Stavka and the General Staff who wanted Eremenko in over-all command and those who thought it better to leave things as they were. Along with both orders went a BODO directive to the two front commanders:

BEAR IN MIND—AND THIS GOES FOR COMRADE EREMENKO AS IT DOES FOR COMRADE GORDOV— THAT DEFENSE OF STALINGRAD AND DEFEAT OF ENEMY APPROACHING STALINGRAD FROM WEST AND SOUTH ARE OF DECISIVE IMPORTANCE FOR WHOLE OF OUR SOVIET FRONT. SUPREME HIGH COMMAND ORDERS COLONEL GENERAL EREMENKO AS WELL AS LIEUTENANT GENERAL GORDOV NOT TO SPARE THEIR STRENGTH AND

NOT TO SHRINK FROM ANY SACRIFICE TO DEFEND STALINGRAD AND DESTROY ENEMY.[1]

Caucasus on the Russian left

Confused flight. On Wednesday the Germans took Stavropol, 180 miles south of Rostov. On Thursday they occupied Armavir, and on Sunday, the day of the meeting at Stalin's dacha, they seized Maikop, the first oil field in their path. While Russian troops retreated in disorder toward reserves massing behind them, commanders reported they had few tanks, no antitank mines, only ten to fifteen shells per gun, and five to seven bombs per mortar. They were short of food, fuel, and entrenching tools and handicapped by civilian refugees crowding the roads.[2]

To meet this situation Stavka released from the Moscow area for service in the Caucasus two Guards rifle corps and eleven independent rifle brigades, then cabled these instructions to Marshal Budenny of the North Caucasus front:

IN VIEW CURRENT SITUATION, MOST IMPORTANT AND DANGEROUS SECTOR FOR NORTH CAUCASUS FRONT AND BLACK SEA COAST IS FROM MAIKOP TO TUAPSE.[3] SHOULD ENEMY TROOPS REACH TUAPSE AREA, 47TH ARMY AND ALL FORCES OF FRONT EMPLOYED IN KRASNODAR REGION WOULD BE CUT OFF AND TAKEN PRISONER.

STAVKA CATEGORICALLY ORDERS YOU TO MOVE 32ND GUARDS RIFLE DIVISION IMMEDIATELY AND HAVE IT, TOGETHER WITH 236TH RIFLE DIVISION, STRADDLE MAIKOP-TUAPSE ROAD THREE OR FOUR LINES IN DEPTH. IT IS YOUR RESPONSIBILITY NOT TO ALLOW ENEMY TO REACH TUAPSE AREA UNDER ANY CIRCUMSTANCES.

77TH RIFLE DIVISION IS TO BE TRANSFERRED IMMEDIATELY FROM TAMAN AND USED PROMPTLY

---

[1] Samsonov, p. 117.
[2] Grechko, p. 62.
[3] Stavka feared an enemy rush from captured Maikop to Tuapse on the Black Sea coast.

TO REINFORCE DEFENSE OF NOVOROSSISK. DEFENSE OF TAMAN PENINSULA IS TO BE ENTRUSTED TO SHORE UNITS OF BLACK SEA FLEET.[4]

On Monday, the day after the conference at Stalin's dacha, Moskalenko drove eighty miles from Stalingrad to meet at Frolovo station the 1st Guards Army coming down from Vologda via the Moscow area. The four recently encircled divisions of the 62nd were still cut off west of the Don, and the commander, Col. Ivan P. Sologub, of a fifth division, the 112th, was killed trying to free the four.

Late that night Churchill and his party took off from Cairo on the second leg of their mission to Moscow.

Tuesday, August 11

Churchill, resting at Teheran, had lunch with the Shah.

In the Caucasus the Germans took Krasnodar, a petroleum and industrial center the defense of which, a Russian officer later complained, was complicated by the fact he had no map of the town.

In Moscow Stavka decided to send Vasilievsky the next day to iron out command problems in the Stalingrad area.

Wednesday, August 12

Shortly before five o'clock in the afternoon three American B-24s, which were among the heaviest and latest bombers in the American arsenal, flew low over Moscow with an unexpected roar. Coming in from the southeast, they passed six hundred feet over the Kremlin towers, banked to the right, and headed for the city's central airport in the northern part of town. What was *this* all about? Stalin knew. It was Winston Leonard Spencer Churchill arriving secretly as planned, but people in the streets looked up in astonishment. Russian planes never flew over the Kremlin, and there had not been a German raid since late April.[5]

---

[4] Grechko, p. 78.

[5] Although Churchill's visit was not made public until after his departure, Russian censorship was so tight and the government's control over communications so complete that no special effort was made to conceal his presence. After the war it was said that German intelligence had an agent in Moscow whose cover name was Max, but, although Gehlen and Halder had some confidence in Max, there is no evidence he signaled Churchill's arrival,

A half hour or so later a line of black limousines came slowly down Gorki Street, Moscow's busiest thoroughfare, and turned into Manezhnaya Square between the red brick walls of the Kremlin and the old American Embassy. I was standing on that corner by the National Hotel and in the back seat of the first car recognized Molotov, Russia's impassive Foreign Minister, who like all of the Kremlin mighty was rarely seen in public. Next to him, smoking a freshly lit cigar, sat Churchill. Churchill, who wore a dark business suit and a gray hat pressed squarely on his head, was looking about him with the eager curiosity of a tourist. Significantly, Harriman, the American, rode in one of the following cars, his trip having been arranged by Churchill, at Harriman's request or suggestion, the week before.

"I should greatly like to have your aid and countenance in my talks with Joe," Churchill had wired Roosevelt from Cairo. "Would you be able to let Averell come with me? I have a somewhat raw job. Kindly duplicate your reply to London. Am keeping my immediate movements vague."[6]

---

and there is reason to believe he was a phony or a dupe or an agent who was caught and turned around against his employers. I lean to the third possibility because on the two occasions when Max's reports appear in the published German record the information they contained was totally false. One, dated July 13 and passed on to Halder by Gehlen on the fifteenth, told of a "council of war" allegedly held that day and attended by Stalin, Molotov, Voroshilov, Shaposhnikov as "Chief of the General Staff," and an American, a British, and a Chinese liaison officer (*Kriegstagebuch des Oberkommandos der Wehrmacht*, Vol. II, p. 1238). For what the Germans thought of this report, see Carell, p. 532: "The Soviet General Staff had made it clear to Stalin that he could not afford any more battles like Kiev and Vyazma (1941)—in other words, that holding on at all costs was out. Stalin had accepted their view. He endorsed the decision of the Great General Staff which was expounded by Shaposhnikov at the meeting of July 13. The Soviet troops would withdraw to the Volga and into the Caucasus; there they would offer resistance, forcing the Germans to spend the coming winter in inhospitable territory. All key industries would be evacuated to the Urals and to Siberia. From the middle of July the German General Staff had known from an agent's report about this important meeting, but Hitler had regarded it as a canard." It was a canard. No American, British, or Chinese officer ever attended a Kremlin council of war. Vasilievsky, not Shaposhnikov, was Chief of the General Staff on July 13. And Russian strategy then as before was not to withdraw until compelled to do so.

[6] *Roosevelt and Churchill*, p. 231.

Roosevelt, who had said no to Harriman once, gave in. He replied the same day:

"I am asking Harriman to leave [London] at the earliest possible moment for Moscow. I think your idea is sound, and I am telling Stalin Harriman will be at his and your disposal to help in any way."[7]

At Stalin's disposal? At Churchill's? Or as a representative of the United States? Harriman received no instructions.

He later recalled he wanted to go to Moscow to "vouch for the combined decision to abandon Sledgehammer and invade North Africa." He wrote: "My concern was that Stalin would not believe a word of what Churchill was telling him. He would think that the British alone had blocked the second front."[8]

They had blocked it "alone." As late as July 31 Marshall and King, back from London, had tried to persuade the President to reverse the North African decision, and the President, now going along with Churchill, had turned them down in what Sherwood called "one of the very few major military decisions of the war which Roosevelt made entirely on his own and over the protests of his highest-ranking advisers."[9]

Now, because of Harriman's presence, Churchill for better or worse would deal with Stalin in the name of both governments, a most unusual diplomatic arrangement and in this instance one of questionable wisdom because the Americans and British did not see eye to eye on all matters that would come up at the conference or in any private Churchill-Stalin talks that would be held in Harriman's absence. One such matter stands out.

As has been seen, the American Chiefs of Staff now believed the invasion of North Africa excluded not only a landing in France in 1942 but full-scale invasion of France in 1943; and although Churchill knew this,[10] he did not say so or hint of any doubt about 1943 in speaking to Stalin. On the contrary, as spokesman for

[7] Ibid., p. 232.
[8] Harriman, p. 146.
[9] Sherwood, p. 615.
[10] Message from Dill to the Prime Minister August 1, 1942: "In the American mind, Round-up in 1943 is excluded by acceptance of Torch. We need not argue about that. A one-track mind on Torch is what we want at present. . . ." (Churchill, *The Hinge of Fate*, p. 451.)

both governments he "gave Stalin to understand" (Churchill's words) that the great attack would indeed come in 1943. Stalin, though unhappy about the delay, was satisfied.

"This marked the turning point in our conversation," Churchill later reported. It also marked the beginning of a misunderstanding that would deepen with the passage of time.

*

Churchill was so eager to see Stalin on his first day in Moscow that he barely had time for a bath and a bite of supper before he was on his way to the Kremlin accompanied by Harriman and the British ambassador, Clark-Kerr, but not the American ambassador, Admiral Standley, King's predecessor as Chief of Naval Operations. There, where they were met by Stalin, Molotov, and Voroshilov, three old Bolsheviks who had been through a lot together, the formalities were brief, about long enough for the Prime Minister to note that while he was only five feet six he was a half inch taller than Stalin. About seven o'clock Stalin indicated with a wave of his hand that Churchill had the floor. This was all right with Churchill. Although he had been up since dawn and on the plane from Teheran for ten and a half hours, he was ready for the fray. Superb salesman that he was, he knew what he would say and how he would say it. He would show his wares one by one, first the bad news, then the good news. He would make each point sound somewhat better than it was and save to the last the thought he believed would be most pleasing to his Russian host.

Churchill built his case skillfully. Refraining from any mention of North Africa, he said that while a small landing in France that year was possible it would "greatly injure" full-scale invasion that was being prepared for 1943. A "million" American troops would arrive in Britain. The "big transportation" would come in October, November, and December. By spring there would be twenty-seven American and twenty-one British divisions in England, nearly half of them armored.

In the beginning Stalin listened attentively, then became "restless." Now he opened up. His view of war was different. A man who was not prepared to take risks could not win. Why were the Americans and British so "afraid" of the Germans?

The time had come to reveal the plans for North Africa. Churchill explained Torch in detail.

When? Stalin wanted to know.

"Not later than October 30, but the President and all of us are trying to pull it forward to October 7."[11]

More questions. Churchill argued on:

"If North Africa were won this year, we could make a deadly attack upon Hitler next year."[12]

"Could make," not "would make." The words may have been carefully chosen. There was still no promise in the matter.

Now for his trump card, one Churchill and the President had been looking at for a month with increasing enthusiasm. The United States and Britain, he said, were exploring the possibility of sending an air force to the Caucasus after Rommel was defeated in Egypt. How would Stalin receive such a suggestion? "Gratefully," said Stalin, obscuring for the time being what he really thought, which was that he would not allow it.[13]

After that first meeting Churchill went to bed "with the feeling that at least the ice was broken and a human contact established,"[14] but not before first suggesting to Harriman that much as he valued his presence in Moscow it would be better if Harriman stayed away from the Kremlin the next day.[15] For a reason that is not entirely clear he wanted to talk to Stalin out of American earshot. Perhaps he proposed to "promise" him a second front in 1943, which he evidently did two days later when he saw Stalin alone.[16] In any event he hoped to go to the Kremlin accompanied only by Sir Alexander Cadogan, the Permanent Under-Secretary of the Foreign Office, Brooke, the C.I.G.S., Sir Archibald P. Wa-

[11] Churchill, *The Hinge of Fate*, p. 481. Unavoidable delays put off the invasion until November 8.

[12] Ibid., p. 482.

[13] See pp. 109–11 below.

[14] Churchill, *The Hinge of Fate*, p. 483.

[15] Harriman, p. 155. In his memoirs Churchill did not refer to this incident. All he recalled was that Molotov asked whether he wished to bring Harriman to the second session and that he said yes.

[16] This was Brooke's understanding. See Bryant, *The Turn of the Tide*, p. 433.

vell, the commander of the British army in India, and Sir Arthur William Tedder, who headed the Royal Air Force in the Middle East.

Stalin would have none of it. Just as Harriman was sitting down the next evening to a lonely supper in the guest house where he was staying the Prime Minister called to say Stalin insisted Harriman attend.[17] Accordingly, Churchill, Cadogan, Brooke, Wavell, Tedder, and Harriman soon found themselves at the Kremlin discussing not what Churchill had in mind, whatever that was, but Sledgehammer vs. Torch, for the initiative was Stalin's and he handed out a memorandum that argued against Torch and for Sledgehammer, a meaningful document that began: "It will be easily understood that the Soviet command built their plan of summer and autumn operations calculating on the creation of a Second Front in Europe in 1942." And so originated a myth somewhat akin to the stab-in-the-back claim that was widely believed in Germany after 1918, except that this was more subtle and, to Russians, more compelling because its target was London and Washington and not the home front.

Churchill and Harriman were taken aback. They did not explore the claim or seek to contest its substance. They might have said: "No, we do not 'easily' understand what you are saying. What plan of operations? We know of none. In what ways did you count on a second front in Europe this year? What would you have done differently if you had known differently? You asked for a second front. We tried to give you one and found we could not. But from beginning to end you have kept us in the dark. You have told us nothing about your forces or plans. You have told us nothing of what you know of German forces or plans. Under the circumstances, any suggestion of bad faith on our part is unacceptable. To this day we have no idea what is going on at the front or even where it is. If even now, at this late date, you want a coordinated war against Nazi Germany, let us know and we will get down to business." Instead, still believing in Russian weakness and German power, they contested only the justice of the Soviet claim. They based their position on the British aide-mémoire handed to Molotov in June and said in effect that if the Russians had counted

[17] Harriman, p. 155.

on a second front in 1942 it was their own fault because the British had told them in no uncertain terms there could be no "promise" in the matter. It was another missed opportunity. Once again, as in the spring, no one put to the Kremlin the hard questions. How many divisions do you have? How many on the line? How many in reserve? Stalin volunteered nothing.

A standoff. Stalin needled Churchill and Churchill dug in his heels, warning that the decision in favor of Torch was final and Russian reproaches were vain.

And now came a change in Russian tactics. Having brought the conference almost to the breaking point, Stalin shifted gears. If the hot breath of anger and disdain would not work, he would try the cool breeze of courtesy and reinforce it with a whiff of trust in his British ally. He sought to convince Churchill the Red Army was stronger than he realized (no specifics of course). He offered to put on a demonstration of his secret rocket weapons, called Guards mortars by the Russians, that Churchill and Harriman took to be trench mortars, which they were not. He agreed to a meeting the next day of British and Russian generals. Taking advantage of the new mood, Churchill asked about the Caucasus, a major British concern.

Would Stalin defend them? With how many divisions? Brooke listened intently. On his flight from Teheran he had looked out of the window to see what kind of defenses there were before Baku and was troubled by what he saw: a working party of a hundred men and two horse-drawn wagons and one half-completed anti-tank ditch, otherwise not a man, gun, truck, tank, or weapon of any kind.

Would Russia defend the Caucasus? Certainly, said Stalin. With how many divisions? Twenty-five.

Brooke did not believe him, though Stalin had more than he disclosed—not twenty-five divisions but twenty-nine rifle and eight cavalry divisions, fifteen rifle and eight tank brigades.[18] And on the way from Central Russia were the two Guards rifle corps and eleven rifle brigades released from the strategic reserve the Sunday before. In short, two days of talks at the summit had done nothing

[18] Russia's true strength in the Caucasus is shown in a careful reading of Grechko.

to dispel Russian suspicion of the British or British distrust of the Russians, for even as Stalin understated his strength, Brooke thought he exaggerated it, and on this note the formal work of the conference ended. There remained only a banquet at the Kremlin Friday night and Churchill's farewell to Stalin on Saturday.

Meanwhile, battle raged in the Stalingrad area. On Friday the 62nd Army reported: "No new information has been received from the 33rd Guards and the 181st, 147th and 229th Rifle Divisions. Some small units have crossed to the east bank of the Don in the sectors of the 112th and 131st Divisions."[19] On the same day there was a strong German attack on the 4th Tank Army to the right of the 62nd. The 4th's command post at Rodionov was overrun about noon, which forced the Russians to throw in part of their still-arriving 1st Guards—two divisions to the left of the 4th, one division to the right.

This, to be sure, was known to the Russians but not to Churchill's party and members of the American and British Embassy staffs when they arrived at the Kremlin for the Friday evening banquet. Churchill, apparently in something of a fury because of Stalin's attitude of the evening before, came wearing a suit of blue coveralls; and if there was any question about his mood, he soon dispelled it. To the astonishment of all, he remained slumped in his chair when the British ambassador stood up and proposed a toast to Stalin. His Majesty's ambassador, he said coldly, should have toasted Molotov, the minister to whom he was accredited.

It was an awkward evening with toasts in Russian fashion to everyone and everything until at 1:30 Churchill, now tired, decided he had had enough. He got up, said good-by, and was some distance down the crowded room when Stalin came hurrying after him. This would not do. The new tactics called for unimpeachable manners. Stalin accompanied his guest "an immense distance through corridors and staircases" to the front door, where they shook hands.

Saturday was another difficult day in the Stalingrad region. At 4:20 A.M., not long after the banquet of the night before, Stalin sent a blistering message to Eremenko, who by this time had full command of his own southeast front and Gordov's Stalingrad

[19] Samsonov, p. 124.

front: Get help to the surrounded divisions—you have the strength and means and to rescue them is a matter of honor—break through the enemy's lines—bring them out. Eremenko was still trying when at seven o'clock that evening Churchill, without Harriman and alone except for a British interpreter, went around to the Kremlin to take his leave.

"We had a useful and important talk," he wrote later without going into details. Once again he asked about the Caucasus. Could Russia hold the mountain passes? Could it prevent the Germans from reaching the Caspian Sea, taking the oil fields around Baku, and driving southward through Iran or Turkey?

"We shall stop them," said Stalin. "They will not cross the mountains."

It was eight o'clock, time for the Prime Minister to go, but Stalin was not finished. He had not yet been "promised" a second front in 1943. He invited Churchill to his private apartment, where they had drinks and supper and sat around talking until 2:30 in the morning, much longer than they had in Harriman's presence on Wednesday and Thursday put together.

About what? Small talk in part but matters of substance, too, as Churchill told London and Washington: ". . . Stalin . . . revealed to me other solid reasons for his confidence, including a counteroffensive on a great scale . . . and . . . he gave me a full account of the Russian position, which seems very encouraging."

Did he?

"We have bowed and scraped to them, done all we could for them, and never asked for a single fact or figure concerning their production, strength, dispositions, etc.," Brooke told his diary before leaving Moscow.[20] Commenting on his daily notes at a later date, he wrote: "During the whole course of the war I never received a Russian order of battle showing their dispositions." Finally, in the published record of their wartime correspondence there is no message from Churchill in which he passed on to Roosevelt this "full account of the Russian position," nor did Churchill in his memoirs disclose what that position was as he heard it. In sum, it would seem that Stalin, secretive as always, did

[20] Bryant, *The Turn of the Tide*, p. 378.

not think it necessary or advisable to lay his cards on the table and that Churchill still thought he had none worth exposing.

What else did they talk about?

Almost certainly about a second front, and almost certainly Churchill, reversing his field though he got nothing in return, gave Stalin a promise in the matter for 1943. He did not so report to Roosevelt (according to their published correspondence) nor to Harriman (to judge from Harriman's memoirs), but he so told Brooke in a private conversation more than two months later, in early December.[21]

And on this strange note the summit conference ended. At six o'clock on Sunday morning, August 16, the Prime Minister, Harriman, and the others left Moscow in a rainstorm, a half hour before the following report was entered in the war diary of the 62nd Army:

"Have not succeeded in establishing communications with 33rd Guards and 181st, 147th and 229th Rifle Divisions. They do not answer radio calls; they do not appear to be receiving."[22]

Yet for all his unawareness of what was going on at the front—for all the inconvenience and effort and the haggling and the strain and pain of negotiating in awkward circumstances—Churchill considered his trip successful. He was "sure," he promptly told Roosevelt and the War Cabinet in London, only he "personally" could have brought the disappointing news of North Africa instead of France "without leading to a really serious drifting apart." The Russians, having made their protest, were "entirely friendly."[23] Words of praise poured in. King George VI congratulated him. Gen. Jan Christiaan Smuts of South Africa spoke of his "really great achievement." "Your introduction of air assistance for Caucasus was a shrewd point," wrote Smuts, "and well worth pursuing with Roosevelt."

But Churchill's visit had an immediate and inauspicious aftermath of which he was unaware. Two or three days after his departure, on Tuesday, August 18, or Wednesday, August 19, Stalin turned his attention to the Caucasus as if Churchill's and Brooke's

[21] Ibid., p. 433.
[22] Samsonov, pp. 124–25.
[23] Churchill, *The Hinge of Fate,* p. 502.

searching questions had set him to thinking. On one of these two evenings (the day is not clear in Shtemenko's account), Col. Sergei M. Shtemenko, who became Chief of the General Staff after the war, and Col. K. F. Vasilchenko, both of the operations department, were summoned to the Kremlin to attend their first session of Stavka.[24] Present besides Stalin were Molotov, Georgi M. Malenkov, and Anastas I. Mikoyan, all members of the Politburo and State Defense Committee. Also present were F. E. Bokov, commissar of the General Staff, who sat in for Vasilievsky when Vasilievsky was away at the front, Bodin, head of the operations department since the recall of Timoshenko from the Stalingrad front and his own recall as Timoshenko's Chief of Staff, and Fedorenko of the armored forces directorate. The subject under discussion was the Caucasus, Shtemenko's specialty.

What was the situation down there? What could be done about it? Shtemenko laid it on the line. Like Brooke he was unhappy about the defenses on the road from Makhachkala along the west bank of the Caspian to Baku. He was also uneasy about the measures that had been taken to block the passes over the mountain range. So evidently was Stalin though not entirely for the same reason.

"Keep an eye on Baku," he told Bodin. And later: "When you go down there, take this colonel with you."

Bodin and Shtemenko left the following Saturday, curiously just one day after Beria, the head of the NKVD and a member of both the Politburo and the State Defense Committee. Lavrenti P. Beria, like Stalin, was born in the Caucasus. Having served for a while as secretary of the Communist party in Transcaucasia, he looked on the area as his personal province, and one of his men, Gen. Ivan Maslennikov, commanded all military and police forces around Mozdok, Ordzhonikidze, Makhachkala, and Baku.

Arriving at Tbilisi (Tiflis), the capital of Georgia, about midnight, Bodin and Shtemenko went directly to the headquarters of Gen. I. V. Tyulenev, the commander of the Transcaucasian front (Budenny had the North Caucasus front). There they explained their mission, which was to speed the mobilization of reserves and

[24] Shtemenko, pp. 56–58.

otherwise strengthen the mountain passes. Against the Germans only? On leaving, Bodin turned to Tyulenev:

"Do you know our allies are trying to take advantage of the tough situation on our front to wring from us agreement to the entry of British troops in Transcaucasia?"

Tyulenev did not know. Bodin went on:

"That of course will not be allowed. The State Defense Committee considers the defense of Transcaucasia a state task of the highest importance, and it is our responsibility to take all measures necessary to repulse the attack of the enemy, bleed him white and annihilate him. The hopes of Hitler and the lust of the allies must be buried."

It would seem that some such thought as this was running through Stalin's mind on the night he told Churchill and Harriman he would "welcome" an Anglo-American air force in the south. But then he was careful. He did not yet have the promise he sought for 1943.

Mutual distrust and suspicion die hard. They were alive and kicking in the allied camp as the German High Command gathered its strength in the second and third week of August for a knockout blow to the east.[25]

[25] As late as 1971 Marshal Grechko, the Soviet Minister of Defense, referred to the allied offer and its rejection by Russia in the following terms: "But the Soviet Union had no use for such 'assistance' and it was not long before London and Washington realized the Soviet Government would never agree to the plan 'Velvet,' which was nothing more than a plan for the occupation of the Caucasus. . . . And so, at the most crucial phase of the fighting on the Soviet-German front the allies, being more concerned with weakening the Soviet Union than genuinely assisting it, were conniving behind the back of the Soviet Government." (See the Moscow-published, English-language version of his book, *Bitva za Kavkaz,* pp. 86–87.) He of course said nothing about the Russian power Stalin concealed from Roosevelt and Churchill. As for operation Velvet, be it noted it was never rejected by the Kremlin in so many words. It died for want of an answer out of Moscow.

2

On August 16, the day Churchill left Moscow to return to London by way of Cairo, there was an intriguing development at the headquarters of the German High Command, which was housed in two compounds near the village of Strishevka ten miles north of Vinnitsa. Here on the Zhitomir road, surrounded by barbed wire and mine fields, Hitler and his closest associates, including Gen. Wilhelm Keitel, the chief of OKW, and Gen. Alfred Jodl, the head of his operations staff,[1] lived and worked in mobile barracks, huts, log cabins, and blockhouses, and here the Fuehrer held the situation conferences to which Halder, coming out from his OKH command post in Vinnitsa, reported at noon each day. On that Sunday Hitler in Halder's presence worried about his extended left flank on the middle Don. What if the Russians mounted a major counteroffensive toward Rostov in the south in an effort to cut off all German forces in the Stalingrad and Caucasus directions?

What, indeed? The Fuehrer had few reserves, and with 6th Army and 4th Panzer collecting their strength for an early thrust to Stalingrad city the protective line of the Don was of vital impor-

[1] Keitel and Jodl were among Nazi leaders hanged for war crimes at Nuremberg on October 16, 1946.

tance. It was thinly held now by the 2nd Hungarian Army (Col. Gen. Gustav von Jany) on the left, a newly arrived Italian 8th (Col. Gen. Italo Garibaldi) in the center, and 11th Corps of 6th Army on the right.

A Russian counteroffensive? For the first time, according to the surviving record, there was concern about Russian power, about reserves that were thought to be insignificant before the campaign, about reserves that were appearing on the middle Don and before 6th Army and 4th Panzer. Other questions come to mind. What did Halder tell Hitler and when did he tell him? What did Hitler know and when did he know it? We cannot be sure, for so many German records of so much of 1942, including OKW's war diary (*Kriegstagebuch*), were destroyed in 1945, the day after Hitler committed suicide and seven days before the end of the war, and the evidence in the documents that have been preserved is slim, tantalizing, and partly negative.

We have Halder's daily notes to himself which contain only brief and occasional references to Russian capabilities and intentions, as if he were so aware of them he felt no need to write them down or thought them of little interest or considered it more prudent not to call attention to an intelligence failure of which he was as guilty as the Fuehrer. Halder kept them in shorthand for his personal use.

We have OKH situation reports (*Lageberichte*) from January 1 to February 6 and from May 1 to December 31. These reports went to Strishevka each day for inclusion in OKW's war diary, but they, too, spoke rarely of Russian operations. The copies we have were saved by the German navy.

We have stenographic notes summarizing the discussions (*Lagevortrage*) that opened the situation conferences at OKW for the period August 12 to December 31 but none for fourteen days in September, eleven in October, three in November, and twelve in December. These notes were taken down by Helmut Greiner, the OKW war diarist, who significantly did not attend the conferences himself but received what he recorded from Gen. Walter Warlimont, Jodl's deputy. Greiner says that on orders from Gen. August Winter, Warlimont's successor, he turned over the typed war diary to Heinrich Himmler's SS police troops and that the diary, which included the *Lageberichte* and *Lagevortrage,* was burned on May 1, 1945, at Hintersee, a village five miles from Berchtesgaden.

Finally, for the period February 7 to March 31 we have only Halder's diary and for April only Halder and the situation summaries prepared by Col. Walter Scherff's historical section.

This is relatively thin stuff, only a fraction of what existed, yet it tells an entirely different story from the one that has come down to us in the recollections of German generals and staff officers. According to their memoirs and the information they vouched for after the war, they constantly warned Hitler of Russian power and he would not listen to them.

Gehlen:

"As our armies, principally the 6th Army under General Paulus, advanced farther and farther toward Stalingrad that summer, General Halder and I had cast anxious eyes on the lengthening left flank along the Don, and Halder repeatedly warned of the possibility that Moscow would launch a counterattack on this flank, most probably across that part of the Don that extended between the Khoper tributary and the great bend at Kremenskaya, for this sector was held not by hardened German forces but by our Romanian allies."[2]

Perhaps. But there is no indication of any such warning in Halder's diary and no reference to possible danger from that quarter in OKH situation reports. Furthermore, there were no Romanian allies in that sector until mid-September when Hitler ordered them there.

In any event, according to Greiner's wartime notes, Hitler at his situation conference on August 16 directed that 22nd Panzer Division, which was supporting 6th Army, be transferred to back the Italian 8th on the middle Don. At the same time he ordered two infantry divisions, the 294th and 298th, out of the Caucasus for eventual use in the same area.

This was only the beginning. See Halder's diary:

August 17

"Fuehrer report: Discussion of the projected formation of a Romanian Army Group on both sides of Stalingrad."

[2] Gehlen, p. 55.

August 18

"General Hauffe (Bucharest): We discuss the planned formation of a Romanian Army Group on the Don and Volga."

Hitler was not only worried but alarmingly so, for when he heard on the twenty-third, according to Greiner's *Lagevortrage,* that 22nd Panzer had sent only a brigade to the middle Don he insisted on the immediate transfer of the entire division.

Why? He knew now the Russians were stronger than he had thought in the beginning. Was he beginning to suspect they were still stronger than he had come to believe? That he had made a mistake in penetrating so deeply into the Russian heartland? Or was it the heat which Keitel and Warlimont thought had something to do with the fury that gripped him from late August on?

Warlimont[3]

"The summer sky was cloudless, the heat stifling, and Hitler, one was given to understand, was particularly affected by it. This probably contributed to the disagreements and explosions which reached an unprecedented height in the weeks and months which followed."

Keitel[4]

"His unbearable irritability had to a great extent been brought on by the hot, continental climate at Vinnitsa, which he could not stand and which literally went to his head, as Professor [Theodor] Morell[5] several times explained to me. Medicaments were useless against it, and even the permanent humidifying installation in his bunker and in the conference chamber only temporarily alleviated his discomfort."

If not the heat, were Hitler's concern and anxiety brought on by a feeling he was inadequately informed about the true situation at the front? The generals give no hint of that.

"Almost every day," wrote Keitel in his Nuremberg cell a month before he was hanged, "Halder was waiting with new statistics on the formations still available to the enemy as a strategic reserve and on the enemy's tank and spare parts (data provided by

---

[3] Warlimont, p. 246.
[4] Keitel, pp. 182–83.
[5] Hitler's personal physician.

General Thomas[6]) and on the capacity of the enemy's armaments industry in the Urals (Thomas again) and so on; again and again the Fuehrer was provoked to refute the statistics."[7]

If so, one wonders why Halder never told his diary about his warnings and why there is no reference to them in any of the situation reports he sent to OKW (barring what may have been included in those of July 12 and August 2, which are missing).

What did Halder say about the Russians? Here are the pertinent extracts from his diary as translated by the historical section of the United States Army:

July 6

"The actual picture of the enemy situation is not yet clear to me. There are two possibilities. Either we have overestimated the enemy's strength and the offensive has completely smashed him, or the enemy is conducting a planned disengagement or at least is trying to do so in order to forestall being irretrievably beaten in 1942."

July 10

"It is not clear whether the enemy Reserve Armies appearing in our radio picture are intended for the buildup of a Don defense line and the attempted bolstering of the northern wing against 40th Corps. . . . Enemy situation on the east bank [of the Don] is obscure."

July 19

The enemy is making "efforts to form a grouping of forces for the protection of Stalingrad."

July 21

"Paulus (6th Army) is advancing at a promising rate in the direction of Stalingrad, where the enemy is trying to form a concentration with troops now being moved in from the northwest by rail and on trucks."

(From now on, there is a change in tone in the diary—little that is specific but a change that is sufficiently strong to enable one to

---

[6] Gen. Georg Thomas was head of the economic warfare department at OKW from October 1, 1942, on.
[7] Keitel, p. 183.

infer that Halder was beginning to realize what he was up against. For example, he blew up on the twenty-third, apparently because Hitler, according to Greiner, decided that day to take the SS Panzer Grenadier Grossdeutschland Division out of action on the eastern front and send it to France. The outburst has often been cited by military historians as an indication of Halder's true feelings throughout the campaign, but he never repeated it, nor did he explain it now.)

July 23

"This continual underestimation of the enemy is gradually becoming both ludicrous and dangerous. It is becoming more and more intolerable. It is impossible to do serious work. The hallmark of this so-called 'leadership' is a pathological reaction to the impressions of the moment and complete misconception of the mechanism of command and its limitations."

July 26

"Maj. Count Kielmannsegg: Report on his tour of AGp. A [Army Group A under Wilhelm List that had just taken Rostov and was moving on the Caucasus]. Graphic portrayal of the demoralization of the enemy as well as our own difficulties due to vehicle and fuel shortages."

August 2

"Lt. Col. Gehlen: Computation of enemy strength and newly activated Armored units—in July, 54 new Infantry Divisions and 56 new Armored Divisions."

(This is a fascinating entry, for Halder did not comment on the figures which were so much higher than anything foreseen at the onset of the campaign, nor were they included in the routine situation reports that went to OKW, nor did Gehlen mention them years later. In the German edition of Halder's diary for the next day, however, a report, which is presumed to be the one referred to on August 2, is published in full with the notation: "[Notiz:] Dem Führer vorgetragen 3. 8. 1942 [Delivered to the Fuehrer August 3, 1942]." But what Hitler thought of it or whether he discussed it with Halder or what Halder thought of it may never be known. Greiner's notes for this period as well as his typed reports are said to have been destroyed. The substance of the August 2 estimate was that the Russians might bring in another thirty rifle divisions before winter but that they were losing tanks as fast as they could be produced or brought in from the United States and Great Britain. Incidentally, Halder, or his German editor, evidently made a mistake in writing of 56 armored divisions [*"56 neue Pz. Div."*]. The document of the next day says 56 armored brigades [*"56 neue Pz. Brig."*].)

August 9

"Lt. Col. Gehlen: Computation of enemy forces still available."

(Halder did not say what this "computation" showed, nor was it mentioned in the situation report, nor did Gehlen later refer to it.)

August 12

"Enemy reinforcements on Hoth's front."

(These reinforcements would have been the four Siberian divisions, the two divisions of the new 57th Army to the left of the Russian 64th, and some artillery and tank-destroyer regiments from Stavka's reserve.)

August 17

"Hoth's and Paulus's attacks are making good strides. Front against Paulus has been reinforced with good troops."

(These "good troops" would have been the recently activated 1st Guards Army and six independent rifle divisions from the reserve, three of them from Siberia.)

This is about all Halder put down about the Russians for his eyes only, but what he told Hitler remains uncertain and none of it is to be found in the OKH situation reports which were vague documents that up to this time identified Russian units on only three occasions: 8th Cavalry Corps on July 3, 16th Tank Corps on July 5, and 62nd Army and 1st Tank on August 12 (1st Tank was dissolved on August 6).

It is clear, however, that on August 16 and from then on and for whatever the reason—the heat, what he knew, or what he was coming to suspect or fear—Hitler was a disturbed man, disturbed enough to engage in violent disagreement with his generals but not to call off the campaign. A gambler who believed in his star, he would go for Stalingrad anyway with Paulus's 6th Army attacking from the west and Hoth's 4th Panzer from the southwest.

*

Meanwhile, Stalin and Stavka went on fighting the war in their own secretive way and according to a plan that had taken shape after July 23 when the German 6th first crashed into the Russian 62nd in the Don bend. From then to August 22 they reinforced the Stalingrad area with ten divisions and sent fifteen more to harass the German left flank on the middle Don, actions that have been viewed in some Western accounts of the war as less responsive to military considerations than to emotional urges on Stalin's part brought on by the fact his name was associated with the region. But although it is true that no city, mountain, river line, or geographical obstacle of any kind is of strategic importance in itself, Stalingrad played a meaningful role in the Russian scheme of things. The aim was the destruction of German forces, and the place to give battle was wherever conditions were most advantageous for the Red Army. They were considered most advantageous around Stalingrad because it was the hub of a communications network and because it could be supplied and defended and was suitable for counterattack. Besides, this was good holding country, which was important to the Russians who were not yet sure whether the Germans intended to go all out for the city or with Paulus's 6th Army swing north over the Don in a stab at Moscow's deep rear.

Accordingly, as it watched and waited for the enemy to show his hand, Stavka held the 8th, 9th, and 10th Reserves at Saratov, Gorki, and Ivanovo and fought to pin down German forces far away to prevent their transfer to the critical area. It attacked on the middle Don and west of Moscow and authorized for action southwest of the capital its strongest formation. This was the uncommitted 3rd Tank at Kozelsk, the only reserve tank army available after the destruction of the 5th in early July.[8]

Paulus of the German 6th slowed his attack. In the third week

---

[8] Third Tank went to battle with Zhukov's forces on August 11. It did not fight at Stalingrad.

of August he smashed two divisions of the 62nd in the little elbow of the Don,[9] hammered at 4th Tank to his left, and roughed up the arriving regiments of the Guards. But the appearance of the Guards on each side of 4th Tank and the approach of other Russian reinforcements led him to look for a softer spot some miles to the south. Objective—Stalingrad, and he liked what he saw on the Don from Panshino down to Vertyachi and Peskovatka. He especially liked what he saw around Vertyachi, and I can understand why because I visited this farming and fishing village on the east bank of the river in the summer of 1972.[10] Here a gunner on the steep cliffs of the west bank, which are cut by ravines that are passable for tanks and trucks, looks down the throat of a Vertyachi defender only a hundred yards away. At Vertyachi bulrushes run from the water's edge to high wicker fences around the houses and barns. Behind the houses tilled land rises gently to a ridge line about three miles to the east, and beyond the ridge line there is open, undulating country all the way to Stalingrad and the Volga thirty-four miles away.

Regrouping, Paulus on the nineteenth issued orders for the assault:

"The enemy will defend the Stalingrad area stubbornly. He holds the high ground on the east bank of the Don and west of Stalingrad and has built defensive positions there in great depth.

"It must be assumed he has assembled forces, including armored brigades, ready to counter-attack, both in the Stalingrad area and in the area north of the isthmus between Don and Volga.

"Therefore in the advance across the Don toward Stalingrad the Army must reckon with enemy resistance in front and with heavy counter-attacks against the northern flank of our advance.

"It is possible that the annihilating blows struck during the past

---

[9] *Pa Dorogam Boivoi Slavi,* a Volgograd guidebook to the battlefield that was published in 1971, reads: "Here at Podgorski, Khmelevski and Zimovski khutors [isolated farms] on the steep bank of the Don the remnants of the 192nd and 184th Divisions fought to the last. Very little is known of these units. Try to learn more [from the peasants] as you go."

[10] The Great Bend of the Don and the area immediately east of it are under military control to this day. To visit this region I needed for every village a separate military visa good for a specified day and then only if accompanied by an officer. So did my Moscow guide, Colonel Plotnikov.

weeks will have destroyed the enemy's means of fighting a defensive action."[11]

On the twenty-second, infantry widened the bridgehead, and now under cover of darkness and a thin mist that hung over the river, Paulus shoved in his battering ram. It was Gustav von Wietersheim's 14th Panzer Corps, which consisted of 16th Panzer and the 3rd and 60th Motorized Divisions.

With first light on Sunday the twenty-third the 14th struck in a move that rocked the Kremlin.

[11] Schröter, p. 24.

3

In the files of the Soviet Ministry of Defense at Podolsk there are documents that explain how 14th Panzer Corps broke out of its bridgehead along the Don and raced thirty-four miles cross-country from the ridge line behind Vertyachi to the Volga and the northern suburbs of Stalingrad. They have not been published and they may never be, for there are matters official historians pass over in silence and this evidently is one of them. It is not that the Germans in a burst of explosive energy cut the Russian armies in two by driving through the city's outer, center, and inner defense lines, although this happened within a few hours. This is known. It is that the power of the attack before the Russians expected it, in a direction they had not anticipated, and before they were set to meet it paralyzed their response. On that day and that day only Eremenko, Vasilievsky, who was in the area, and Stavka lost control, so much so that it appeared this was the beginning of the end for the Russians instead of for the Germans, which in fact is what it was. The case for loss of control rests on some astonishing developments:

—Although friendly forces were not far away, no help reached the 98th Division around Vertyachi, which bore the full weight of the initial German assault.

—Nikolai I. Biryukov and his 214th Division were only five miles to the north. Early that morning he heard the sound of battle to his left and saw in the summer haze the flash of artillery fire and the smoke of exploding bombs. It was not, however, until after nightfall—after the Germans had reached the Volga behind him— that he learned the 98th had collapsed.

—Vasilievsky was at 62nd Army headquarters that day, though whether he did anything more than report to Stalin by radio we do not know.

—The 62nd moved its command post once during the morning and again in the afternoon, thereby creating periods when it was out of touch with its front-line and reserve divisions.

—Although Eremenko, the front commander, says he knew by eight o'clock in the morning the Germans were headed for Stalingrad, the Russian units that met them in the city suburbs were taken by surprise.

—Because of confusion in the Kremlin the 8th Reserve Army at Saratov, two hundred miles up the Volga, set out toward Stalingrad without formal permission from the high command.

Vasilievsky, who knew the full story but never told it publicly, referred after the war to this Sunday as the "tragic 23rd of August." It was "tragic" for the Russians who might have averted it if they had foreseen the danger and reinforced the Vertyachi sector as had been their original intention.[1] Instead, they were led to believe by Paulus he would strike farther to his left—more to their right.

*

Kotluban village is about midway between Vertyachi and Stalingrad. Shortly before noon that day Gen. Vasili A. Glazkov of the

[1] Biryukov's 214th Division was scheduled to go to Vertyachi but the order was countermanded on the sixteenth. Glazkov's 35th Guards was also supposed to go there but its instructions were changed on the eighteenth.

35th Guards Division and his deputy, Col. V. P. Dubiansky, were standing in the doorway of a warehouse west of the railroad station watching a line of German attack planes sweep low on a bombing and strafing mission. Air assault had been heavy the evening before and all morning. Sheds were on fire. Smoke poured from burning freight cars. Trucks zigzagged through the fields with shells for the antiaircraft guns, and along the tracks the village of Samofalovka was in flames when out of the dust and confusion three jeeps pulled up at the warehouse and a general stepped out. He was K. A. Kovalenko, Gordov's deputy for the Stalingrad front.

"What!" he called out in amazement. "You still here? You were told to stop the Germans from crossing the Don at Peskovatka and Vertyachi." The order had not been received, apparently because the courier bearing it had been shot down on the way.

Kovalenko ordered the 35th and the 169th Tank Brigade to move out, then set up his command post in the warehouse. His instructions were to take over all Russian formations in the area and block the German thrust.

Several hours later Glazkov set out in the blazing sun through the wheat fields to the south. Out to the left was the 100th Regiment, to the right the 102nd, and in one of them was a machine-gun company led by Capt. Ruben R. Ibarruri, the young son of the Spanish communist Dolores Ibarruri, who was known to veterans of the Spanish Civil War as "La Pasionaria" (the passion flower).

Peasant women and children standing by their farm carts waved as the men walked by. Like their mothers the girls wore blouses, skirts, and white kerchiefs to keep the dust from their hair. The boys wore dark cloth caps like their fathers, white shirts, and dark shorts. They all knew what the soldiers knew—that German planes were out in great numbers—nothing more.

Dust clouds ahead!

Glazkov's scouts drew fire and stopped. A regimental commander pushed a battalion forward and soon word came back that hostile tank and motorized columns were moving east toward Stalingrad on the ridge line three miles out.

Glazkov turned the direction of his advance to the west. Perhaps he could get to Borodin village, a state farm with about twenty houses and barns and a duck pond, and from there move south along the center defense or "K" line and get in behind the enemy columns.

Borodin was in German hands. Glazkov attacked it, got into the village, and was driven out. In a second assault Ibarruri's commander was hit and he took over the battalion. In a third attack Ibarruri was mortally wounded. He died ten days later in a field hospital on the far side of the Volga.[2]

Late in the afternoon the 35th by-passed Borodin and fought its way south along the "K" line to Zapadnovka, where the Russian 87th was engaged. Moving up a slow rise, it attacked and took Hill 137.2, which dominated Borodin, the "K" line, and Zapadnovka, cutting off 14th Panzer from the rest of 6th Army.

*

About 4:30 that afternoon Aleksei Chuyanov was in his office at party headquarters in Stalingrad city when he received a telephone call from his friend K. A. Zadorozhni, the director of the tractor plant. Zadorozhni was excited.

"Aleksei Semeonovich," he shouted, "do you know the enemy has broken through our front?" Chuyanov did not know. What is more he doubted it because he was a member of Eremenko's Military Council and would have been informed.

"No," he said. "I do not know."

Zadorozhni blurted it out. "Tanks and infantry are not more than a kilometer and a half from the factory [about a mile]."

Chuyanov, who prided himself on being a mortal foe of *panic,* could not believe it. "You are not mistaken?" he asked.

"No, Aleksei Semeonovich. I can see them from my window."

*

At about the time of the telephone call to Chuyanov the men of the headquarters company of a rocket battalion were resting on a

[2] Every year on the anniversary of her son's death Dolores Ibarruri, who lived in Moscow, laid a wreath at her son's grave. As I was driving from the airport into the city in 1972, she was coming out from the ceremony. Police cars with sirens wailing preceded and followed her car, and traffic going both ways was stopped until she had passed.

tennis court in the northwest suburbs of the city. Supper was over, and they were writing letters home or cleaning their equipment when Lieutenant Babko, one of the company commanders, called in from an outlying position. Captain Sarkisian picked up the receiver.

"Comrade Captain, permit me to report."

"Report."

"There are tanks stopped on the hill before us. Their guns are pointed toward the city. Whose they are I do not know."

Sarkisian told him to investigate, not because he thought they were German but because Soviet Russians are suspicious by nature. They dislike the unknown or unidentified and when in doubt about something they check it out.

Taking along four men, Babko started up the hill on foot. As he neared the top he may have noticed the halted tanks, troop carriers, and scout cars were masked with camouflage netting, and this would have troubled him because the Russians rarely used it. Telling his men to stand where they were, Babko went on alone. When close to the lead tank, he called out.

"*Kommandir kolonni, ka mne.*" (Column commander, come to me.)

The hatch opened slowly and someone wearing the blue coveralls and black leather helmet of a Russian tankman stood up. He spoke Russian poorly and with a thick accent.

"Pass—please," he yelled. "No bother us."

Babko was sure now. They were Germans. He whirled and gave an order—his last. Minutes later the entire battalion opened fire.

The fight for the city was on.

*

A half hour later—why so much later I do not know—a siren sounded in the tractor plant. It was a new alarm, and the men and women in the machine shops, unaccustomed to it, wondered what was going on. So did the young men of the factory militia and its 1st Destroyer Battalion as they streamed out of the buildings wiping their hands on their work clothes. In the yard K. A.

Kostuchenko, who was both militia and battalion commander, told them Germans had broken through to the city and were only a mile or so away, perhaps around Rinok to the north, possibly as close as Spartanovka. They would move out as they had in training the night before and so often before that—infantry followed by the antitank gunners of the battalion—and take up positions on the far side of Mokraya Mechetka. The men knew Mokraya Mechetka. That was the "wet" Mechetka, a deep gorge nearby through which a narrow stream of the same name flows to the Volga. Beyond it was Sukhaya Mechetka, the "dry" Mechetka, a wide ravine on the near side of Spartanovka.

Soon the factory gates swung open and Kostuchenko and the rifle company passed through in a half dozen trucks. The trucks turned right for three blocks, then left and over the long bridge that spans Mokraya Mechetka. The others followed on foot, six hundred Russians in cloth caps and dark coveralls, some with rifles and carbines, others with machine guns and antitank rifles, all with ammunition and antitank grenades. Afterward some of them wryly remarked they had marched in step although no one told them to. Just habit they thought. They, too, turned at the gates along Lenin Prospect. To their right was the high brick wall of the factory. To their left were the white apartment houses where they lived. Children, their own, maybe, were playing in the dirt before the buildings. Laundry, their own, maybe, was drying on the balconies.

Kostuchenko set up his command post on the far side of Mokraya Mechetka ravine. He sent patrols toward the "dry" Mechetka, and then the city came under strong air attack. As the men laid down their grenades and reached for their entrenching tools, a few German shells exploded in the factory grounds behind them.

Work continued in the factory, but on the exercise ground within the plant complex the commander of the 99th Tank Training Brigade tried to squeeze a week's instruction and equipment verification into an hour or two. He had a company of infantry and two armored battalions, each with twenty-five medium T-34 tanks that had just come off the assembly line. Also headed for Mokraya Mechetka was a composite battalion of marines that was gathering on the far side of the Volga.

*

About this time Gen. Hans Hube of the 16th Panzer Division sent the following radio message to corps headquarters that had stopped for the night somewhere between Glazkov's division on the "K" line and Stalingrad city:

BATTLE GROUP 79TH PANZER GRENADIER REGIMENT FIRST GERMAN TROOPS TO REACH VOLGA 1835 HOURS. ONE COMPANY 2ND PANZER REGIMENT OCCUPIED SPARTANOVKA. ENEMY RESISTANCE INITIALLY WEAK BUT STRENGTHENING. STRONG ATTACKS FROM THE NORTH EXPECTED. OUTSTANDING SUPPORT BY VIII AIR CORPS.

*

The evidence suggests Eremenko was slow reacting to the German breakthrough until he received clearance or a free hand from Stavka. Otherwise his failure to alert Biryukov, Glazkov, Chuyanov, the factory director, the rocket battalion, and the factory militia is a puzzling question. He did inform Stalin as soon as he heard of the breakthrough and sent to the western outskirts of town the 269th and 272nd Regiments of Col. A. A. Sarayev's 10th NKVD Police Division, neither one of which had field artillery or antitank guns because the 10th was essentially a force to keep order and defend the factories. He also called up two battalions of cadets at the Stalingrad Military-Political Academy as if he were preparing to round up stragglers from his own 62nd Army instead of getting ready to meet a panzer thrust by the German 6th. And it would appear the Kremlin, too, underestimated the danger, for about noon Eremenko received the following radio message from Moscow:

ENEMY HAS BROKEN THROUGH YOUR FRONT WITH SMALL FORCES. YOU HAVE STRENGTH TO DESTROY HIM. CONCENTRATE AIR POWER OF BOTH FRONTS AND SEND IT AGAINST HIM. MOBI-

LIZE ARMORED TRAINS AND SEND THEM INTO ACTION ON CIRCULAR STALINGRAD RAILWAY. USE SMOKE TO CONFUSE ENEMY. FIGHT HIM DAY AND NIGHT. USE ALL YOUR ARTILLERY AND AIR. MOST IMPORTANT OF ALL DO NOT PANIC. DO NOT BE AFRAID OF IMPUDENT ENEMY AND REMAIN CONFIDENT OF OUR SUCCESS.

The Supreme was suggesting an old trick.[3] Armored trains with machine guns and artillery mounted on flatcars were a favorite weapon of the young Red Army in the civil war years that followed the 1917 revolution, and some of them were used at Stalingrad, then called Tsaritsyn, where Stalin represented the Bolsheviks in a struggle against "counterrevolutionaries." The idea was to deceive the enemy into thinking there were more trains than there were by having them move about and intentionally belch forth smoke to attract attention.

In the early afternoon Stalin sent Malenkov to Stalingrad to represent the State Defense Committee.

*

By Red Army standards General Kalinin at fifty-one years of age was something of an old war horse. A World War I veteran and an army man since the revolution, he had seen action in the early days of the Battle of Moscow and later taken command of the Saratov Military Region, where his duties were largely administrative. It was, then, with mixed feelings of bureaucratic caution and a quickening of the blood that late on the twenty-third he talked to Komarov, Communist party secretary for the Saratov area. Komarov put it straight to him.[4]

"What do you know about the fascists having reached the Volga?"

"Nothing," said Kalinin.

"Sailors tell me the enemy is on the Volga bank [near Stalin-

---

[3] Eremenko had six armored train battalions: the 28th, 30th, 40th, 51st, 59th, and 377th.

[4] Kalinin, pp. 209–12.

grad]. He is firing on our boats. What do you think they know about this at Stavka?"

Kalinin had no idea.

"Then, telephone Stavka. Something has got to be done right away."

Kalinin was not so sure. The report might not be true. "Why spread panic?" he asked.

"What do you mean—panic?" Komarov exclaimed. "Germans are shooting up our Volga boats. There are losses. Permit me. I will talk to Moscow on your vetch." He got through instantly.

"Germans on the Volga are firing on our ships," he reported. The officer at Stavka took the news calmly.

"Where are you calling from?"

"From the office of the commander of forces in the region."

"And where is the commander?"

"He is here." Komarov passed the phone to Kalinin.

"Where and when did the enemy reach the Volga?" Kalinin said he did not know but that he was about to send out a reconnaissance plane, a thought that may have just occurred to him. The war horse was beginning to look alive.

"Good. Call back in an hour. Report exactly where the Germans have broken through to the Volga."

Kalinin sprang to action. His orders: (1) alert the 8th Reserve Army, (2) fortify the hills around Saratov, (3) fortify the hills around Kamishin, which was halfway between Saratov and Stalingrad.

Stavka called back. "What forces can you send to the front right away?" Not everyone at Stavka knew of the existence and whereabouts of the reserve armies. Kalinin said he had the 8th and that its six divisions with supporting arms were ready for combat.

"Who commands it now?"

"No one."

"How long will it take you to turn over your job, take command of the 8th, and move out?"

Kalinin was getting excited. "Two or three hours," he said.

"Good. An order approving your appointment will be signed immediately. Where do you plan to concentrate the army?"

"Around Kamishin. The army staff is already on the way."

"Telephone us from Kamishin."

Kalinin took leave of his family and set out by car. On the way it occurred to him what a strange world this is. Here he was about to do battle with the Germans and yet the peasants in the nearby watermelon fields had no idea the enemy was so near. One division followed him by boat, two on the partially constructed railroad from Saratov down to Kamishin. The other three left on foot.

Kalinin worked hard that evening. He traveled about, inspected a position that would be occupied by the first regiment that pulled in, and conferred with his staff. Then:

Stavka calling.

Gen. E. A. Shchadenko was on the line, and Shchadenko was a *very important person,* an army commissar first class. His voice was cold, unfriendly.

"Why did you leave your region?"

"Because of an order from the Supreme High Command." Shchadenko was unimpressed.

"Tell Saratov immediately," he said, "that you will be returning to your post. For the present run your region from Kamishin. The order naming you to the army will be revoked. I will report to the Supreme High Commander today."

Kalinin tried to explain. "But . . ." Shchadenko cut him off. "Wait till the new commander arrives, then return promptly to Saratov."

Several days later General Malinovsky, former commander of the now-liquidated south front, took over the 8th Reserve, which was activated as the 66th.

Kalinin recalled years later: "Sad as it was to part with a cherished dream—to fight the enemy myself—now all my thoughts were directed to the region and the formation of reserves."

*

Hours after Kalinin parted with his "cherished dream" the work of other men went for nothing. Gen. V. F. Shestakov, chief of engineers, and Gen. N. P. Anisimov, the quartermaster, of the southeast front, reported to Eremenko they had completed construction of a pontoon bridge over the Volga to the tractor plant. They had been given twelve days to build it and finished it in ten, a job that would have taken army engineers with suitable equipment less than a day.

"Very good," said Eremenko. "Thank the people who built it and the commanders, including Comrade Stepanov, who directed them. Now I order you to destroy it."[5]

He feared the unlikely possibility the Germans would cross the river, and in the coming weeks about everyone in Stalingrad would regret the bridge was not in place.

*

After a heavy air raid that night it looked from the far side of the Volga as if the whole city and the river itself were on fire in some kind of distant, muffled, painless, peacetime disaster. On the near side, however, the streets were like flaming corridors in a hell dominated by the color, the sound, the smell, and the touch of war. Telephone poles snapped, power lines sagged. There were explosions everywhere. Splintered rafters and crumpled plaster crashed three or four stories to the cellars. There were incoherent shouts from running men and women. A lost child stared about him in open-mouthed horror. A peasant screamed at a horse that had fallen in the traces. A company of infantry marching to the front walked heads down to keep flying cinders from their smarting eyes. Or so men say. We cannot be sure. There are not many survivors today, and the recollections of the few around are hazy, confused, uncertain. It all seems so long ago. They say that on that Sunday night when the Germans broke through to Stalingrad the pain was agonizing, that it was not so much the first wound or burn that hurt as the second or third that made the first almost unbearable.

What could a man do? Not much for now except go to the factory where he might be needed. What if the planes came back? Go to the shelter of a nearby building? The buildings were full of smoke. Get behind a shaky wall? A fragment of brick could pierce the brain. The gutters? They were open sewers from broken water mains.

[5] Eremenko, pp. 131–32.

Try the river—the sheltered riverbank. But the streets to the Volga were barred by armed militiamen.

"Nobody goes through."

"Why not?"

"Nobody goes through." It was the only answer anyone got. What about the side streets? They, too, were blocked.

Throughout the night eight launches went back and forth over the river carrying hospital workers and the wounded. At six o'clock on Monday morning the bombers returned and the raids went on all day. The tractor plant and the Barricades and Red October factories were hit again and again as the City Defense Committee headed by party secretary Chuyanov ordered the evacuation of "nonessential" (i.e., nonworking) women and children but stopped the departure of doctors and nurses and construction workers who would be needed to restore vital services.

At midnight a state of siege was declared, and black-and-white posters went up all over town:

ANYONE CAUGHT DISTURBING SOCIAL ORDER AND PEACE WILL BE SHOT AT SCENE OF CRIME WITHOUT INQUIRY OR TRIAL, AND ALL OTHER MALICIOUS PERSONS VIOLATING PUBLIC ORDER AND SECURITY IN CITY WILL BE HAILED BEFORE MILITARY TRIBUNAL.[6]

The raids continued on Tuesday and Wednesday when the Defense Committee appealed for volunteers. Up went more posters, and their words were the words or rhetoric of war and revolution:

Dear Comrades!

Native Stalingraders!

Frenzied bands of enemy have reached walls of our native city.

Once again, as 24 years ago, our city is living through difficult days.

Bloody Hitlerites are striving to reach sunny Stalingrad and great Russian river—Volga.

Troops of Red Army are selflessly defending Stalingrad. All

[6] Samsonov, p. 152.

approaches to city are strewn with corpses of German-fascist occupiers.

Super-bandit Hitler is rushing more and more of his cutthroats into battle and trying to take Stalingrad at any cost.

Comrade Stalingraders!

We will not give up our native city, our native home, our native land. We will turn every street in city into impenetrable barricade. We will make impregnable fortress of every home, every building, every street.

Everybody, come out and build barricades. Organize brigades. Barricade every street. To build barricades, use whatever is at hand—stones, logs, iron, streetcars.

We will build barricades quickly so soldiers can annihilate enemy from barricades built by us.

Soldiers of the Red Army! Defenders of Stalingrad!

We will do everything so you can hold Stalingrad. Not a step back. Fight enemy without mercy. Take vengeance on Germans for every hearth destroyed, for every brutality committed, for bloodshed and tears of our children, our mothers, and our wives.

Defenders of Stalingrad!

In terrible year 1918 our fathers held Red Tsaritsyn from band of German mercenaries. In year 1942 we will hold Red Banner Stalingrad. We will hold it so you can throw back and then destroy bloody band of German occupiers.

Everyone to building barricades!

Everyone who can carry gun—to barricades—to defense of our native city, our native home.[7]

The barricades went up. They ran from the wall of an office building or apartment house to a wall on the other side of the street with a gap in the center barely wide enough for a car or truck to pass.

In and near the tractor factory 3,000 workers, organized into fifty-two brigades, repaired bomb damage and built defense lines—

[7] Ibid., pp. 152–53.

mostly trenches and bricked-up doors and windows. Men of the Red October plant restored the water system, from another factory the power lines.

Death and suffering were all about. For Monday, Tuesday, and Wednesday the casualty lists showed:

>*Tractor District*
>68 killed, 247 wounded
>
>*Barricades District*
>200 killed, 120 wounded
>
>*Red October District*
>62 killed, 126 wounded
>
>*Dzerzhinsky District*
>70 killed, 68 wounded
>
>*Yermansky District*
>302 killed, 257 wounded
>
>*Voroshilov District*
>315 killed, 463 wounded
>
>*Altogether*
>1,017 killed, 1,281 wounded[8]

The official figures are suspiciously precise and pitifully incomplete. On Wednesday night alone, three steamers, the *Mikhail Kalinin,* the *Paris Commune,* and the *Joseph Stalin,* left under cover of darkness for Gorki far up the river. The first two got through but the third ship in the line came under attack as it passed Rinok north of the city. Tracer bullets set it on fire, and it is said that of its 1,200 passengers and crew about 150 got out alive.

By that Wednesday evening the armies defending the approaches to the city were so weakened that a call for men went out from Eremenko's command post in the Tsaritsa bunker near the center of town. Mobilization orders were broadcast by radio and

---

[8] Ibid., p. 149. Stalingrad proper was divided into six administrative districts as they are listed here from north to south. The southern suburbs including Beketovka formed a seventh, Kirovski.

poster with every man from eighteen to fifty subject to immediate service.

Only a few thousands were taken that evening. Formed into detachments, they were marched to the front dressed as they were in pants, a shirt, a cap. Tens of thousands more were soon enrolled. Combat units were organized. The lucky ones got a uniform and several days' training before going to battle.

There were no individual mobilization orders. No telegrams went out from the war office. No letters.

A woman could never tell. She might see her husband or a son being marched through the streets. She might walk alongside him for a mile or more—there was so much to talk about. Or she might find a farewell note on the table at home.

Total war had come to Stalingrad.

4

The German lunge to the northern suburbs of Stalingrad which split the Russian armies, cut their communications along the Volga, and rattled the Kremlin had a decisive impact on the course of the summer campaign that was not immediately apparent at Hitler's headquarters near Vinnitsa. At first sight it looked like a brilliant stroke that would lead to capture of the city by Army Group B and indirect support for Army Group A that was beginning to run into trouble in the northern Caucasus. But there were drawbacks. For one, it solidified Hitler's determination to take Stalingrad and the Caucasus at the same time. For another, in the Stalingrad region it narrowed the field of battle to an area no larger than the state of Delaware where the war of movement, a German specialty, would give way to a war of attrition, a Russian specialty. There was still a third drawback. In committing 6th Army to the Volga, the German High Command compelled or permitted the Russian High Command to release the bulk of the forces it was holding out for an emergency. Before the week ended, Stavka would activate its 8th and 9th Reserve Armies, two tank corps that had been re-formed and re-equipped after the early struggle west of Voronezh, and five independent rifle divisions, altogether some 200,000 men.[1]

This is not to suggest that in the beginning the new tactical situation was any more clearly understood in the Kremlin than it was at Vinnitsa. Indeed, from an order Stalin issued at 4:50 A.M. on Monday, August 24, it would appear he underestimated the German drive or overestimated his own ability to deal with it. Addressed to Vasilievsky, Eremenko, and Malenkov of the State Defense Committee who reached the city some time during the night, the message went by radio because telephone circuits were severed by the German corridor:

> SUPREME HIGH COMMAND ORDERS YOU
>
> FIRST, FIRMLY AND WITHOUT FAIL TO CLOSE GAP THROUGH WHICH ENEMY HAS MOVED TO STALINGRAD. SURROUND HIM AND DESTROY HIM. YOU HAVE ENOUGH STRENGTH. YOU CAN AND MUST DO IT.
>
> SECOND, HOLD YOUR POSITIONS WEST AND SOUTH OF STALINGRAD WITHOUT FAIL. DO NOT MOVE TROOPS FROM FRONT TO LIQUIDATE ENEMY. WITHOUT FAIL KEEP ON COUNTERATTACKING WITH AIM DRIVE ENEMY BACK BEYOND STALINGRAD'S OUTER DEFENSE LINE.[2]

In short, with your forces on the Russian right destroy 14th Panzer Corps in its thinly held corridor to the Volga; on the Russian left hold 62nd and 64th Armies where they are (in a dangerously exposed position out on the Don and the Mishkova to the west and southwest of the city).

This, however, was far from the Kremlin's final word. Although the order was responsive to Russian military instinct, which is to

---

[1] About this time G-2, the intelligence section of the War Department, advised the White House that Stalingrad could be written off as already lost to the Germans (Sherwood, p. 627). The American and British officers I knew in Moscow were more hopeful, though they realized their optimism was based on an instinctive understanding of the imponderables in the east, not on hard information.

[2] Samsonov, p. 140.

stand fast until forced to retreat and to counterattack wherever possible with whatever is available, Stavka took more far-reaching measures on Monday, Tuesday, and Wednesday and followed them on Thursday with a reorganization of its command structure in the field. Kremlin action took the form of four related orders and three new assignments:

To Moskalenko

Break off contact with the enemy in the little elbow of the Don and pull back 1st Guards Army for an attack on the corridor from the north.

To Malinovsky

Take command of the 8th Reserve, herewith renamed the 66th, and join Moskalenko.

To Kozlov

Take over the 9th Reserve, hereafter to be called the 24th, and move it down from Gorki to support Moskalenko and Malinovsky.

To Gordov

Move out of Stalingrad city and direct the assault by Moskalenko, Malinovsky, and Kozlov on the northern side of the corridor.

In sum, the plan taking shape called for a mighty counterattack out of the north, the idea being to break through to Stalingrad and restore the ruptured Russian line. If it succeeded, the city would be saved and Army Group B brought to a shattering halt. If it failed, no one could tell what might happen. There were two problems, one inherent in the situation, the other man-made by Stalin himself. The inherent problem was that the initiative was still in German hands and time was short. The Russians needed a week or more to mount the assault. Would the Germans wait? Hoth's 4th Panzer was not far away, and it was not their style. The man-made problem grew out of a determination on Stalin's part to play a more active role in the struggle. Heretofore, with occasional lapses during which he interferred with the conduct of an operation, he had been content to formulate and direct military policy, appoint and remove commanders, approve, amend, or reject their plans, and concentrate much of his attention on the production of weapons, the cracking of bottlenecks, and the creation of his strategic

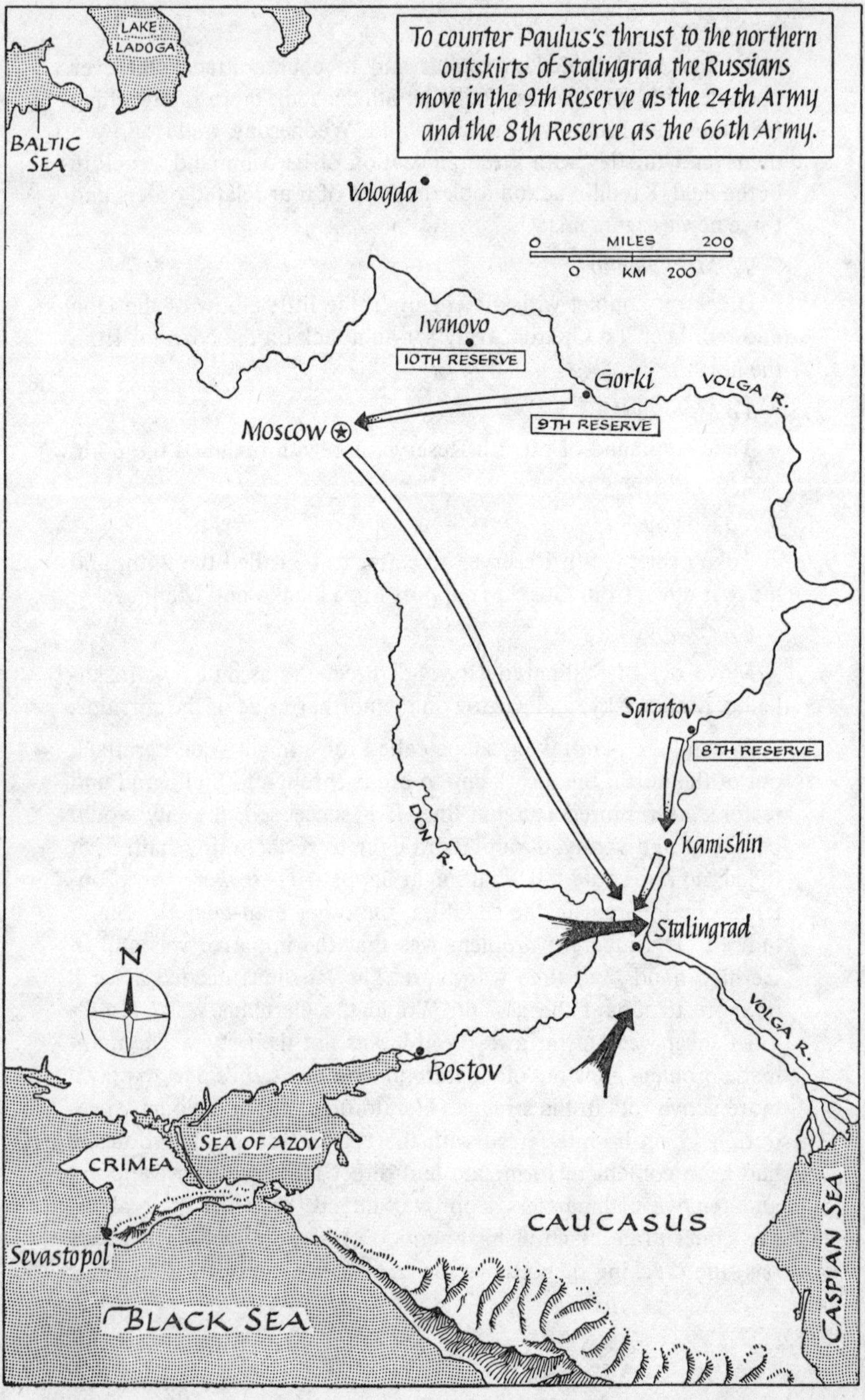

To counter Paulus's thrust to the northern outskirts of Stalingrad the Russians move in the 9th Reserve as the 24th Army and the 8th Reserve as the 66th Army.
LAKE LADOGA
BALTIC SEA
Vologda
0 MILES 200
0 KM 200
Ivanovo
10TH RESERVE
Gorki
VOLGA R.
Moscow
9TH RESERVE
Saratov
8TH RESERVE
DON R.
Kamishin
Stalingrad
N
VOLGA R.
Rostov
SEA OF AZOV
CRIMEA
CAUCASUS
Sevastopol
BLACK SEA
CASPIAN SEA

reserve. Now he wanted control of troops and the uninhibited power to decide not only the day and the direction of a blow but the hour and the forces to be employed, and so there arose one of those sensitive political problems the Supreme handled the way a squirrel handles a nut. His usual approach was forceful. If he felt strongly about an issue that came up during a Stavka session, he expressed his opinion and that settled it; there was no further debate. If he did not care one way or the other, he told those supporting opposing views to get together and come up with an agreed solution, which he would accept. But if he intended to impose a change of policy, especially one that would enhance his authority, he maneuvered warily. He examined the matter, weighed it in his mind, and then put it away until he was ready to take a second look. Meanwhile he "consulted" with his associates so that his decision when he was ready to announce it had all the earmarks of a collective act. He talked first to one man, then to another, perhaps first to Molotov or Beria, then Voroshilov or Vasilievsky. Until his mind was made up and he had the "votes" the subject would not be raised at a formal meeting. This is how he made himself Supreme High Commander in the early weeks of the war. It is how he overcame resistance before it massed against him, and this, I understand, is how he went about the business of making certain that in the days to come every major decision would be his alone. On this occasion he came up with an ingenious plan that was somewhat revolutionary in concept. He reasoned:

1. Neither Eremenko nor any other field commander could fight on both sides of the German corridor, so the battle would have to be controlled by Stavka of the Supreme High Command.

2. For Stavka to control it from such a distance (six hundred miles away) its representatives would have to be frequently in the field.

Therefore, he proposed:

1. That Vasilievsky while retaining his position as Chief of the General Staff be named Stavka representative at Eremenko's southeast front headquarters in Stalingrad city with responsibility for overseeing the execution of Stavka orders south of the corridor.

2. That Zhukov, giving up his post as commander of the western front before Moscow, be appointed Stavka representative at Eremenko's Stalingrad front headquarters north of the corridor, and

3. That Zhukov, to enhance his authority, be appointed Deputy Supreme High Commander, a newly created title.

From Stalin's standpoint the decision was a cunning stroke, for he became a field commander under circumstances that made this illogical arrangement sound logical to his colleagues. In any event my understanding is that his plan was accepted with only a few clarifying questions like:

Will Eremenko continue to serve as commander of both fronts?

In principle, yes; in practice, he will command in the south while his deputy Gordov leads the armies out of the north under Stavka's (Stalin's) direction and Zhukov's supervision.

What are Zhukov's rights and responsibilities as Deputy Supreme High Commander?

He will be more a deputy *to* the Supreme High Commander than Deputy Supreme High Commander; i.e., he will report to and receive orders only from Stalin but he will not have the right to give instructions of his own to Stavka or the General Staff.[3]

And so it came about that on Thursday, August 27, four days after 14th Panzer Corps of 6th Army reached the northern suburbs of Stalingrad, Zhukov was ushered into Stalin's presence for a conversation about which years later he was in one respect intentionally vague. Stalin told him of his new appointment and of his first assignment, which was to see to it that Moskalenko's 1st Guards Army attack the northern side of the German corridor on September 2 and that the 24th and 66th Armies, just transferred to the Stalingrad front, join the 1st as soon as possible. Zhukov in his memoirs, however, slurred over the 24th and 66th. In keeping with Soviet policy he did not identify them as having been reserve armies until two days before.[4]

[3] Shtemenko confirms the limitations on Zhukov's authority: "The General Staff was the working organ of Stavka and obeyed only the Supreme High Commander. Even the deputy Supreme did not have the right of access to the General Staff" (p. 113).

[4] Zhukov, pp. 408–9. In their published recollections and histories of the war Soviet generals and writers do not appear to cloud Russian battle strategy

*

Zhukov wasted no time. After a day studying reports and situation maps he left Moscow by plane early Saturday morning, August 29, flew to Kamishin on the Volga above Stalingrad, and from there drove with Vasilievsky to Gordov's new command post at Malaya Ivanovka and farther on to the headquarters of Moskalenko's still-gathering Guards army.

At 6:30 that morning, however, about the hour Zhukov was leaving Moscow central airport for the first massive counteroffensive of the summer campaign, Hoth's 4th Panzer launched a punishing attack toward Stalingrad out of the southwest.

---

by inaccurate statements, but essential details are omitted as if they were left out on instructions or stricken by censors from manuscripts.

5

With 6th Army in the northern outskirts of Stalingrad and 4th Panzer racing for the southern suburbs one would expect that a thrill of elation or accomplishment ran through the Fuehrer's headquarters in the distant Ukraine. The contrary was the case. Halder was uneasy, Hitler increasingly anxious, apprehensive, as is shown by Halder's restrained notes to himself and the memoranda Greiner took for OKW's war diary. First, Halder:

August 22

Hoth's 4th Panzer is showing "signs of fatigue."
(No details. No explanation. No comment.)

August 26

"Severe nervous strain on the responsible commanders. Von Wietersheim wanted to withdraw his advanced outpost on the Volga, but was prevented by Paulus."

(In its thin corridor to the river Wietersheim's 14th Panzer Corps was now cut off from the rest of 6th Army and suffering from a shortage of ammunition.)

August 28

"Situation easier in 6th Army; regrouping in 4th Panzer. Something is brewing on the left wing of 6th Army."

(According to Greiner and Warlimont, Hermann Goering, Reichsmarschall and head of the Luftwaffe, appeared at the briefing conference this day and reported to the Fuehrer the findings of Gen. Freiherr Wolfgang von Richthofen,[1] who had talked to Paulus and Hoth and whose air observers had studied the Stalingrad region. Warlimont, quoting Goering quoting Richthofen: "There was no question of major enemy forces being in the area. During reconnaissance northwards, the Luftwaffe had had difficulty in finding any enemy forces at all, although the country was completely without cover."[2] Halder ignored this report as if he did not believe a word of it.)

August 29

"Trouble is beginning to develop on its [6th Army's] left wing."

(Halder was paying increasing attention to Russian capabilities and intentions. Here he referred to forces assembling north of the corridor.)

Now for Greiner's notes and what Halder did not put down:

August 27

Hitler wants the 294th and 298th Infantry Divisions, which on August 16 he ordered out of the Caucasus, sent by plane and truck to aid the Italian 8th Army on the middle Don where Russian action still troubles him.

August 29

Hitler expresses "indignation" about what he calls *stillstand* (inaction or deadlock) in the Caucasus. He blames List, the commander of Army Group A.

August 30

"The Fuehrer is very discontented (*sehr unzufrieden*) about the development of the situation at Army Group A and will speak to General Field Marshal List at Fuehrer Headquarters tomorrow."

[1] Richthofen commanded the 4th Air Fleet (4th and 8th Air Corps).
[2] Warlimont, p. 255.

But Greiner, who got his information on the situation conferences from Warlimont, who got his from Jodl, who attended them, heard or recorded only part of the story and nothing like what Halder wrote the same day:

"Today's conferences with Fuehrer were again the occasion of abusive reproaches against the military leadership abilities of the highest commands. He charges them with intellectual conceit, mental inadaptability, and utter failure to grasp essentials."

Now what? It could not have been the heat this time, for the temperature, according to OKH situation reports, was running about 70° Fahrenheit.

Was Hitler overcome by nervous exhaustion or by the psychic tension that is found in most forms of mental disorder? One would think so from a reading of Halder's notes and the recollections of Keitel, Warlimont, Gehlen, and others. But there is no solid evidence to this effect, and the views or suggestions of the generals who survived him would have a clearer ring if they included anything but occasional and fleeting references to the actual predicament of the German High Command at the end of August.[3]

Or were Hitler's concerns of the past two weeks hardening to a fear he again faced defeat such as he had suffered before Moscow when the Russians threw in more and more unexpected reserves? Unless with 6th Army and 4th Panzer he went for broke in the Stalingrad region? Unless before it was too late he put the feet of his generals to the fire?

Questions flood the mind. What did he know and when did he know it? What did Halder do and when did he do it? There are few answers in the surviving documents. OKH situation reports were still blandly uncommunicative. No one told much of anything to Greiner. His notes for September 6 are missing if there were any. There are none for September 10, 11, and 12. There are none for September 19, 22, 23, 24, 25, 26, 27, 28, 29, and 30 or for October 1 and 3. Yet these were the days when the dam burst—when Hitler broke permanently or temporarily with generals he had lifted to positions of high responsibility. Halder:

[3] There is a candor about Halder's wartime diary—something like the truth but not the whole truth—that is less evident in the memoirs of other German generals.

September 9

"1630. Field Marshal Keitel comes to see me. List must resign: Hints of more changes in high places, including mine."

September 11

"Fuehrer situation conference takes place in icy atmosphere."

September 12

"Von Weichs and Paulus come in. Decision to adopt the 'central' solution."

(Up to this time there had been some discussion [all rather academic] whether, after taking Stalingrad, an effort should be made to push back the Russians to their old "O" defense line above the city [this was called the "big solution"] or in this sector to stay about where they were [the "central solution"].)

September 15

". . . gratifying advances inside Stalingrad."

September 16

"Fuehrer is still greatly worried about the Don front."

September 17

Blumentritt to the west to replace Zeitzler[4] "so that I may expect arrival of my successor here about September 20."

September 20

". . . we are beginning to feel the approaching exhaustion of our assault troops."

September 23

"At Stalingrad slow progress."

September 24

"After situation conference, farewell by the Fuehrer: My nerves are worn out, also his nerves are no longer fresh. We must part. Necessity for educating the General Staff in fanatical faith in the

---

[4] Guenther Blumentritt was Deputy Chief of the General Staff under Halder. Kurt Zeitzler was Chief of Staff of German forces in western Europe and had attracted Hitler's attention because of successful resistance to the allied raid on Dieppe on August 19.

[Nazi?] Idea. He is determined to enforce his will on the Army."

And later that day:

"After 1700. My farewell to the several groups: Gen. Staff.—Gen. Qu.—Arms Chiefs—individual callers."

This is the last entry in Halder's diary,[5] but since *what* happened is clearer than *why,* we have to go back to 4th Panzer's assault of August 29 and the turbulent events that accompanied and followed it, including an incipient revolt in 14th Panzer Corps of 6th Army and the Russian counteroffensive against 6th Army's corridor.

They were terrifying days for front-line troops on both sides of the line.

*

Hoth's August 29 strike toward the southern outskirts of Stalingrad was a tactically brilliant operation that had no impact on the outcome of the campaign. It wounded the enemy, compelled him to take action he had not planned, killed men, but though the Germans had the brains and the ability and the mobility to inflict casualties and gain ground, they did not have the strength to take Stalingrad and the Caucasus at the same time. On that Saturday 4th Panzer cracked the outer defense or "O" line on the Mishkova and reached the center defense or "K" line on the Chervlennaya. The next day it crossed the steep-sided Chervlennaya, which was dry after the long summer drought, then turned north toward Bassargino Station. Now if Paulus moved down out of the corridor to meet Hoth, the entire right wing of the Russian 64th Army and all of the 62nd would be trapped.[6] Message, transmitted by radio at noon, from Baron Maximilian von Weichs of Army Group B to Paulus of 6th Army:

[5] Halder retired to his home in Bavaria where he remained until his arrest on July 21, 1944, the day after the bomb attempt on Hitler's life. Halder was held but not tried for complicity in the plot.

[6] The 62nd and 64th were vulnerable because of Stalin's August 24 order directing them to hold their exposed positions on the river line.

IN VIEW OF THE FACT THAT 4TH PANZER ARMY GAINED BRIDGEHEAD AT GAVRILOVKA AT 1000 HOURS TODAY, EVERYTHING NOW DEPENDS ON 6TH ARMY'S CONCENTRATING THE STRONGEST POSSIBLE FORCES IN SPITE OF ITS EXCEEDINGLY TENSE DEFENSIVE SITUATION . . . IN ORDER TO DESTROY THE ENEMY'S FORCES WEST OF STALINGRAD IN COOPERATION WITH 4TH PANZER ARMY. THIS DECISION REQUIRES THE RUTHLESS DENUDING OF SECONDARY FRONTS.[7]

Hoth drove on to Bassargino Station where he cut the east-west highway and railroad that were the 62nd Army's main lines of supply from Stalingrad. But there was no sign of Paulus, who was paralyzed in the "tense defensive situation" in the corridor. There Wietersheim's 14th Panzer Corps, isolated and harassed by Russian forces, was just about out of ammunition, fuel, food, and water. There was no question of its moving south to join Hoth. General Hube of 16th Panzer Division thought only of retreating to the west, and he so informed his officers the next morning in defiance of Hitler's order to stay where he was.

"The shortage of ammo and fuel," he told them, "is such that our only chance is to break through to the west. I absolutely refuse to fight a pointless battle that must end in the annihilation of my troops and I therefore order a break-out to the west. I shall personally take responsibility for this order, and will know how to justify it in the proper quarters. I absolve you, gentlemen, from your oath of loyalty, and I leave you the choice of leading your men in this action or of handing over your commands to other officers who are prepared to do so. It is impossible to hold our positions without ammunition. I am acting contrary to the Fuehrer's orders."[8]

The withdrawal was called off when 250 supply trucks, escorted by tanks and motorized infantry, got through to 16th Panzer, but by then it was too late. Eremenko was pulling back his armies to the inner defense or "S" line. His order:

[7] Carell (a pseudonym for Paul Karl Schmidt), p. 601.
[8] Schröter, p. 31.

1 September 1942   *Active Army*

Comrade fighters, commanders, and political workers, valiant defenders of Stalingrad!

For month there has been fierce struggle going on for Stalingrad city. Germans have lost hundreds of tanks and planes. Over mountains of their own corpses, soldiers and officers of brutal Hitlerite bands are trying to get to Stalingrad, to Volga.[9]

Our Bolshevik party, our people, our great Motherland have charged us not to allow enemy to Volga, but to defend Stalingrad city. Defense of Stalingrad has decisive meaning for entire Soviet front.

Unsparing of our strength, despising death, we will not allow Germans to Volga, we will not give up Stalingrad. Each one of us must understand that seizure of Stalingrad by Germans and their reaching Volga will strengthen our enemies and weaken our own forces.

Not a step back!

Military Council demands of every fighter, commander, and political worker, of all defenders of Stalingrad, selfless courage, firmness, and heroism in battle with presumptuous enemy.

Enemy must and will be destroyed on approaches to Stalingrad.

Forward against enemy! In merciless battle, comrades, for Stalingrad, for Great Motherland.

Death to German occupiers!

Late that evening 4th Panzer, alone and without 6th Army to its left, turned east toward Voroponovo[10] only five miles from Stalingrad. And late on the following night Eremenko moved his command post out of the city to the far side of the Volga. He was in trouble, and his best hope for holding out rested with Zhukov, Gordov, and Moskalenko, whose forces were gathering in the

---

[9] Until now and for months to come the Russians would not admit publicly the Germans had reached the Volga on August 23.

[10] Voroponovo was renamed Maxim Gorki after the war. Before turning to writing, Gorki worked in the machine shops here as a young man.

north. Before crossing to the safe bank Eremenko fired Lopatin of the 6th Army as he had Kolpakchi before him and replaced him with Gen. Nikolai Krilov, the army's Chief of Staff. Months later Krilov, the army's third commander in less than four weeks, told me he had a brother in the United States Army he had not seen since childhood when the family was separated by revolution and civil war.

*

General Moskalenko, a wiry little man with lidded eyes and a tight mouth, had enough divisions shot out from under him to know the dimensions of the problem he faced. Since the first of the year he had commanded the 6th Cavalry Corps (mauled in winter battle near Kharkov), the 38th Army (punished in its July retreat through the steppe country of the Don Cossacks), the 1st Tank Army (pushed around in late July west of the Don and soon liquidated), then the 1st Guards (bloodied in late August in the little elbow of the Don). Now he had what looked to him like a Guards army in name only and a mission of crushing proportions.

On paper, as Stalin would have seen it during his Stavka sessions in the Kremlin, the Guards appeared solid enough. It consisted of:

> 38th, 39th, and 41st Guards Divisions
> 24th, 84th, and 315th Rifle Divisions
> 64th and 116th Rifle Divisions
> 4th, 7th, and 16th Tank Corps
> Two rocket regiments
> One regiment of army artillery
> One regiment of corps artillery
> One tank destroyer regiment
> Two bridge-laying brigades
> One sapper battalion

But Moskalenko in the field saw something else. The 39th Guards had not arrived from the Don. The 38th and 41st were in the vicinity but not fully concentrated. The 24th, 84th, and 315th were crippled after piecemeal attacks on the corridor. So were the 4th and 16th Tank Corps, each of which instead of two hundred tanks was down to a composite brigade of about seventy.

Stalin had already delayed the assault for one day. Would he agree to another? If not, Moskalenko would go into action with only two of his eight divisions, the 24th and 116th, and two of three tank corps, the fresh 7th and the weakened 16th.

No. Hoth and Paulus were too close to the western outskirts. Stalingrad might fall any day.

Accordingly, artillery preparation, which was unusually light, began at seven o'clock on Thursday, September 3, as planned, and a half hour later the men moved out and up through open fields to the heights 14th Panzer Corps had seized in its August 23 rush to the Volga. Catastrophe. It was a case of one mile forward and one mile back. Explaining to Stalin what had happened, Zhukov said not much could be accomplished until Kozlov's 24th and Malinovsky's 66th Armies reached the field, which would not be before Saturday. Stalin was indignant. Vasilievsky had telephoned from Eremenko's new command post to say the enemy was only about two miles from the city and that 62nd Army could not hold out on its own. What about the Guards divisions? Stalin wanted to know. What about the other rifle divisions? The Supreme turned to the BODO with a fiery message for Zhukov:

SITUATION WORSENED. ENEMY THREE VERSTS[11] FROM STALINGRAD. STALINGRAD CAN FALL TODAY OR TOMORROW WITHOUT QUICK HELP FROM NORTHERN GROUP. INSIST THAT COMMANDERS NORTH AND NORTHEAST OF STALINGRAD STRIKE ENEMY QUICKLY AND BRING HELP TO STALINGRAD. DELAY NOW AMOUNTS TO CRIME. RUSH ALL AIR TO STALINGRAD'S HELP. VERY LITTLE AIR IS LEFT IN STALINGRAD ITSELF. REPORT IMMEDIATELY RECEIPT [of this order] AND MEASURES TAKEN. 3.9.42. 2230 HOURS.

[11] About two miles. A verst is 3,500 feet.

Soon after midnight he sent another message to Zhukov:

IF ENEMY LAUNCHES GENERAL ATTACK ON CITY DO NOT WAIT FOR FINAL CONCENTRATION OF TROOPS.

Moskalenko tried again on Friday, the fourth, and on Saturday the fifth all three armies hit the corridor and Paulus's 6th Army for the first time although at different hours of the day: the Guards at 6:30 A.M., Malinovsky's 66th at 9 A.M., Kozlov's 24th at 3 P.M. Soon the loss of life on both sides was frightful. Day after day the Russians attacked and day after day the Germans, who were so near their goal and yet so far, drove them back.

On one occasion the Germans were so close in they used Stalingrad's telephone network. An instrument rang at Communist party headquarters. Chuyanov picked up the receiver.

"*Kto eto?*" (Who is it?). Chuyanov was a power in the town and not to be disturbed without good reason.

The voice of a Russian woman came over the wire.

"The German High Command is interested in you," it purred. "I can tell you that you and your associates are going to be hanged."

Chuyanov lost his cool.

"Who hangs whom," he shouted, "remains to be seen. But you, you fascist buzzard, will certainly be hanged from a post."

And he rang off.

On another occasion Wietersheim informed Paulus his 14th Panzer Corps could not keep going.

"Sir," he reported, "I can work out the exact day on which I shall lose my last man if the situation is allowed to continue like this."

Paulus barked back.

"Are you commanding 6th Army, Wietersheim, or am I?"[12]

*

By September 9 things might have looked a little better to Hitler if what disturbed him—the "heat" according to Keitel and Warli-

[12] Schröter, p. 33.

mont, "nerves" according to Halder—could have been alleviated by tactical success in the field. On the sixth, German forces captured Novorossisk on the Black Sea coast; it was not much, but it was something. On the seventh, they warded off Russian attacks in the Stalingrad area and moved on to Gumrak airport outside the city so that by nightfall both 6th Army and 4th Panzer were in the western suburbs. The Fuehrer, however, was unappeased. His was a deeper concern. Apprehension had turned to hot anger, which was his mood on the ninth when he fired List and let Halder know he was on his way out, and there followed two decisions in quick order, one noisy, the other silent. In the first, which he promptly announced, he personally took over List's post as commander of Army Group A in the Caucasus. Now he was Commander in Chief of the Armed Forces High Command (OKW), Commander in Chief of the Army High Command (OKH), and a field general if only in name. In his second decision he secretly ordered to OKW headquarters about a dozen stenographic reporters from the Reichstag in Berlin. These he put in uniform, swore in, and assigned to make a verbatim report of every military conference he attended from then on.

Both actions are revealing. The one shows defiant anger—an empty gesture toward generals he had accused of "intellectual conceit, mental inadaptability, and utter failure to grasp essentials" (Halder, August 30). The other shows angry suspicion, as if he thought they misquoted him or ignored an instruction or had not told him something they insisted they had.

Why? We may never know for certain because the few surviving generals who might have been aware of all that went on later professed ignorance, the stenographic records were burned after Hitler's death, and the charred fragments that remain date from December 1, more than two months later.

In any event the Fuehrer was now determined to go for Stalingrad city at whatever the price. It was higher than anyone at the time thought possible.

6

The soldiers, the workers, the old men, and the women and children were at work in Stalingrad before dawn on Thursday, September 10, digging trenches, building underground shelters, filling sandbags, hauling water, and carrying ammunition. They knew the assault on the city would come any day now because everybody said so and everybody was usually right because everybody was the grapevine and the grapevine as elsewhere in Russia was swift and astonishingly accurate. It went something like this: A man who had a brother whose wife had a sister who was a typist at party headquarters passed on what he heard to the man next door whose mother told a nurse who confided in an orderly who kept the stretcher bearers informed. In return the stretcher bearers reported what they learned from a wounded sergeant who had a friend who was a runner for a battalion commander. This was no rumor factory. It was that mysterious channel of underground communications that in a totalitarian state protects the weak. People respected the grapevine. To betray the network by injecting into it something untrue was looked on as the betrayal of a trust, almost a crime against humanity, for without a reliable grapevine there was no early warning system, no means of anticipating official pronouncements and avoiding *trouble*. In this instance the grapevine confirmed what the leaders said. The Germans, now close in, would come over the hills and through the defiles and along the roads, perhaps tomorrow or the next day or the day after that.

There was much to be done. For a little boy there were bomb and shell fragments to be hidden away to show to other boys. For a girl there were errands to be run. Their mothers sawed wood, cleared the streets of debris, righted overturned trucks, carried telephone poles, pushed heavy carts, and helped soldiers pull the guns. It was prudent to be busy. Men who wandered away from their companies were rounded up by field police and assigned to replacement companies. They hated that; it was better to go into action with friends than with strangers. Civilians who appeared to be doing nothing were collected into labor battalions and marched off to unload river barges or clear fields of fire for machine guns and antitank artillery. They hated that; days might pass before they were released.

On this morning as on all clear days the sun rose abruptly out of the steppe on the far side of the Volga. Its first rays tipped Mamayev Kurgan or Hill 102.0[1] where Krilov's 62nd Army command post was lodged on the summit in a warren of trenches and dugouts. Hill 102.0 dominated Stalingrad. To Krilov's left were the town's business district and its central railroad station with its clock tower on Moscow time.[2] Behind him was the river with oil storage tanks on the embankment and shipyards with barges tied to their moorings. Islands cut the Volga into channels upstream and downstream but here the river was about half a mile wide with no bridge to the far side which was low, flat, sandy, covered with scrub pine, and for the most part uninhabited.[3] To Krilov's right was the factory district, first the Red October steel factory, then the Barricades metallurgical plant, then the Dzerzhinsky tractor plant that had turned out half the tractors in the Soviet Union before the war.

From Hill 102.0 or Mamayev Kurgan the sun's rays touched

[1] 102.0 meters above the level of the Volga at Stalingrad where the river itself is below what is customarily thought of as sea level.
[2] All Russia fought the war on Moscow time.
[3] The present dam with its highway to the far side was built after the war.

the heights just beyond to the west—Hill 133.4 off to the left, Hills 126.3 and 143.4 straight ahead, Hill 144.3 to the right. Minutes later the sun struck the chimneys of the factories and the charred walls of apartment houses and office buildings. Soon all was bathed in light—companies of marching infantry, horses hauling the guns, men stringing barbed wire, engineers laying mine fields, workmen bricking up windows and cutting embrasures in factory walls. From Mamayev Kurgan or any of Stalingrad's hills soldiers saw entire city blocks of blackened chimneys and twisted iron bedsteads. Behind them launches towed barges over the river.

All was quiet along the front a few miles to the west. Russians in faded brown uniforms and Germans in field gray lay concealed in gullies or broken trenches that looked from the air like the fingers of a hand with firing points at their tips. The idea was to see and not be seen, to plot the position of enemy guns, to locate his lines of supply and communications, to find out when and where he gathered for meals, to observe any unusual concentration of troops. By dawn this Thursday recruits from the replacement companies that had filled out the ranks during the hours of darkness were deepening trench fingers and looking about them apprehensively at the unfamiliar landscape. They saw nothing but wheat fields, grazing ground, the embankment of Stalingrad's circular railway, and a few suburban brick buildings that had been gutted by fire.

Preparations for defense went on all day. They were light in the apple orchards on the west side of town—mostly trench fingers, gun emplacements, barbed wire, and mine fields. They were fairly heavy in the workers' settlements behind the orchards—deep trenches in the gardens and embrasures with sandbags at cellar and upper-story windows. They were strenuous at the factories and along the riverbank—thick, antitank barriers made of steel girders, fields of fire for large-caliber guns, damaged tanks dug into the ground to serve as stationary pillboxes.

Oddly, the implications of the not-a-step-back directive, however unnerving to those who hoped for escape, had something of an exhilarating effect. Veterans, recruits, the men, and the women were told and believed that what was coming was the decisive struggle, that whether the war was won or lost would be determined here, by them, in this destroyed building, on that torn street, or in the field beyond; and in this fertile atmosphere two sentiments took hold and increased in intensity. One was a feeling for the *rodina*—the motherland or native land. The other was a sense of identity with Russian military tradition. Both have their counterparts elsewhere but in Russia they are rooted in the history of a frontier society.

To a Russian the *rodina* has special meaning. It is not the state or the regime, and it is more than the country or its people. It is their manner of speech, the ground they walk on, the sturgeon that swim in the Volga, the quiet waters of the silent Don, the birch trees on the outside of town, the dark smell of rain on a dusty road. It is a song, a proverb that hits the mark, the excitement of small pleasures in a hard, often stormy life. It is what they are used to. Russians are moved by the *rodina*.

They are stirred, too, by a military tradition only they are familiar with. It speaks to them with a voice that says death is inseparable from war and war inseparable from victory. Non-Russians rarely understand it.

Louis Philippe de Ségur, who accompanied Napoleon on his invasion of Russia in 1812, was astonished to find that "not one" of the 20,000 Russians wounded at Borodino "uttered a groan." "Perhaps when they are far from their homes," he wrote, "they look less for compassion. But certainly they appeared to support pain with greater fortitude than the French; not that they suffered more courageously, but that they suffered less; for they have less feeling in body and mind, which arises from their being less civilized."[4]

Writing of the Crimean War and the Battle of Inkerman in 1854, a British author[5] declared:

"Again the thick-skulled Muscovite appeared dazed by the audacity of his [British] foe."

He quoted an officer who reported a Russian attack was accompanied by "that horrible, jackal sort of rasping, screeching, discordant yell which with the Russians takes the place of our manly British cheers."

The Russians of course tell it differently. They say it was not the

[4] *History of the Expedition to Russia* (Philadelphia, 1825).
[5] W. Baring Pemberton, *Battles of the Crimean War* (New York: The Macmillan Company, 1962).

cold but Russian arms that defeated Napoleon in 1812 and by way of evidence point out that he began his retreat from Moscow on October 19 with 110,000 men and was down to half as many before winter set in. And as they recall the Crimean War they held off a combined British, French, Turkish, and Sardinian force for an entire year and finally compelled it to withdraw.

In any event their feeling for the *rodina* and their awareness of military tradition were strong in Stalingrad on Thursday, September 10. An army girl from another town wrote a letter home:

Dear Mother:

Expect my return only when victory has been won. When you hear victory has been won, come out to meet me.

With the warmest greetings of a Red Army fighter, I am your daughter

A. Vasilenko

Men and women dug tank traps across all roads leading in from the west. Batteries of field artillery were moved in during the night, the guns camouflaged before daybreak. Buildings on the outside of town were occupied and organized for all-round defense. Gullies and the Tsaritsa River that sliced through to the Volga were mined.[6]

At the tractor plant men repaired tanks. Guns were still being turned out at the Barricades factory. The Red October plant, destroyed by air attack, was readied for defense.

On Mamayev Kurgan activity was feverish. At the top a labor battalion improved Krilov's command post. On the near slopes women dug communications trenches to the summit. Ammunition was carried by hand and stored in underground shelters on the way up.

There was movement everywhere. On the Square of Fallen Heroes in the center of town a militia company of high school students practiced the art of storming and defending an apartment house. Down by the Tsaritsa ravine there was a school for runners

[6] The Tsaritsa, like Tsaritsyn as the city was called before it became Stalingrad (1925), was named not for the tsars (czars) but by ancient Tartars who called it "Sari-su" (Yellow River) as they did the old site "Sara-chin" (Yellow Island). In its course to the Volga the Tsaritsa divides old or lower Stalingrad from the new or upper town.

and couriers. Nearby a police detachment trained dogs to run with explosives on their backs toward enemy tanks.

Thursday, September 10, was a day of preparation and expectation in Stalingrad. Young boys, orphaned in the bombings or lost, attached themselves to combat companies and did whatever the soldiers let them do.

On the following day General Chuikov, the deputy commander of the 64th Army that was now well entrenched in the southern suburbs, was summoned across the river to Eremenko's headquarters. There he was given command of the wavering 62nd and ordered into the city. At forty-two years of age he became the army's fourth commander in two months—just as the battle reached its most spectacular stage.[7]

[7] General Krilov, who had been Chief of Staff at Odessa and at the siege of Sevastopol, stayed on as Chuikov's Chief of Staff for the long, hard pull through to February.

7

The stillness before the storm that would bring the Battle of Stalingrad to a swift, bloody, and unexpected climax came on September 12. On that ominous Saturday when for the first time since late June there were no major engagements and no ground of importance was gained or lost, both Adolf Hitler and Joseph Stalin called in their senior commanders in the field. Hitler summoned Weichs and Paulus and gave the order for the "final assault." Stalin summoned Zhukov to the Kremlin and approved plans for a more powerful offensive out of the north. Clearly it was a day of critical military importance. How critical we know. How the rival Supreme High Commanders viewed it is less certain because the record is incomplete and the testimony of associates who survived them is sometimes less than candid.

A German version holds that Hitler, irrationally and unlike his generals, thought victory was near, because he ordered the seizure of Stalingrad in an assault to begin the following day and for that purpose added to 6th Army three divisions of Hoth's panzer force. Keitel, writing in his Nuremberg cell in 1946, said: "Halder, like Jodl and myself, was waiting to see where the Russians' strategic reserves would put in an appearance."[1] Halder, though he wrote nothing about it in his diary, said later he pointed out "very clearly" what would happen when Stalin unleashed a "million and a half troops against Stalingrad and the Don front."[2] But Hitler, as we have seen, was not in a triumphant mood. He had fired List on the ninth and let Halder know he, too, was about through. On the eleventh, stenographic reporters from the Reichstag arrived from Berlin to make verbatim transcripts of all high-level military discussions from then on. Still, having advanced three hundred miles in seventy-seven days and with only two or three more to go before Stalingrad was his, he was determined to move on, given the awesome alternatives which were to stand where he was in the unsheltered steppe for the winter or pull back. And having decided to move on, he may well have resolved to exude confidence, whatever his true feelings. All leaders are actors to a degree, and the Fuehrer as leader-actor could put on an astonishing performance to conceal a fear or a doubt or intimidate those around him. In any event he had no purely military need to see Weichs and Paulus that day. Plans for the attack had already been approved and 6th Army regrouped to launch it.

For Stalin the problem was of a different order. He had the men and the machines and every reason to think he could hold his own and more. But the counteroffensive until now had been a dismal failure, the loss of life horrendous, although the circumstances would appear to have been different than Zhukov recalled them in his memoirs. Zhukov says that on the tenth he told Stalin by telephone:

"With the forces at the disposal of the Stalingrad Front we cannot break through the corridor and join the troops of the Southeast front. The Germans have significantly strengthened their defensive line with units recently arrived from Stalingrad. Further attacks with these forces and this deployment would be useless, and the troops would inevitably suffer great losses. Reinforcements and time to deploy them for a more concentrated frontal assault

---

[1] Keitel, p. 182. Most of them had already "put in an appearance."
[2] The Russians had nothing like a million and a half reserves at this late date.

are needed. Blows by individual armies will not be enough to topple the enemy."[3]

The implication is he criticized the Supreme for his conduct of the operation. Zhukov goes on:

"Stalin said in reply it might be well for me to fly to Moscow and report in person."

In the files of the Soviet Ministry of Defense, however, there is a document Zhukov does not mention which indicates he was not alone in his efforts to persuade Stalin to stop the bloody assault. It shows he acted in concert with Vasilievsky and Malenkov of the State Defense Committee, that they were more diplomatic than Zhukov recalls, and that all three went out of their way not to upset the Supreme. In the Kremlin as elsewhere honey caught more flies than vinegar; vinegar had a way of turning to hemlock in the hands of anyone who offered it.

On the twelfth, according to this document, Zhukov and Malenkov, evidently in response to a severe rebuke from Stalin, sent the following teletype to Moscow:

COMRADE STALIN:

WE ARE NOT DISCONTINUING OFFENSIVE OF 1ST, 24TH AND 66TH ARMIES BUT ARE PRESSING IT PERSISTENTLY. AS WE HAVE REPORTED TO YOU, ALL AVAILABLE FORCES AND RESOURCES ARE PARTICIPATING IN CONTINUING OFFENSIVE.

(It would seem that Stalin had accused them of failure to press the attack energetically.)

LINK WITH STALINGRADERS COULD NOT BE ESTABLISHED BECAUSE WE WERE WEAKER THAN ENEMY IN ARTILLERY AND AIR. OUR 1ST GUARDS ARMY, WHICH INITIATED OFFENSIVE, DID NOT HAVE ONE ADDITIONAL ARTILLERY REGIMENT OR ANTITANK OR ANTIAIRCRAFT REGIMENT.

SITUATION NEAR STALINGRAD COMPELLED US TO SEND IN 24TH AND 66TH ARMIES BEFORE

---

[3] Zhukov, pp. 412–13.

THEY WERE FULLY ASSEMBLED AND BEFORE ARRIVAL ARTILLERY REINFORCEMENTS. RIFLE DIVISIONS WENT INTO BATTLE STRAIGHT FROM 50-KILOMETER [30-mile] MARCH.

SUCH INTRODUCTION OF ARMIES INTO BATTLE UNIT BY UNIT AND WITHOUT ADDITIONAL RESOURCES DID NOT ENABLE US TO BREAK THROUGH ENEMY'S DEFENSES AND UNITE WITH STALINGRADERS, BUT IN RETURN OUR SWIFT BLOW COMPELLED ENEMY TO TURN HIS FORCES AGAINST OUR GROUP, WHICH EASED POSITION OF DEFENDERS OF CITY, WHICH WITHOUT THIS BLOW WOULD HAVE BEEN TAKEN BY ENEMY. WE HAD NO OTHER AIM UNKNOWN TO STAVKA IN MIND.

(The choice of words is defensive, almost obsequious. Zhukov and Malenkov wrote as if they heartily approved Stalin's operational plan and no other had entered their heads.)

COMRADE VASILIEVSKY WILL HAVE REPORTED TO YOU NEW OPERATION WE HAVE IN MIND FOR 17.9. THIS OPERATION AND ITS TIMING ARE RELATED TO ARRIVAL OF NEW DIVISIONS, TANK UNITS, ARTILLERY REINFORCEMENTS AND SUPPLIES OF AMMUNITION.

(They hint at the point without making it as if that were Vasilievsky's mission.)

AS ON PREVIOUS DAYS, OUR ATTACKING FORCES HAVE ADVANCED SLIGHTLY BUT SUFFERED GREAT LOSSES FROM ENEMY ARTILLERY FIRE AND AIR, BUT WE DO NOT CONSIDER IT POSSIBLE TO STOP OFFENSIVE BECAUSE THIS WOULD FREE HAND OF ENEMY OPERATING AGAINST STALINGRAD.

(They want Stalin to stop it and to believe he is stopping it on his own initiative.)

WE CONSIDER IT OBLIGATORY FOR US EVEN UNDER DIFFICULT CONDITIONS TO GRIND DOWN ENEMY WHO, NO LESS THAN US, IS SUFFERING LOSSES, AND AT SAME TIME WE WILL PREPARE BETTER ORGANIZED AND MORE POWERFUL BLOW.

(They hope Stalin will understand it will not be possible to do both at the same time.)

BATTLE HAS ESTABLISHED THAT SIX DIVISIONS—THREE INFANTRY, TWO MOTORIZED AND ONE TANK—ARE OPERATING ON FRONT LINE AGAINST [our] NORTHERN GROUP. IN SECOND ECHELON AGAINST NORTHERN GROUP THERE ARE NO FEWER THAN TWO INFANTRY DIVISIONS AND 150 TO 200 TANKS.[4]

It was only after this telegraphed message reached the Kremlin that Stalin called Zhukov to Moscow and only after the Kremlin meeting the same night, which Vasilievsky and Zhukov attended, that Stalin agreed (or decided) to halt the offensive and resume it with greater power on the seventeenth or eighteenth.[5]

*

Understandably the significance of the twelfth passed unperceived at the White House in Washington and 10 Downing Street in London to which accurate intelligence from the east continued to seep slowly when at all. In Washington, where the War Department had just about written off Stalingrad as lost to the Germans, President Roosevelt was thinking of the coming congressional elections and planning a two-week campaign swing around the country

[4] Samsonov, pp. 160–61.
[5] Zhukov and Vasilievsky say that on the night of September 12 they first suggested to Stalin the strike that turned out to be the great November counteroffensive. Eremenko, on the other hand, says he proposed it in early August, and on August 15 Stalin mentioned to Churchill plans for "a counteroffensive on a great scale."

that would take him to the Chrysler plant in Detroit (now making tanks), the Ford plant at Willow Run (B-24 Liberators), the Boeing plant in Seattle (B-17 Flying Fortresses), the Higgins shipyard in New Orleans, and various training camps. In London, where it was still thought possible the Russians might be defeated or sue for a separate peace, Churchill was pressing with discouraging results the idea of an allied air force in the Caucasus. On August 30 he suggested to Roosevelt an operation that would involve 20 squadrons, 12,000 men, 2,000 vehicles, and 4,000 tons of initial supplies. There was no immediate answer from the White House. On September 6 he wired Stalin saying he was "anxious" to send staff officers to Moscow to discuss the matter. There was no reply from the Kremlin.

8

Adolf Hitler had a feeling for Sunday as if it were a day when his enemies slept. He invaded Russia on Sunday, June 22, 1941. In 1942 he opened his summer campaign on Sunday, June 28; he struck out from Vertyachi toward the Volga on Sunday, August 23; and it was on a Sunday, September 13, that he went for Stalingrad in all-out assault. The attack was a blistering drive that drove back the Russians into the heart of the city.

To be sure, if you had been in Moscow that day as I was, you would have heard nothing about it. Not a line on Stalingrad appeared in the daily press. The radio played soft music, classical compositions, and military marches. News bulletins told of activity on other fronts and of meetings in the arms factories and on state and collective farms. But if you had been at 62nd Army headquarters on the crater-pitted top of Mamayev Kurgan, you would have known early on that this was a decisive day. Chuikov, who had taken command the night before, worked until two o'clock in the morning and then went to sleep. At 6:30 he was awakened by the shock waves of explosions echoing in his dugout. To his right, around Spartakovka and Orlovka above the factory district, action was light; here the Germans sought only to prevent the Russians from transferring troops to threatened sectors. Straight ahead on the far side of Hill 126.3 a mile to the west, gunfire was angry and continuous. To Chuikov's left in the suburbs to the south, it was equally strong. Puffs of exploding shells showed where the battle raged. Black flares fired by German infantry warned away their own bombers and attack planes from advancing lines.

Paulus was a professional. He did not rush in with a hundred thousand or more men and hundreds of tanks. He worked methodically like a surgeon and in two directions. In the center he threw in elements of the 71st, 94th, and 295th Divisions and a combat team from 24th Panzer. He hit the south to his right with 29th Motorized and 14th Panzer. He sliced off a hill here, isolated a building complex there, destroyed a Russian mine field, and laid one of his own to protect a flank. He broke up a concentration of Russian infantry before it could counterattack, occupied a Russian trench, seized a railway siding. First came the artillery, then the planes, then the tanks and automatic-rifle men. They, too, were professionals. Blasting a way through narrow corridors, throwing grenades through windows and doorways, and taking cover when Russian guns and mortars opened up, 6th Army inched forward into a hell of its own making. Dive bombers struck at river barges bringing in troop replacements and at likely targets in the town.

German shells and bombs churned the kurgan, a major objective. Despite counterbattery and antiaircraft fire from the far side of the Volga, they cut into a machine gun–artillery battalion (UR)[1] and the NKVD regiment (269th) that held its forward slope. They tore open underground shelters and flattened trench lines.

Soon there was a control problem. With little information coming in and few orders getting out, Chuikov and Krilov turned to signal lamps, to their one radio transmitter, and to couriers. One runner recalls that as he jogged down the hill toward the river and along a glass-strewn street he spied an upright piano that had been rescued from a burning building: "I slowed down a bit and managed to hit three keys as I went by."

---

[1] A UR (Russian initials for a fortified region) was a peculiarly Russian formation used to construct and hold a fortified area. Commanded by a colonel or a general, it consisted of five to nine machine gun–artillery battalions. An average UR had some four thousand men.

About 7:30 Chuikov got through by radio to the command post of his left-wing division below the Tsaritsa. He talked to Colonel Dubiansky, who had taken over the 35th Guards after the death of General Glazkov five days before.[2]

"Are you the Dubiansky I used to know in the Byelo-Russian Region?" he asked.

"The same, Comrade General."

"I am answering your request. I have no reserves. There will be no replacements. When I get them, I will send them. For now—stand to the end. That is all."

Elsewhere in the city it was the same story. Commanders called for help. They got none. But in truth little is known of what went on out on the line that morning. Most of the men there died, and those who survived can scarcely recall what they saw, what they heard, or how they felt. Like passengers who live through a plane crash the colors they remember are darkness and blinding light. Like men and women who have just escaped from a burning building all they see in the mind's eye are shadowy figures in the smoke. A few recall bizarre details like a broken doll in a gutter or a bleeding horse standing head down in a mine field.

Death came swiftly or slowly in many forms and usually from far away—in a smoking tank, on a dusty street, at a cellar window, behind a wall, in a cherry or a pear orchard, in a trench, in a barge or rowboat crossing the river. The wounded thought mainly of getting away before the bayonets came because as every infantryman knows that is what bayonets are for—to kill the wounded.

Who were they? Who were these Russians? These Germans? To their families and friends they were men and boys. To almost everyone else they were abstractions, visionary notions, *soldiers*.

Back in the long, narrow town along the Volga refugees hurried to the riverbank. There were labor gangs still building barricades and clearing fields of fire. There were replacement companies

---

[2] In the military museum at Volgograd (Stalingrad) there hangs a faded brownish-gray greatcoat that is torn and ripped in 162 places. It was General Glazkov's, commander of the 35th, who died on the southwest approaches to the city after repeated requests for permission to move his headquarters went unanswered. To Glazkov as to Gen. V. Ye. Sorokin of the 126th who died before him, Stalin's directive—"not a step back without an order from higher command"—was iron-clad.

marching to the hollow sound of the guns while scattered units were re-formed for combat in the ravines, in the orchards, on spacious city squares and playing fields. Stragglers were assigned to the nearest division. Those who had time rested and smoked cigarettes they made from *makhorka,* a strong, coarse tobacco, and a strip of newspaper. Others who found a well nearby or a horse trough took off their boots, unwrapped strips of cloth they wore instead of socks, and washed the cloth. They hung the strips to dry on tree limbs, broken fences, whatever was at hand.

One has to guess a bit, as we do when we try to guess what it was like at Troy or Cannae, at Gettysburg or on the Marne. The youngest and most alert looking would have been submachine gunners who had something of the pride of American Marines; they were out ahead. The tallest and strongest would have been antitank riflemen who worked in pairs; one carried and fired the long, single-shot, bolt-action rifle that weighed forty pounds, the other lugged boxes of armor-piercing ammunition. Antitank riflemen marched behind the submachine gunners but they—and the gunners—knew they would stand when the gunners dropped back.

Whatever their ages, the faces of all of them would have been creased with fatigue like those of the civilians of whom some 200,000 were still in the town despite mobilization and evacuation. Civilians received no pay but got hot tea and bread in the morning and perhaps a bowl of *shchi,* or cabbage soup, in the evening, and the wonder and envy of their neighbors are said to have been the self-reliant who in a fashion known only to themselves managed to find in the midst of scarcity a few potatoes or a jar of jam or a piece of fish. Maybe some of them had cat. Vasili Grossman, a Russian correspondent who was in Stalingrad in September, was struck by the large number of Persian cats sunning themselves in time of battle. When I got there in early February the cats were gone.

As the day wore on and communications worsened, control became still more of a problem because the army was no longer the cohesive force it had been weeks before. Two divisions were down to a composite regiment each, another to a composite battalion. Other formations existed only on paper, their men having been killed off, wounded, taken prisoner, or rounded up by straggler lines as they made their way back to the river from the outer, center, and inner defense lines. In this 62nd Army, which was quite different from the neat reserve force of six divisions that first met Paulus in July, there were twenty-three separate units holding a twenty-five-mile front. Reading from right to left, this is how they lined up on the map General Krilov showed Chuikov when he gave up his brief command of the army to become Chuikov's Chief of Staff:

Holding a salient north of the Mokraya (wet) Mechetka

Three regiments of the 124th Rifle Brigade (Col. Sergei F. Gorokhov)

Three regiments of the 149th Rifle Brigade (Lt. Col. V. A. Bolvinov)

The 282nd Regiment of the 10th NKVD Division (Col. A. A. Sarayev)

Two regiments of the 115th Rifle Brigade (Col. K. M. Andryusenko)

A composite regiment of the 196th Division (Col. S. P. Ivanov)[3]

One regiment of the 2nd Motorized Brigade (commander unidentified)

A third regiment of the 115th Brigade (Andryusenko)

A regiment of the 315th Division (Gen. M. S. Knyazev)[4]

A second regiment of the 2nd Motorized Brigade

The fourth regiment of the 149th Brigade (Bolvinov)

The fourth regiment of the 124th Brigade (Gorokhov)

Facing west south of the Mokraya (wet) Mechetka

A composite regiment of the 112th Division (Col. I. E. Yermolkin)

The 6th Guards Tank Brigade (Lt. Col. V. D. Krichmanov)

The 189th Tank Brigade (commander unidentified)

The 38th Motorized Brigade (Col. Ivan D. Burmakov)

The 6th Tank Brigade (Maj. S. N. Khopko)[5]

[3] The only division of the original six still in the line.
[4] General Knyazev was with the rest of his split division north of the German corridor.
[5] Recently moved into the city from 57th Army to the south.

Facing west south of the Tsaritsa ravine
The 42nd Rifle Brigade (Col. M. S. Batrakov)
The 244th Division (Col. G. A. Afanasiev)[6]
The 10th Rifle Brigade (Col. F. A. Verevkin)
The 133rd Tank Brigade (Maj. Nikolai V. Bubnov)
The 272nd Regiment of the 10th NKVD Division (Sarayev)
The 131st Division (Col. M. A. Pesochkin)
A composite regiment of the 35th Guards (Colonel Dubiansky)

In addition, the army had twelve weakened artillery and mortar regiments, a tank destroyer brigade, and, defending Mamayev Kurgan, the machine gun–artillery battalion (UR) and NKVD regiment. Heavy artillery and about five hundred antiaircraft guns were on the far side of the river.

Paulus hit hardest between the wet Mechetka and the Tsaritsa and by four o'clock in the afternoon was still advancing slowly. On the Russian right the 6th Guards Tank Brigade under Krichmanov was driven back through the orchards to the workers' settlements before the Barricades and Red October factories. In the Russian center units were forced out of the hospital and, what was more important, off Hill 126.3, from which the Germans could look down on Mamayev Kurgan. In response Chuikov pulled in from his right the 112th Division's composite regiment and called up a battalion that had just been formed from the remnants of the 399th. From down the line on his left he pulled in Batrakov's brigade to hold the upper side of the Tsaritsa.

There was a problem, too, below the Tsaritsa where the 29th Motorized and 14th Panzer Divisions took Sadovaya Station on the railroad coming in from the west, but the key point that day was Hill 126.3. With fire directed from an observation post on its summit, Mamayev Kurgan became untenable. At midnight Chuikov moved his command post to the security of the Tsaritsa bunker, Eremenko's old headquarters, and on the following day, the fourteenth, the Germans broke through to the Volga in a deafening burst of violence. With one battering ram of planes, tanks, artillery, and infantry they took Kuporosnoye suburb in Stalingrad's southern outskirts and drove a wedge between 62nd

[6] Also recently transferred from 57th Army to the south.

Army and the 64th to its left. With another they grabbed Mamayev Kurgan, almost cutting in two the now-isolated 62nd.

Russians reeled in the smoke of exploding bombs and gunfire. From the high kurgan enemy air and artillery observers now had a clear view of the city and the river beyond. But what they could not see was the 13th Guards Division, a fresh force of 10,000 men that lay concealed in a pine forest on the far side of the Volga or the 92nd Rifle and 137th Tank Brigades that were moving in to join it. And what they did not know was that three other fresh divisions, the 95th, 193rd, and 284th, were off to the northeast and marching by night to Stalingrad's defense.

OKW's war diary for that confusing Monday includes the following entry: "In the area of Army Group B it appears from a report of Col. Gen. Baron von Richthofen that enemy resistance in the Stalingrad area is weakening."

Reacting to this bit of hopeful intelligence, Hitler canceled plans to move the 100th Jäger (Light Infantry) and 22nd Panzer Divisions from the Italian sector on the middle Don to Stalingrad.

9

Some time after midnight, about one o'clock on the morning of the fifteenth, Lt. E. P. Cherviakov of the 13th Guards Division led the reinforced 1st Battalion of the 42nd Regiment out of the pine forest across the Volga from Stalingrad. As the men walked silently toward the river, some of the peasant boys wondered at the desertlike vegetation under their feet. Back on the farm they could tell by the crunching sound whether they were moving through the stubble of wheat or barley or oats. But this was different. It set them to thinking. So did the burning city and the flames reflected in the water before them and the sound and sight of explosions in the darkness. Most of them were new to combat because the division had fought a bloody war. It started out as the 3rd Airborne Corps, had its baptism of fire at Kiev in August 1941, escaped from encirclement, retreated in a running fight, and as the 87th Division fought near Kursk. Renamed the 13th Guards, it took part in the May offensive toward Kharkov and in July, again in retreat, escaped over the Don.[1] Now, under its young commander,

[1] There was panic at the Don crossing. Swimming or using inner tubes, log rafts, and empty fuel barrels, only 666 men made it over to the safe side.

174

Gen. Aleksandr I. Rodimtsev, a veteran of the Spanish Civil War[2] who had led the division for a year, it was going in with replacements as it had so many times before. The men lay down and looked about them. Talking was forbidden. No smoking.

Shortly before two o'clock a chance German shell set fire to a wrecked barge at the shore line, and when a sheet of flame brightened the beach and other enemy guns zeroed in on the fiery target, Rodimtsev decided not to wait for the moon to go down.

Cherviakov led the way to the boats. Lines were cast off, and the launches, many of them towing barges, moved slowly into the current where for the first few minutes there was no enemy fire. Then there were tracers. A shell burst damaged a rudder, and a launch started drifting downstream. More scattered gunfire never quite got the range, but as the boats neared the central landing stage in the lee of the high west bank heavy machine guns and mortars opened up and the men went over the side. They raced from the pump house to the docks, from the docks to the brewery, from the brewery up Moscow Street to the State Bank, where they were stopped by a German strong point. Working their way around the bank, they took the Univermag department store, battled fourteen hours for the Square of Fallen Heroes, and by nightfall had the central railroad station.[3]

Meanwhile, the 34th Regiment and the rest of the 42nd made it in and occupied that part of the city close to the river on both sides of the docks from the Tsaritsa ravine on their left near Chuikov's command post to the riverbank near Mamayev Kurgan on their right. While Rodimtsev established headquarters in an old mine shaft by the water's edge, the third regiment, the 39th, waited on the far side of the river to join an assault on the kurgan the next day.

Things were relatively quiet on the second night. There was

---

[2] Like Rodimtsev ("Pavlito") many Russians who fought at Stalingrad were in Spain under assumed names, among them Malinovsky ("Malino"), Nikolai N. Voronov ("Walter"), Pavel I. Batov ("Pablo"), Kolpakchi, Shumilov, and Biryukov.

[3] Cherviakov was wounded that night and carried back to the riverbank but what happened to the twelve hundred men of the battalion and his replacement has not been determined. Some say they were all killed within a week, others that six got out alive.

some range-finding artillery fire. Signal rockets—blue, yellow, green, red, and white—pierced the dark sky. Here and there a fire fight broke out between combat patrols or a combat and a reconnaissance patrol. While tired troops slept, police and civilians guided officers through factories to show them furnace rooms and machine shops that could be organized for defense. They pointed out conduits that would make concealed lines of approach and withdrawal.

"How," a lieutenant asked, "do we get to the schoolhouse without being seen?"

"Follow the ravine," someone said. "Before you get to Pushkin Street you will see a cellar door low down on your right. That leads to the bakery. There is a trench from the bakery to the schoolhouse."

A sergeant's patrol has to scout the northern approaches to Mamayev Kurgan.

"There is only one way," he was told. "Go back to the river. Hang close to the shore until you get to Banni Gully on this side of Red October. That is the factory over there. Follow the gully until you come to the railroad tracks. Then you are on your own."

"Who holds the tracks?"

"Probably the enemy, but the gully is ours."

Battle flared again with first light on Wednesday the sixteenth, both sides attacking, Paulus to retake the railroad station, Chuikov to recapture Mamayev Kurgan, a spectacular affair. The Russian assault began with artillery fire from the far side of the river on German machine gunners and riflemen on the hill's eastern slope, then the 39th Guards Regiment from over the Volga joined the 112th Division's 416th (composite) Regiment under Capt. V. A. Aseyev. They crossed the rail line between the shore and the kurgan and headed for the water tanks on the summit, which was a favorite place for Stalingraders. In summer they picnicked here and watched excursion steamers, ferries, and great rafts of logs move down the river to Astrakhan. In winter skiers and children on sleds flashed down to the low land between the kurgan and Hill 126.3 to the west.

The Russians made it. In an exploit which when it became known weeks later gave heart to the country, the Guards won undying Russian fame. But something was concealed: that the faceless and unheralded men of the 112th also took part and, indeed, may have been the first to reach the top.[4]

On the same day the Germans, counterattacking in the center of town, took the central railroad station. The Russians got it back. The Germans took it again. The Russians got it back, and although by nightfall the 42nd's 1st Battalion was still clinging to the smoking rubble, it was cut off in a complex of railroad shops from which it never got out.

Meanwhile, at that dreary Ukrainian compound near Vinnitsa, Hitler was wallowing in a morass of self-pity. Nothing helped—not Richthofen's cheerful intelligence, which was false, not the fact List was gone and the Fuehrer himself was Commander in Chief of Army Group A in the Caucasus, not even his determination to get rid of Halder and bring in Zeitzler as Chief of the Army General Staff. They were not enough. Nothing was enough. Things were going wrong, and, he felt, it was all so unfair. He personally had worked out the plan of campaign. He personally had executed it. Yet he was bogged down in the Caucasus, not getting very far in Stalingrad, and threatened on the middle Don. He'd get even. He'd punish his generals. How? He'd sulk; that's how. They'd see. They'd find out. He wouldn't shake hands with them any more. He

[4] Little is known about the mysterious 112th except that it is usually referred to in Russian history by the name of its already-dead commander, Colonel Sologub, that it fought in the city longer and almost certainly suffered more casualties than any division but the Guards, that it was in battle until the end of December, and that it received no unit decoration whatsoever. Time and again Colonel Yermolkin, who commanded "Sologub's division," held together the nucleus of a combat force, expanded it with replacements, and took it into the fight until once more it was ground down to next to nothing. Such reticence about such a division suggests its ranks were filled out repeatedly with punitive or punishment battalions which were used by both sides on the eastern front. Marshal Rokossovsky wrote of an entire brigade (3,000 men?) that came under his command in the summer of 1942. He called it the "uneasy brigade": "In August we got a rifle brigade formed of men who had been convicted of various criminal offenses. Yesterday's prisoners had volunteered for the front to atone for their guilt by feats of arms. The government believed in their eagerness for action, and so the brigade arrived. The troops quickly familiarized themselves with the military situation, and we satisfied ourselves they could be entrusted with serious missions. Frequently the entire brigade carried out a reconnaissance in force. It fought impetuously and forced the enemy to disclose his system of fire." (Rokossovsky, p. 135.)

wouldn't eat with them as had been his practice. He'd cancel the noon situation conferences. He wouldn't go to the map room. On second thought he wouldn't go out at all until after dark. He'd stay in his blockhouse. See how they liked that. He'd hold the evening situation conferences in his own hut, and the few officers he permitted to attend would know soon enough what he thought of them and all the others. They'd learn they couldn't tell him one thing one day and the opposite the next; he'd always have two stenographers present taking down every word. He'd have it on paper. And if they thought he'd soon forgive them, they were wrong. He'd hold out.

So it happened.

"It was not until 30th January, 1943, that he deigned to shake hands with Jodl and myself," wrote Keitel in his Nuremberg cell in 1946.

Warlimont added a few details. Hitler only left his "sunless blockhouse" after dark—the map room lay deserted—briefing conferences took place only in Hitler's hut—there were few officers present—the atmosphere was glacial. Ever since the French campaign he had gone to the officers' mess—no more—he never appeared in the mess again—his chair remained empty until his deputy, Martin Bormann, took it in early October.

Still no explanation. Still no analysis of the problem that was gripping the German High Command—Russian reserves continuing to gather at a time when its own were exhausted. On the seventeenth the 92nd Rifle and 137th Tank Brigades pulled into Russian staging areas across the Volga from Stalingrad. Behind them, strung out in the steppe country 50 to 150 miles away, were three rifle divisions moving on Stalingrad by forced march. They were Col. Vasili A. Gorishny's 95th, Nikolai F. Batiuk's 284th, and Fedor I. Smekhotvorov's 193rd. Also coming on foot because the rail line from Nizhnye Baskunchak was reserved for food, fuel, and other supplies were replacement companies that would be fed into the lines to replenish depleted units.

The Germans had nothing to spare. To help in Stalingrad they first ordered, then canceled (September 14), then ordered again (September 23) the 100th Jäger Division from the middle Don where it was also needed. On the sixteenth the process of weakening the Caucasus group to strengthen the middle Don was continued. On that day the 3rd Romanian Army was directed to take over a hundred-mile sector between the Italian 8th and German 6th Armies.

There was no respite for either side. On the eighteenth, the Russians in the north launched their last convulsive offensive bid to break through to the city before November. After a five-day rest, reluctantly granted by Stalin at the urgent request of Vasilievsky, Zhukov, and Malenkov, the 1st Guards and 24th and 66th Armies, reinforced with fresh divisions, artillery and antitank regiments, and some antiaircraft, attacked to the south. Point of main effort: both sides of the Moscow–Stalingrad railway in a sector held by the Guards.

Another failure. The Guards, operating on the Russian right, moved out at 7 A.M. By noon they had Kilometer Station 564, the village of Borodkin, and Hill 154.2. The Germans counterattacked and took back all three. Kozlov's 24th in the center and Malinovsky's 66th on the Russian left near the Volga fared no better, although for a few hours there was some excitement at Eremenko's headquarters when ten of Malinovsky's tanks hacked their way through to the city in a night strike that looked like the beginning of a breakthrough. German forces, however, closed in behind them and sealed off the breach.

And so it went for five painful days that recall some of the disastrous offensives on the western and eastern fronts in World War I when men's lives and limbs and eyesight were exchanged for control of a ruined farmhouse or a ridge line or some other slight rise in the land that was presumed to have tactical importance.

On the third day three divisions from Stavka's reserve, the 258th, 260th, and 273rd, were thrown in and cut to ribbons by German air and artillery. The 120th attacking along the Volga bank ended up with thirty to forty men in each of its nine battalions.

In the city itself the battle increased in intensity as the Germans struggled for control of Stalingrad below the Tsaritsa and from the Tsaritsa up to the kurgan, a sector thinly held by the 13th Guards.

Before dawn on the eighteenth, the 137th Tank Brigade crossed the river and took up a position to the right of the 39th Guards Regiment that was being harried in a hopeless effort to hold the hill. At the same time the 92nd Rifle Brigade, recently filled out with marines from the northern fleet, moved by boat to Golodni Island and from there on a new foot bridge to the Stalingrad side in an attempt to free the 42nd Brigade, which was now cut off below the Tsaritsa. Late in the day the Germans blew up the ammunition dump of the Guards, and the situation became so threatening above the Tsaritsa that Chuikov moved army headquarters from the Tsaritsa bunker to a narrow strip of pebbly beach between the Volga and the Red October factory.

But new and stronger reserves were at hand. During the night of the nineteenth, Gorishny's 95th Division, the first to follow the Guards, got two of its three regiments over the river. They attacked and missed taking the kurgan the Guards lost the afternoon before. Now the battle became a horror of company-size action. Field artillery, tanks, and self-propelled guns blasted holes in the walls of brick buildings. Flame throwers spewed burning oil through cellar windows. A clawing dust from crushed stone and mortar dried the throats of soldiers and civilians alike. Men yelled for the water boys and the women with buckets hanging from yokes on their shoulders.

Slowly the law of survival dictated new tactics, for the only certainty about battle is that it never develops exactly as foreseen by commanders and their staff officers. Circumstances which were thought to obtain at the onset turn out to be unrealistic, and the conflict degenerates into a scramble wherein significant decisions are taken by junior officers and noncoms. Later on, an attempt will be made to correlate their actions as if something has occurred as anticipated. If the objective is achieved, the operation is held to have been soundly conceived and capably executed. If something goes wrong, lack of initiative on the part of subordinates is suspected. Battles, as the saying goes in a Russian barracks, are won by generals and lost by soldiers.

The new tactics involved swift action by small groups of heavily armed men. Acting on information that may have come from a schoolboy who knows the block the way you know your own back yard, a detachment rushes a grocery store at the corner of an apartment house. Several men are cut down as they race across the street. Others are dropped as they go through the door. If the store is cleared, another unit comes up to consolidate the position. If it is not, no one gets out alive. In another part of town two

8 Russian women emerge from a bomb shelter or underground building. In the upper right: smoke from a burning building. SOVFOTO.

9 A German mortar squad in a bomb crater near a destroyed Russian tank. BUNDESARCHIV, KOBLENZ.

10 An uneasy General Paulus (TO THE RIGHT), shown here with General Seydlitz-Kursbach, the day after his 6th Army was surrounded. BUNDESARCHIV, KOBLENZ.

11 As the days grow colder, Russian infantrymen change to padded jackets and felt boots *(valenki)*. DEUTSCHE PRESSE-AGENTUR.

12 Russia's last line of defense west of the river was a narrow strip of stony beach between the embankment and the Volga. SOVFOTO.

13 Field Marshal Paulus as he looked when I saw him after his surrender. To the left is Colonel Adam, his adjutant; to the right Colonel Schmidt, his Chief of Staff. SOVFOTO.

14 German prisoners of war line up for the long, painful trek to Siberia. DEUTSCHE PRESSE-AGENTUR.

men crawl to a basement window. If they find an unoccupied storeroom, one waits while the other goes for reinforcements. In time isolated actions are co-ordinated. City combat becomes a system.

Late on the nineteenth, dark clouds gathered in the Stalingrad sky, and there was rainfall off and on until Sunday morning. It was easier this way. In the unusual darkness the Russians got Gorishny's third regiment over the river sooner than expected, which gave them a chance to take out more of the wounded in the returning boats. In the chilly air the troops felt better though five or six hours might pass before the women with the yokes on their shoulders came by.

Strange there should be such thirst with the wide Volga flowing one or two hundred yards away! But no one went to the river without permission, and permission was rarely given. All roads led to Stalingrad; none led away except for the seriously wounded, men under orders, and designated women and children when the opportunity arose.

"For us," the men used to say, "there is no land beyond the Volga." For most of them there was none. A man who got too close to the high Stalingrad bank heard a sentry's challenge, and if the sentry were not satisfied with the response, his reaction was certain:

"*Lozhityes!*" (Lie down.)

A challenged soldier who did not fling himself to the ground could be shot. This was standard operating procedure in the Red Army. Once at Stalingrad airport I saw a sentry compel a major to lie down. The dialogue between sentry and prone major proceeded from there.

By the twentieth, a Sunday, the Germans had cleared the mouth of the Tsaritsa and had undisputed possession of Stalingrad from the Tsaritsa down to Kuporosnoye suburb.

Monday, September 21

Thanks to more cloudy weather and a concealed moon, the Russians got about eight thousand replacements over the river—nine hundred of them for the Guards—and the rest into the lines between Mamayev Kurgan and Red October to the right. With their help Chuikov tried an attack to the west and southwest to throw

Paulus off balance and ease the pressure on Gorishny's 95th and Rodimtsev's Guards Divisions. The attack failed.

Still hammering from the Tsaritsa up to the kurgan, German assault battalions broke through to the Volga in two places. They separated the 42nd and 92nd Brigades from the Guards and in the area of the Guards split the 42nd Regiment from the 34th.

Chuikov from near Red October was now paying close attention to German tactics, and late in the day he issued a general order:

IT HAS BEEN ESTABLISHED THAT ONCE ENEMY SEIZES BUILDINGS ALONG STALINGRAD STREETS HE QUICKLY ORGANIZES THEIR DEFENSE. IN BATTLE WITH ENEMY HOLDING SUCH STRUCTURES I ORDER WIDEST POSSIBLE EMPLOYMENT OF HAND GRENADES, MORTARS, ARTILLERY OF ALL CALIBERS, AND SAPPERS WITH FLAMETHROWERS AND EXPLOSIVES.

House-to-house fighting was widespread. There were times when the Russians held a kitchen, the Germans the living room, or the Germans the first and second floors, the Russians the third and fourth. Once when the Russians took the ground floor of a print shop the enemy retreated to the second floor; and when the Russians took the second floor the Germans went back to the first.

The frightening roar of battle was continuous. By day smoke palled the sun. At night flaming houses and factories reddened the sky. Shattered walls lurched grotesquely. The paneless windows of gutted apartment houses stared blindly at the turmoil.

No place was safe from bomb explosion and shellfire. Whole streets disappeared. Others, littered with wreckage, were almost impassable.

Women and children hid in cellars or tried frantically to dig tunnels from the center of town to the riverbank where lay the bodies of those who were burned to death or drowned while trying to escape by ship in late August.

Tuesday, September 22

A significant day.

First, two regiments of Batiuk's 284th Division, the third from the strategic reserve to reach the city in eight days, were brought over the river under a smoke screen and sent between the Guards and Gorishny's 95th to its right.

Second, Smekhotvorov's 193rd formed up for a crossing as soon as boats were available.

And third, the Kremlin in a sudden change of method called off the costly offensive out of the north. The effort to cut through to Chuikov and 62nd Army was abandoned. Full attention was turned to plans for a counteroffensive against both German flanks, one of them on the middle Don in the area that would be occupied by the 3rd Romanian Army.

Coincident with this decision went an order from Stavka that sent three veteran divisions from the northern group of armies to Stalingrad in a roundabout way. What remained of the strategic reserve would be used not for defense of the city but for the great drive that it was hoped and expected could be launched about November 10. Accordingly, from September 22 until the end of the battle in early February Stalingrad got only one more division from Stavka's private force—the 45th in late October.

Clearly in Stavka's judgment the turning point had come or was at hand.

What Hitler thought is less certain. There are no Greiner notes for the last week of the month. Zeitzler replaced Halder on the twenty-fourth, and on the twenty-seventh the Fuehrer pulled out for Berlin in his first absence from headquarters since June 24, four days before the summer offensive.

10

On September 23 Joseph Stalin, who now knew where he was going and how he proposed to get there, received at the Kremlin the first American visitor he had seen in a year, excluding Ambassador Standley and Harriman. The visitor was Wendell L. Willkie, the Republican candidate for President that Roosevelt defeated in 1940; and although Willkie, who was on an airborne tour of the world to see what he could do for the war effort, talked to Roosevelt before his departure, he was about as poorly briefed as a man could be. He knew nothing of allied plans for the invasion of North Africa, which Stalin was familiar with, and nothing about Churchill's discussions with Stalin in August.

"I just want to warn you," Roosevelt is reported to have told him before his departure from Washington. "I know you've got guts, but you may get to Cairo just as Cairo is falling, and you may get to Russia at the time of Russian collapse."[1]

[1] I cannot vouch for the accuracy of this quotation which comes from *Russia at War 1941–1945,* the recollections of Alexander Werth, a British reporter who cited Willkie as his source. Werth took it as an accurate reflection of the President's views at the time, but I am inclined to think that if Roosevelt said what he is reported to have said he was engaging in a little good-humored

Willkie went to Cairo and found it in one piece. He arrived in Russia on the eighteenth and found it alive if not well. Then began a study of Russia's war plants, collective farms, libraries, and any other areas of interest the Russians would talk about or permit him to investigate. By the twenty-first when he flew into Moscow where I saw him at the airport he was coming to suspect there was something about allied thinking he did not like or did not know. Reporters pressed him about the second front, not *whether* there would be one that year or the next but *when,* for outside of a small official circle in Washington, London, and Moscow that was privy to wartime secrets it was assumed invasion of Europe was the next western move. Willkie said only a military man was competent to answer the question, but he went on to give a hint of what he would say in an explosive outburst six days later:

"In my judgment the front at Stalingrad is just as much an American and British front as a Russian front. This war is global in nature. The United Nations cannot be separated, and no nation can protect itself alone and hope to come through this war.

"For the Russians the Second Front has become a symbol of the kind of aid they think they are entitled to from the United States and Great Britain. They appreciate the kind of aid they are getting. On the other hand, they don't feel that it is adequate. They are carrying the brunt of the fight, which they think is as important to the United States as it is to them. They hope we can get more material to them."[2]

Willkie was impressed by what he saw and heard. At the front near Rzhev west of Moscow he asked Gen. Dmitri D. Lelyushenko how large a sector he was defending.

"Sir," said Lelyushenko, "I am not defending. I am attacking."

He visited an aviation factory where 30,000 workers were running three shifts and working sixty-six hours a week, more than 35 per cent of them women, some of them boys Willkie took to be not more than ten years old.

But the high point of his trip and the launching pad for his chal-

---

fooling or teasing at Willkie's expense because by late September there was little question of Cairo falling, and although the President still worried about Russia's ability to hold out, its collapse did not appear imminent even if Stalingrad fell.

[2] The New York *Herald Tribune,* September 23, 1942.

lenge to Roosevelt and Churchill was the two-hour-and-fifteen-minute talk with Stalin on the twenty-third, the day after Stalin called off the attempt to get through to Stalingrad from the north and turned to plans for the November counteroffensive. Stalin, whom Willkie found "desperately tired," said nothing of this development or of the power that would make it possible. Indeed, he indicated the outcome of the battle was in doubt and conveyed to Willkie the impression the United States and Great Britain were dragging their feet. Willkie was outraged.[3]

"Personally," he said in a public statement several days later, "I am now convinced that we can help them [the Russians] by establishing a *real* Second Front in Europe with Great Britain at the earliest possible moment our military leaders will approve. And perhaps some of them will need some public prodding."

Churchill was furious. Roosevelt, who had brought it on himself by not taking Willkie into his confidence, let fall a press conference remark about "typewriter strategists," including an impish imitation of Willkie's pronunciation of several words. And Willkie returned to Washington in a fury of anger at the President.

Only Stalin would have been pleased. He was putting pressure on the allies and at the same time maneuvering himself into a position where he could blame them if Stalingrad fell—not that he would have thought this a likely possibility but one could never be certain, for while the Russians were getting reinforcements the Germans were winning real estate. On the day he saw Willkie a Russian reporter wrote from the besieged city:

"Here the sky burns over your head and the ground shakes under your feet."

The day before, Colonel Batiuk, the thirty-eight-year-old commander of the 284th Division, tried with Gorishny's 95th to take Mamayev Kurgan with one of his two fresh regiments. He failed. With the other he tried on his left to break through along the riverbank to the 13th Guards whose 34th Regiment under Maj. Dmitri I. Panikhin was cut off by a new German thrust to the Volga. He failed again.

[3] So was Ambassador Standley but for an entirely different reason. Angry with Roosevelt and Willkie because he was not asked to sit in on the conversation with Stalin, Standley flew to Washington, where he stayed for some weeks before returning to his Moscow post.

"Enemy is at command post," Panikhin told his division commander by radio. "They are throwing grenades." The words were tapped out on an old Underwood typewriter and inserted in the war diary of the Guards.

On a street under German fire a Russian gunner showed soldiers and civilians where it was safe to cross. Nearby lay the body of the sentry he replaced. At an underground headquarters the eyes of officers and men were heavy with lack of sleep, their faces dark from exhaustion. There was so little oxygen in the place there were times when it was claimed it was barely possible to keep a match going long enough to light a cigarette.

Late that night a shaky foot bridge from the Barricades factory to Zaitsevski Island was finished, and the walking wounded started crossing to friendly land. Still later, some five hundred replacements, mostly Stalingrad boys seventeen to nineteen years old, were brought in by boat to strengthen the Guards, and an overloaded ferry pulled in from the far shore with five truckloads of supplies, more replacements, and nurses.

But it is only in retrospect that one can understand what was happening. To the men in the town this was an unequal struggle for bloodstained rubble. To Eremenko and his command staff, however, it was a deadly game in which they had more than a chance. The 193rd Division was forming up for a crossing. Three veteran divisions from the northern group of armies were on their way. And a formidable force called FAG (Front Artillery Group) was just coming into being. FAG consisted of 250 to 300 guns and several rocket regiments on the safe side of the river. It had its own observation posts in the town and a communications network connected to a brain center from which Gen. V. Ye. Taranovich of Eremenko's staff could mass fire on selected targets. With FAG Eremenko would soon be able to break up an attack before it got going by loosing a barrage lasting up to forty minutes on German assembly areas.

Chuikov, however, had to deal with the present, which was nerve-racking and frustrating. On the twenty-fourth he expected or hoped for all of the 193rd Division but got only the 685th Regiment when the other two regiments were held out for fear the Germans would try to cross the Volga from their foothold south of the Tsaritsa. On the twenty-fifth he learned to his astonishment and anger that Tarasov of the 92nd Brigade was not on the Stalingrad shore as he had thought but directing his crippled unit from Golodni Island. For what he called "lying reports"—i.e., reports that did not say specifically where the command post was—he removed Tarasov and his top commissar, Andreyev, and preferred charges against them before the military tribunal of the army. This did not help. On the next day, a Saturday, what little was left of this brigade and the 42nd were pulled out of the city.

Now the Germans had the Volga bank from Kuporosnoye suburb below the Tsaritsa to the central landing stage above it. They also had Mamayev Kurgan. Next objective—the northern part of Stalingrad, and to block them or upset their timing Chuikov attacked on Sunday morning, the twenty-seventh. He tried along the narrow line from the central landing stage up to the wet Mechetka and gained a little ground. Gorishny's 95th Division took and lost the summit of Mamayev Kurgan. To its right the 6th Guards and 189th Tank Brigades were driven back into the housing settlements near the Red October and Barricades factories. The ubiquitous 112th Division, still farther to the right, was pushed back a mile or more. And once again the army's command post between Red October and the river came under air attack. Telephone communications were disrupted, restored, and broken again. Headquarters lost contact with its division commanders, and to find out what was going on and maintain some measure of control Chuikov went to Batiuk's command post, his Chief of Staff Krilov to Gorishny's, and Commissar Kuzma A. Gurov to corps headquarters of the tank brigades.

That same night, however, the approach from the northern group of armies of the three veteran divisions freed the remaining regiments of Smekhotvorov's 193rd from guard duty on the east bank, and Eremenko with Golikov's help got them over the river with little loss of life. By dawn they were with the tank brigades in the workers' settlement to the west of Red October.

The picture was changing—uneasily in the beginning but increasingly as the days passed and as Stavka's reorganization plans began to take effect.

On Monday, September 28, the northern group of armies, hitherto called the Stalingrad front, became the Don front under General Rokossovsky replacing Gordov. The southern group, heretofore called the southeast front, became the Stalingrad front, with Eremenko still in command.

In time these two forces would crash into the German flanks as D day for the counteroffensive came around, but for the present they would hold their positions, regroup, and absorb reinforcements.

Planning was intensive. A code name was assigned to each commander as follows:

Stalin	:	*Vasiliev*
Zhukov	:	*Konstantinov*
Vasilievsky	:	*Mikhailov*
Rokossovsky	:	*Dontsov*
Eremenko	:	*Ivanov*

New security regulations were exceptionally strict:

(1) Nothing about the counteroffensive committed to paper would leave the Kremlin.

(2) Zhukov would fly on Tuesday, September 29, to Don front headquarters and disclose the operational concept to three men only: to Rokossovsky and the other two members of his military council, Gen. M. S. Malinin, his Chief of Staff, and Corps Commissar A. S. Zheltov.

(3) Vasilievsky would fly the same day to Stalingrad front headquarters and personally inform Eremenko and the four other members of his military council: Gen. G. F. Zakharov, the Chief of Staff, Nikita Khrushchev, Aleksei S. Chuyanov, and Brigade Commissar Nikolai F. Kirichenko.

(4) Individual army commanders with a need to know would be informed at a later date. Chuikov in Stalingrad city was not one of them.

Meanwhile, the three veteran divisions were gathering on the far side of the Volga:

Stepan S. Guriev's 39th Guards (from 1st Guards Army) that would enter the town on October 1.

L. N. Gurtiev's 308th (from 24th Army) that would cross the river on the 2nd and 3rd.

Viktor G. Zholudev's 37th Guards (from 4th Tank Army) that would move in on the 4th.

The Battle of Stalingrad was entering a new stage and at precisely the time when hundreds of miles to the south in the Battle for the Caucasus German forces had just about shot their bolt. By September 25, Russian commanders in the Caucasus had fifty rifle divisions, thirteen cavalry divisions, thirty-six rifle brigades, nine marine brigades, four rifle regiments, two regiments of marines, and supporting troops. They outnumbered the Germans in infantry, artillery, and mortars in mountain country where German tank superiority counted for little.

Seventeenth Army (General Ruoff) with Romanian support had Novorossisk on the Black Sea coast but could not break out along the shore road to Tuapse. First Panzer (General Ewald von Kleist) had Mozdok on the rushing Terek River but could not get to Grozny or Ordzhonikidze or to Makhachkala on the Caspian Sea.[4]

In sum, by the end of September Hitler's anabasis of 1942, his march upcountry, had come to an end.

[4] In this period Leonid Brezhnev was head of the political department of the 18th Army in the Caucasus. Russian history says that several months later he was on a trawler that hit a mine in the Black Sea, that he was hurled overboard and later rescued unconscious from the water. (Grechko, p. 255.)

PART FOUR

1

In October the paved streets of Moscow glistened in the damp darkness. As the days grew noticeably shorter and the nights turned cool to cold, it rained often and with unusual persistence. Pedestrians hugged the buildings. They hurried across street corners, ducked into subways, and waited in doorways for the weather to break. To these city dwellers the rain was an inconvenience, an irritation, but out in the countryside it crippled both armies and brought suffering to the middle Don where rested Russian troops and new forces organized to replace activated reserves were massing for counteroffensive. After the hot, dry summer there was little grass in the flat steppe, and because of a shortage of fodder, horses died by the thousands on the Russian side of the line. Farm tractors, pressed into service, broke down. Heavy guns sank in mud to their axles. Gunners and riflemen stepped into the traces alongside tired animals and with ropes and straps over their shoulders pulled like Volga boatmen in the old days—*pa burlatski* as the Russians say—like barge haulers. They slipped, fell, got to their feet again. To the army it was another *rasputitsa*—the fall season of bad roads. In the snug Kremlin, however, it was a time of secret preparation and a measure of psychological warfare directed at the United States and Great Britain.

"I must inform you," Stalin cabled the Prime Minister on the third, "that our position in the Stalingrad area has changed for the worse since the early days of September."

It had not changed for the worse. But this was Stalin's story as he told it to Willkie and he stuck to it. He wired the President:

"As to the situation at the front you certainly know that in recent months our situation in the south and especially in the region of Stalingrad has worsened due to the fact we are short of planes, especially pursuit planes."

He said he could forgo for now tanks and guns but needed planes—800 a month—from 8,000 to 10,000 trucks, 5,000 tons of aluminum, and 4,000 to 5,000 tons of explosives.

And as if to emphasize his point he let loose that day a subtle blast that had one meaning to the President and Prime Minister and quite another to the Russian people and the world at large.

"What place does the possibility of a Second Front occupy in the Soviet estimates of the current situation?" asked Henry Cassidy, the Associated Press correspondent in Moscow, in the first and most pertinent of three written questions he submitted to the Kremlin.

"A very important place," Stalin replied in his sixth public utterance of any kind since the German invasion fifteen months before and the first in eleven months in which he had spoken of an allied landing in Europe. "One might say a place of first-rate importance."

To outsiders who knew nothing of allied intentions the words seemed restrained enough. To Churchill and Roosevelt, however, they indicated increasing Russian difficulties and mounting Kremlin opposition to Torch only three weeks to the day before American troop ships sailed for North Africa.

Cassidy received Stalin's reply on the fourth and published it the following morning, evidently with some impact on the President, who promptly sent a private message to Churchill which read in part:

"I feel very strongly that we should make a firm commitment to put an air force in the Caucasus and that that operation should not be contingent on any other.[1]

[1] Churchill had been trying for five weeks to get Roosevelt (and Stalin) to act on this proposal. Returning to Washington from his campaign swing around the country, the President now embraced it with enthusiasm. By an

"The Russian front is today our greatest reliance and we simply must find a direct manner in which to help them other than our diminishing supplies. We shall, on our part, undertake to replace in the Middle East all of our own planes which are transferred [to the Caucasus] and assist you in every possible way with your own air problems in the Middle East."[2]

On the eighth the President and Prime Minister answered Stalin's messages of the third, phrasing their cables, in Roosevelt's words, "to leave a good taste in his mouth," but because they concentrated on their thought to put an air force in the Caucasus the taste they left was not to his liking. He acknowledged their messages—no more—with the result that by the twenty-fourth when Montgomery was attacking Rommel in Egypt and ships were leaving American ports for North Africa they were in something of a quandary. They discussed the Kremlin's curious silence:

Churchill to Roosevelt[3]

". . . Have you had any answer to your message [to Stalin] quoted in your [message number] 193? . . . Meanwhile, fourteen days have passed and no progress has been made in the necessary arrangements with the Russians for choosing landing grounds, etc., to enable our twenty squadrons to take station on the Russian southern flank in January. . . . As you see, I have received nothing but this cryptic 'thank you.' Baffling as all this is, we are persevering because of the splendid fighting of the Russian armies. I wonder whether anything has occurred inside the Soviet animal to make it impossible for Stalin to give an effective reply. It may be that the Russian army has acquired a new footing in the Soviet machine. . . ."

Roosevelt to Churchill[4]

"I am not unduly disturbed about our respective responses or lack of responses from Moscow. I have decided they do not use speech for the same purposes we do.

"I have not heard of any difficulty at our end about arrange-

---

"operation not contingent on any other" he meant without waiting for Rommel's defeat in North Africa, which was Churchill's idea.

[2] *Roosevelt and Churchill*, pp. 256–57.
[3] Ibid., pp. 258–59. Sent October 24.
[4] Ibid., pp. 261–62. Sent October 27.

ments for landing fields on the Russian southern flank but I shall explore that from my end at once.

"I feel very sure the Russians are going to hold out this winter and that we should proceed vigorously with our plans both to supply them and to set up an air force to fight with them. I want us to be able to say to Mr. Stalin that we have carried out our obligations one hundred per cent."

Leaving them to ponder his refusal to discuss allied air in the Caucasus, Stalin remained silent while Russian preparations for the November counteroffensive continued. There were many changes, none of which became known to German or allied intelligence:

October 1

Gen. I. V. Galanin replaced Kozlov as commander of the 24th Army on the Don front.

October 6

Ivan Varrenikov became Chief of Staff of the Stalingrad front while Zakharov moved up to replace Golikov as deputy commander and N. I. Trufanov took the 51st Army from T. K. Kolomiets.

October 14

On the Don front Batov replaced V. D. Kruchenkin as head of the 65th (formerly 4th Tank) Army while A. S. Zhadov took the 66th replacing Malinovsky.

October 15

Ivan M. Chistiakov assumed command of the 21st Army on the middle Don replacing A. I. Danilov, who became Chief of Staff of 5th Tank, a new force and now the most powerful formation in the Red Army.

October 23

Malinovsky got a new 1st Reserve Army which would go to battle in December as the 2nd Guards. The 1st had two rifle corps and a mechanized corps consisting of three mechanized brigades and two tank regiments.

October 25

A new southwest front under Vatutin was organized along the middle Don facing the Italian 8th Army and the Romanian 3rd which on the tenth of the month took over the sector between the Italian 8th and German 6th. In the southwest front were included the 21st Army and a revitalized 1st Guards that was moved westward from the Don front.

October 29

The strong 5th Tank Army under Romanenko was assigned to the southwest front.

Other developments included the formation of new tank and mechanized corps, made possible by tank production that was reaching two thousand a month, heavy (KV) tank break-through regiments, brigades of flame-throwing assault tanks, whole battalions of men armed only with antitank rifles, and an undetermined number of independent artillery and tank destroyer regiments. The new Kremlin mood, born of confidence, was a nourishing atmosphere. Suddenly there were new ideas, new tactics, new weapons, new equipment, and new commanders. As Chuikov's 62nd and Shumilov's 64th Armies continued to slug it out in and below Stalingrad, other Russian forces got ready for what was hoped would be the true turning point of the war. They needed only a few weeks, for although there were complex problems to be worked out, like train schedules, night marches to points of attack, the concentration of ammunition and other supplies, and the construction of lead-in roads and rail lines, the over-all plan was quite simple. In its final form it called for a minimum of movement prior to assault, then action by three front commands and twin breakthroughs at the weak sectors on the German flanks.

Southwest Front

COMMANDER: General Vatutin, a young Deputy People's Commissar of Defense and a member of the Stavka staff.

SECTOR: the middle Don from Pavlovsk in the west to Kletskaya in the east.

FORCES: from west to east—a newly organized and improved 1st Guards Army, a new and completely re-formed 5th Tank Army and a reinforced 21st Army.

MISSION: to drive southeast with 5th Tank and 21st Armies and meet the spearhead of the Stalingrad front near Kalach.

Don Front

COMMANDER: General Rokossovsky.

SECTOR: from Kletskaya on the Don to the Volga above Stalingrad in the east.

FORCES: from west to east—the 65th (formerly 4th Tank) Army, the 24th and 66th.

MISSION: attack to the south by the 65th and holding operations by the 24th and 66th.

Stalingrad Front

COMMANDER: General Eremenko.

SECTOR: from Stalingrad south to the country west of Astrakhan.

FORCES: from north to south—the splintered 62nd Army in Stalingrad, the 64th in the outlying suburbs, and the 57th, 51st, and 28th.

MISSION: to drive northwest with 57th and 51st Armies and meet the troops of the southwest front near Kalach.

Over-all Objective

To seal off the German 6th and 4th Panzer Armies in a fiery ring of explosive force and flying metal.

As the days went by, Stalin watched the build-up intently. With Zhukov organizing the offensive out of the north and Vasilievsky working in the south below Stalingrad he wanted to know everything.

"What does Rokossovsky think of that?" he would ask Zhukov on reading a report that affected the Don front.

Turning to Vasilievsky, he wondered: "What does Eremenko have to say?"

He may well have known the answers already, for in his conspiratorial way he talked to both commanders on the vetch from time to time. But he wanted to be sure, and his questions were probing:

Why not one blow over the middle Don, go for Rostov in the south, and cut off all of Army Group B near Stalingrad and Army

Group A in the Caucasus? (This was the possibility Hitler had been worrying about since August 16.) Answer—insufficient forces. Army Groups B and A were stronger than the mobile forces Russia could put in the field.

Why not one strike from the middle Don to the lower Volga? Answer—time. It would take three more days.

How many reserve divisions did the Germans have? Answer—not enough. Six to eight.

Could they bring more from France or other parts of occupied Europe? Answer—not in time.

What if something went wrong? Answer—the 1st Reserve Army (Malinovsky's) and eight independent tank corps with about 1,600 tanks would be held out for an emergency.

How would the final concentration be screened from German intelligence? Answer—in principle, the participating tank and cavalry corps would not cross the Don or Volga until the night before D day, now fixed for November 9 on the middle Don and November 10 south of Stalingrad.

Why not attack the same day on both sectors? Answer—distance. To reach the rendezvous near Kalach the Don forces had twenty-five more miles to go and would need an extra day.

The Supreme was persistent. How thick would the ice be on the middle Don? On the Volga? Some answers satisfied him; others did not. He worried about air cover. He looked into the organization and use of armor which were failures in the June and July fighting west of Voronezh.

Meanwhile, the battle raged inside Stalingrad itself and October 14 was one of the most terrible days for the defending Russians. But that, it can be seen in retrospect, was local action continued by the German High Command for psychological purposes and reasons of a practical nature, for by then both OKW and OKH knew the campaign was a failure. They knew Russia would not be destroyed in 1942. They knew it would not be cut in two. They knew there would be no Caucasian oil for Germany's war machine. They knew the army faced another winter on Russian soil, an awesome prospect given the horror of the first winter and the likelihood of some kind of American and British action in the west. The evidence in the slim surviving records is stubbornly compelling.

On the ninth the situation conference at Hitler's headquarters was opened with an ominous declaration by Zeitzler, the new Chief of the General Staff. Greiner summarized his remarks in these terse sentences:

"The Chief of the General Staff of the Army states: The absolute quiet on large sectors of the eastern front cannot yet be explained. Either the Russian has sent his forces away from the front for a rest, or he has removed them and is massing them in other places, perhaps for use within the framework of a winter offensive. Under the circumstances the formation of reserves of our own is especially important."

The words stand out in OKW's war diary and give added significance to a secret order Hitler issued to his generals five days later. On the fourteenth in *Operational Order No. 1* he called off the 1942 campaign. Hailing it as successful, he announced a new strategy of strategic defense except for continuing operations (in Stalingrad city) and projected offensive action of a local character. The Russians, he said, had suffered great losses. It was time to hold the line and get ready for 1943. This winter would be easier than the last. The coming year would witness the "final destruction" of "our dangerous enemy." He would "personally" see to it his front-line soldiers got some rest:

"But I expect officers and men to enter upon the winter campaign of 1942/1943 with pride based on results already achieved, with firm faith in their own strength and with the unshakeable will to destroy the enemy wherever in this winter campaign he tries to break through our front.

"The fundamental requirements are:

"1. Winter positions to be held at all costs.

"2. Defense to be active everywhere, giving the enemy no respite and misleading him as to our true intentions.

"3. In case of enemy attack not to withdraw one step or make a retreating maneuver of an operational character.

"4. With counterattacks and counter-blows to liquidate quickly local breakthroughs.

"5. To localize large breakthroughs and at all costs turn stabilized sectors into bastions that would ease the execution of counter-measures.

"6. Cut-off and encircled units to defend themselves until help arrives."

The meaning was clear. Whatever troubled him in September—whatever he feared in early October—Hitler realized by the middle of the month he could not go on. He could not get Leningrad, which he had worked on for months. He could not attack in the Moscow region. There remained one hope. By calling off offensive operations everywhere except in Stalingrad the city might yet be his. Getting it might rouse the German spirit and cover the year's failure. Announcing its seizure might stimulate his Italian, Hungarian, and Romanian allies and dampen the fires of liberation that were beginning to burn in occupied Europe. Holding it would give 6th Army and 4th Panzer cellars to stay in and brick to build shelters with for the winter. Otherwise they were condemned to the freezing cold of the wind-swept steppe—or worse.

Accordingly, the war between the armed might of Nazi Germany and the Red Army of Communist Russia narrowed almost overnight to a fight for two destroyed factories on the high Volga bank in the northern part of town. Red October and the Barricades plant were the largest scrap heaps around but military prizes for all that. If Hitler took them, he could say he had all of Stalingrad. He would say it anyway although the Russians clung to the northern suburbs, the two factories, a part of Mamayev Kurgan, and the distant suburbs in the south to Krasnoarmeisk and beyond. If Stalin held them, he would pin down 6th Army, a matter of critical importance to Stavka in view of the coming offensive. And so for both reasons and out of sheer momentum and because armies are difficult things to turn around, the fight continued, though not on the scale that had characterized the struggle for the approaches in July and August or for the city in September. Paulus now moved for the northwest corner of one factory, for the southwest corner of another, for a cellar, a conduit, for a few hundred yards at the water's edge. Russians in groups of thirty to forty men backed by heavy artillery from over the river battled behind barbed wire and mine fields.

The last big push began on the fourteenth, Eremenko's fiftieth birthday and the day Hitler virtually acknowledged failure in *Operational Order No. 1*. The Germans crashed through two Russian divisions, took the huge tractor plant to the right of the Barricades, broke through to the Volga, and separated Gorokhov's group in the northern suburbs from the rest of the army. In this action Gorishny's 95th Division and Zholudev's 37th Guards lost 75 per cent of their men.

Paulus turned to the two factories. He overran the right wing of Smekhotvorov's 193rd Division in the Red October district and threatened Gurtiev's 308th[5] in the Barricades, which the Russians promptly strengthened by transferring Ivan Lyudnikov's 138th Division from the 64th Army on their left.

At 10:30 on the morning of the twenty-third, an officer reached the commander of the 39th Guards with a written message from the commander of the 193rd:

GURIEV:
ENEMY HAS BROKEN THROUGH LEFT FLANK OF MY 883RD RIFLE REGIMENT. REQUEST YOUR HELP IN DESTRUCTION OF THIS FORCE. MY RESERVES ARE EXHAUSTED.

SMEKHOTVOROV

Chuikov was now running the battle from his fifth and last command post. He had started out on September 12 on Mamayev Kurgan, moved down to the Tsaritsa ravine the next day, gone to the riverbank by the Red October factory on the eighteenth, moved upriver closer to the tractor plant on October 5, and finally settled into a hiding place hollowed out of the Volga bank between Red October and Mamayev Kurgan. Headquarters consisted of sixteen or seventeen dugouts with five, six, or seven men in each one and military and police sentries guarding the approaches.

I saw him there some time later. Though it was bitterly cold outside, he was working in shirt sleeves by the light of kerosene lamps that were made by stuffing wicks into the flattened heads of empty shell casings. The close air smelled of burning oil.

[5] Except for the 112th ("Sologub's division"), Colonel Gurtiev's 308th was the only Russian division fighting in Stalingrad after the middle of September that was neither promoted to Guards status nor awarded a unit citation. The inference is that it, too, may have been filled out with replacements from punitive battalions.

"In early November," he told me, "I knew we would hold out. The Germans were smart, they were tough, and there were a lot of them, but they did not have the strength to throw us into the river."

Outside of Moscow many years later I met him again. I was ushered into his office by a young lieutenant and saw before me a Marshal of the Soviet Union who looked taller, broader in the shoulders, and only slightly heavier than I had remembered him. Chuikov spoke highly of the technical qualifications and combat ability of the German 6th Army.

"Their method," he said, "was to surround and strike but there was too much system to their method. We could foresee what they would do next and react in time."

He took off his dark-rimmed glasses and pointed both bows toward me.

"To forestall encirclement," he said, "it is not necessary to meet both attacking forces."

He covered one bow with a large hand.

"Stop one attack, and there is no encirclement."

He thought his major contribution to the battle was the imposition of Russian tactics on the enemy.

"They liked to fight by day and sleep by night. We made them fight at night. They liked to fight in the streets. We kept them empty. They tried to drive us into the open and hit us with air. We got so close to them they hit their own troops."

He said there was no enemy maneuver that took his army by surprise.

"Our intelligence was very good. We did not know their written plans but we knew very well when they concentrated for an attack. That was the time to hit them."

In general he thought the German High Command attached undue importance to seizure of the town and may well have put so many units into it that they interfered with each other.

Or so it appeared to him twenty-seven years later.

How did it appear to Adolf Hitler whose forces in Egypt were attacked at El Alamein on October 23 in an action that heralded the opening of Anglo-American operations in North Africa?

All we know is that on the last day of the month he closed down his headquarters in the Ukraine and returned to East Prussia.

2

In early November there were two distinct D days on the military calendar. The first, which was known to the Russians, was the allied landing in North Africa that was launched on the eighth and completed on the eleventh when French opposition stopped with the German seizure of unoccupied France. The second, which was unknown to the United States and Great Britain, was the Russian counterstroke in the Stalingrad direction that was planned initially for the ninth, then put off, first to the seventeenth, then to the nineteenth.

The Russian D day was still fixed for the ninth when Zhukov, accompanied by officers from Stavka and the General Staff, arrived at Serafimovich on the third. Serafimovich is a Cossack fishing and farming town on the middle Don and the heart of the area from which two armies would move down to meet two others driving up from the lake country below Stalingrad. Vatutin of the new southwest front was there. Rokossovsky came over from the Don front. With them were officers who heard for the first time details of the counteroffensive plan.

Two days later, while General Eisenhower was flying from England to Gibraltar and the vanguard of the allied armada was sailing through the strait into the Mediterranean, Zhukov went on to

Raigorod on the Volga south of Stalingrad and held another briefing session for commanders who would attack to the northwest. On both occasions he was laconic, asking, the men said later, more questions than he answered.

Zhukov flew back to Moscow, reported to Stalin, returned to Serafimovich, and made one more trip to the south, this time to 57th Army headquarters at Tatianka on the Volga. Everywhere he found commanders who felt the need for more time. Gen. N. N. Voronov, Chief of Artillery of the Red Army, worried about training 13,500 officers for his 13,500 guns. Front and army commanders said supplies and equipment were not arriving on schedule. Although six branch lines with 725 miles of track had been laid from the north to the middle Don, the country's rail network was overtaxed, and some divisions still had 200 to 250 miles to go on foot before they reached their assigned sectors. Other delays were unavoidable. German air caught some units at Volga crossings and held them up for days.

There were other problems. Rokossovsky was unhappy about the few replacements allocated to his front. Like other generals in the same predicament, he raided rear areas and brought back from hospitals and other quiet installations all the soldiers he considered fit for service.

So the Russian D day was postponed to the seventeenth and then for another forty-eight hours because it was felt that air units assembling for the assault might not be ready.

Meanwhile, the German High Command, now back in East Prussia, was floundering in a sea of uncertainty and half-measures as if it expected to be attacked in the east or west or both but did not know where or with what. On the third, Hitler ordered 6th Panzer and two infantry divisions from France to the eastern front. He was right about this. On the fifth, there were reports of allied warships and transports near Gibraltar but nothing much was done about them. He was wrong about that. Then, on the seventh, the General Staff came in with a message allegedly received from a German agent in Moscow to the effect the Russians were planning some kind of early offensive action. What Hitler thought about this is not known. Evidently not much, for he left the same day by train for Munich to deliver a political speech the next night, but Gehlen of Foreign Armies East, who passed it on to Zeitzler, viewed it as a remarkable piece of intelligence, so much so that in his memoirs years later he printed in full the signal received from "Max"—"the office controlling the Abwehr agents in Moscow." "Max" was full of information, all of it either wrong or of no value whatsoever to the German High Command, similar in both respects to the faulty July report.[1] Gehlen quoting "Max":

> On November 4 Stalin presided over Council of War [the odd German word *Kronrat* (Privy Council) was used in the original text] in Moscow, attended by twelve marshals and generals. Following basic principles were laid down at this council:
>
> (a) operations to be executed cautiously to avoid heavy casualties;
>
> (b) loss of ground is unimportant;
>
> (c) it is vital to salvage industrial and public-utility installations in good time by evacuation, which explains orders issued for dispersal of refineries and machine-tool factories from Grozny and Makhachkala to New Baku, Orsk, and Tashkent;
>
> (d) rely only on oneself, don't count on getting aid from allies;
>
> (e) take sharp measures to prevent desertion, either by better propaganda and rations or by firing squads and tougher GPU supervision; and
>
> (f) all the planned attack operations are to be executed before November 15 if possible, insofar as weather permits. They are primarily from Grozny toward Mozdok; at Nizhnye-Mamon and Verkhnye-Mamon in the Don basin; and at Voronezh, at Rzhev, south of Lake Ilmen, and at Leningrad. The necessary troops are to be brought out of reserve and up to the front line.[2]

"Events over the following months," wrote Gehlen, "showed that this report must have been genuine."

On the contrary, they suggest it was as false as it sounds and

[1] See footnote on p. 100.
[2] Gehlen, pp. 57–58. Grozny to Mozdok was three hundred miles south of the Volga mark. Nizhnye-Mamon and Verkhnye-Mamon were a hundred miles upstream from the critical Don sector.

that it may have originated with British or Russian intelligence, for "Max" put his finger on just about every sector of the Russian front except the two along the Don and Volga where the blows would fall.

"Max," however, did not upset Hitler's plans. Taking Keitel and Jodl with him, he headed for Munich, arriving there on the afternoon of the eighth, hours after American and British forces landed in Morocco and Algeria. Now he was in a deeper bind. Rommel, who was taking a beating from Montgomery, was threatened in his rear by the allied invasion, and Gehlen was beginning to receive tactical intelligence that indicated early Russian action on the middle Don. In this confused situation the Fuehrer could do no right. Having shuffled the cards and stacked them against himself, he rushed troops into Tunisia and unoccupied France on the eleventh and the next day ordered Keitel's and Jodl's OKW staff from East Prussia to Salzburg. By a bizarre coincidence it arrived by train on Friday the thirteenth, the day the Russians approved their final plan for the counteroffensive. The plan, Operation Uranus, called for:

D day
Thursday the nineteenth for attack out of the north and Friday the twentieth for attack out of the south.

Primary Operations
The 5th Tank and 21st Armies to drive out of the Serafimovich bridgehead and cross the steppe toward Kalach.

The 51st and 57th Armies to break through the lake defiles below Stalingrad and move up toward Kalach.

Secondary Operations
The 65th in the north and the 64th in the south to press the Germans in the ring.

The 62nd to hold the line in Stalingrad.

The 66th in the north to liberate the 62nd if all went well.

An outer ring to be established some miles from the inner ring of encirclement to prevent the German High Command from extricating the surrounded force or going to its rescue.

*

207

Nothing can look colder than the wide, white-capped Volga on a gray day in November when the waters turn dark and surly. Ice floes grumble as they grind together, break apart, and again bang into each other. On such a day the Russians wait for the river to freeze. It may take a few days or a week or two. On the lower Volga it may take two or three weeks, and so it did at Stalingrad in the late fall of 1942.

On Tuesday, November 3, the following report was entered in Chuikov's war diary:

"Volga full of chunks of ice. Crossing is paralyzed. Not one boat or launch arrived. No ammunition was received. Wounded could not be evacuated."

On Wednesday and Thursday a few boats made it in. On Friday, Saturday, and Sunday nothing moved. On Monday and Tuesday six fast cutters got through, and such were the conditions when on Wednesday the eleventh Paulus of 6th Army launched his last desperate attack. As he had for several weeks, he ignored Rodimtsev's 13th Guards and Batiuk's 284th Divisions near Mamayev Kurgan, and in a final bid for control of the factory district went for Red October and the Barricades plant. Against Red October on the Russian left he sent a regiment of infantry reinforced by the 336th Sapper Battalion that had just been flown in from Magdeburg, Germany. Against Lyudnikov's 138th in the Barricades he sent two regiments supported by the 45th Sapper Battalion that was trucked in from Millerovo in the German rear. At about this time, three other sapper battalions specially trained for house-to-house warfare, the 50th, 162nd, and 294th, were rushed to the city from other fronts.

The fight went on all that day and the next and the day after that, and when it quieted down on Friday the thirteenth Lyudnikov was cut off from the rest of the army, which was now divided into three parts. North of the tractor plant and the wet Mechetka lay Gorokhov's group. Since October 15 it had been supplied by air. In the Barricades was Lyudnikov's force. Men called his sector the "island" because the Germans ringed it on three sides and kept the ice-filled river behind him under fire. Chuikov was with the main force of the army which held a line that ran from Red October to the south for a few miles.

This is how it was, and this is how it remained for many weeks to come. Yet out in that ruined city with shells and bombs bursting around them there were still some 30,000 civilian men, women, and children, surviving by some combination of circumstances that defies the imagination.

Rodimtsev told me later on that the most useful were schoolboys ten, eleven, twelve, and thirteen years old. Briefed by intelligence officers and plain-clothes police agents who ringed his command post, the boys wandered in and out of no man's land. They entered German lines, ate with German troops, and talked to German officers whose names, ranks, and attitudes were soon known at Rodimtsev's headquarters.

So the clock ticked on to Russia's D day and to the counteroffensive that was of such force and so unexpected that for years it was looked on as something of a miracle, which it was anything but.

3

In the early hours of Thursday, November 19, a cold, blinding fog hugged the high country in the land of the Don Cossacks. The afternoon before, General Vatutin of the southwest front telephoned a cryptic message to Romanenko and Chistiakov, whose 5th Tank and 21st Armies would strike the main blow out of the north. Rokossovsky of the Don front wired the same to Batov's 65th:

>SEND THE PERSON WHO IS TO
>RECEIVE THEM FOR THE FUR GLOVES.

To all of them and to Vasilievsky, the Chief of the General Staff, who had set up headquarters at Chistiakov's command post near Kletskaya, it meant:

>START INFANTRY ATTACK 19.11.42 0850 HOURS.

It was the signal for the assault that would be followed the next day by attack out of the south, but as Romanenko, Chistiakov, and Batov looked at field and weather reports that morning they saw problems. Planes were grounded. Tanks could not move. From their concealed forward positions artillery observers gazed into an impenetrable haze.

Army commanders turned to front commanders, front commanders to Vasilievsky, Vasilievsky to the Kremlin. The recommendation—to go ahead anyway. The decision—to go ahead.[1]

At 7:20 A.M. Russian rockets opened up on previously plotted targets. Streaks of flame ripped through the gloom and the predawn darkness.

At 7:30 A.M. the guns started. They fired on Romanian trench lines and artillery emplacements in one of the heaviest barrages of the war and kept it up for an hour and twenty minutes.

And at 8:50 the infantry moved out of the bridgeheads along the south bank of the Don where the men had slept in the open or lain there wondering if they could do what they had to do. The only comforting thought that occurred to many of them was that if they could not see the enemy the enemy could not see them.

Everywhere the method was the same—rockets, artillery, then infantry through the first and second lines of defense—and everywhere there was competent, aggressive Romanian defense that

[1] Despite all precautions, the counteroffensive, except for its precise timing and objective, did not come as a complete surprise. The German High Command knew something was in the wind, perhaps an assault on the Romanians to force back 6th Army from Stalingrad. The Russian people knew nothing and everything. Although censorship was tight and there were no published leaks, through their remarkable grapevine they expected a major attack, and I felt sufficiently sure of the possibility to file a story on it to the New York *Herald Tribune* on the fourteenth, five days before. Other correspondents may well have done the same. Even so, Winston Churchill was still concerned about the Russian front, sufficiently concerned to dictate a minute to his Chiefs of Staff on the eighteenth pointing out that Torch was no substitute for the invasion of France. It was in this memorandum that he made known for the first time so far as I know that there was a "promise" in the matter. ". . . we have given Stalin to understand," he wrote, "that the great attack on the Continent will come in 1943, and we are now working on a basis of thirty-five divisions short of what was purposed in the period April–July, or, in other words, little more than a quarter. . . . My own position is that I am still aiming for Roundup retarded till August. I cannot give this up without a massive presentation of facts and figures which prove physical impossibility. . . . I never meant the Anglo-American Army to be stuck in North Africa. It is a springboard and not a sofa." (Churchill's *The Hinge of Fate*, pp. 650–51.) In the published correspondence there is no trace of a message to Roosevelt in which he expressed himself so resolutely for France in 1943.

compelled the Russians to send in the tanks sooner than they expected or intended.

As the morning wore on, the freezing fog thinned out, then lifted. Romanenko of 5th Tank ordered in his 26th Tank Corps about noon. An hour later Chistiakov of the 21st released his 4th Tank Corps and followed it about three o'clock with the 3rd Guards Cavalry Corps. All were headed for the Don at and above Kalach, not knowing that straight ahead in the fishing village of Golubinski was the greatest prize of all—the command post and headquarters of the German 6th Army. General Paulus, unaware he was in the line of a Russian advance, was living in a cluster of houses and barns, the home of a collective farmer, Yevgeni Ivanovich Semenov.[2]

Curiously, the Russians were now following the steps of 6th Army when it first hit the Russian 62nd in the Great Bend of the Don in late July. It was as if there were some kind of huge revolving door—first the Germans driving east over the steppe toward the Don, now the Russians breaking through the Romanian 3rd Army and coming in behind the German 6th through the same dreary villages and over the same dirt tracks. If all went well, they would reach the river at the close of the second day—the cavalry to the north of Golubinski, 4th Tank in the center, and 26th Tank to the south opposite Kalach; and if all went well from then on, 6th Army would be isolated on the third day.

Baron von Weichs, the commander of Army Group B on which 6th Army, 4th Panzer, and their satellite Hungarian, Italian, and Romanian forces depended, foresaw the danger early on. At ten o'clock that first night he issued the following order from his headquarters at Starobelsk in the deep rear:

THE SITUATION DEVELOPING ON THE FRONT OF THE 3RD ROMANIAN ARMY DICTATES RADICAL MEASURES IN ORDER TO DISENGAGE FORCES

[2] The reader will understand the care with which an army conceals the location of its command post or nerve center from enemy intelligence. The Russians concealed theirs from just about everyone. I once told General Chuikov that when I was in Stalingrad after the battle was over it had taken me two hours to find his 62nd Army headquarters. He laughed and said that it had taken him as long to find Eremenko's headquarters on the far side of the Volga when he reported in on September 12 to take command of the army.

QUICKLY, TO SCREEN THE FLANK OF 6TH ARMY AND TO ASSURE THE PROTECTION OF SUPPLIES IN THE LIKHAYA-CHIR SECTOR OF THE RAILROAD. IN THIS CONNECTION, I ORDER:

1. ALL OFFENSIVE OPERATIONS IN STALINGRAD TO BE STOPPED EXCEPT FOR ACTIVITY OF RECONNAISSANCE UNITS WHOSE INFORMATION IS REQUIRED FOR ORGANIZATION OF DEFENSE.

2. 6TH ARMY TO DETACH IMMEDIATELY FROM ITS FORCES TWO MOTORIZED FORMATIONS, ONE INFANTRY DIVISION, IF POSSIBLE AUXILIARY MOTORIZED UNIT OF 14TH PANZER CORPS AND IN ADDITION THE STRONGEST ANTITANK FORCES AVAILABLE, TO CONCENTRATE THIS GROUP ON ITS LEFT FLANK AND ATTACK TOWARD THE NORTHWEST AND WEST.

Weichs did not know at that hour the Russians would hit his right flank the next day.

Far behind him the German command structure was in disarray. Zeitzler was in East Prussia with the Army High Command. OKW's operations staff was at Salzburg. And Adolf Hitler, the Commander in Chief of the Armed Forces, the Army, and Army Group A in the Caucasus, was at Berchtesgaden with Keitel, his OKW Chief, and Jodl, the head of OKW's operations staff.

*

Friday, November 20, was a problem day for the Russian High Command. The northern group was delayed by strong counterattacks in the snowy steppe, and the initial assault of the southern group was put off for an hour by the same icy fog that had covered the Don sector the day before. Foot soldiers operating with independent tank brigades in the south finally got off and were working their way through Romanian defenses when the fog lifted about ten o'clock. Time to send in the armor.

But none was available. The 4th Mechanized Corps attached to Trufanov's 51st Army on the Russian left and the 13th Mechanized attached to Fedor I. Tolbukhin's 57th on the Russian right were not fully concentrated. In each corps there were three mechanized brigades and two tank regiments, which were new combinations of armor, motorized infantry, and self-propelled guns, but they were late, having been held up at the Volga crossings by air attack, floating ice, weak bridges, and a night fog that made the roads almost impassable.

Trufanov consulted Popov, deputy commander of the Stalingrad front who was at his headquarters that morning, then ordered General Volski's 4th Mechanized to take off at eleven o'clock. Trouble. The 4th, like the 13th to its right, could not comply. Noon came and went. Still it had not moved out. Exasperated, Trufanov and Popov drove over to Vasili T. Volski's area and found him refueling. Anger. Shouts. Hot words. And when at last the corps moved out, it was past four o'clock in the afternoon, almost dark. Still, infantrymen looked gratefully on as they stepped off the roads to let it by, and by nightfall, although still far behind schedule, the tanks were approaching the Chervlennaya, opposite Stalingrad's old center defense or "K" line. According to plan they would meet the Don group the next day, 4th Mechanized to link up with the 26th Tank Corps, the 13th with 4th Tank, but because in war almost nothing goes according to plan, the question now was not whether the timetable could be adhered to but whether the objective could be achieved at all—whether the Don and Volga groups could sever 6th Army and 4th Panzer from all other Axis forces before Paulus and Hoth reacted in an organized way.

*

They could. On Saturday, realizing the danger that threatened his headquarters at Golubinski, Paulus wrote out a hasty message asking the High Command for permission to move his army back from Stalingrad to the Don. Then he and his Chief of Staff, Gen. Arthur Schmidt, took a light plane and flew to Nizhnye Chirskaya forty miles to the southwest. At about the same time General Hoth moved 4th Panzer's command post from Verkhnye Tsaritsinski to Buzinovka, which came under Russian shellfire before he could reestablish communications with his scattered army. In the late afternoon he turned over his men to 6th Army and flew to Tsimlianskaya on the lower Don to await instructions.

Now, with his two field commanders on the run Hitler got a grip on himself. He summoned his operations staff from Salzburg to Berchtesgaden and characteristically, without full consultation with the Army High Command, reached a fateful decision, which he radioed to Paulus:

> THE COMMANDER IN CHIEF WILL PROCEED WITH HIS STAFF TO STALINGRAD. THE 6TH ARMY WILL FORM AN ALL-ROUND DEFENSIVE POSITION AND AWAIT FURTHER ORDERS.[3]

Several hours later there was another message for Paulus from the Fuehrer:

> THOSE UNITS OF THE 6TH ARMY THAT REMAIN BETWEEN THE DON AND VOLGA WILL HENCEFORTH BE DESIGNATED FORTRESS STALINGRAD.[4]

The order could not have been more to Stalin's liking if he had written it himself.

And perhaps for this reason no commander who saw it believed it meant what it implied—that Hitler had taken a step of incalculable consequences, that he was determined to hold 6th Army in the Stalingrad area, that he would not allow it to fight its way out, and that although he had no other solution to propose for the present he would find one. That night the entire Berchtesgaden entourage got ready to return to East Prussia the next day, Hitler, Keitel, and Jodl by train to Leipzig and from Leipzig to the Wolf's Lair by plane, others by train to Berlin and air from there on, still others by plane all the way.

*

By early Sunday morning the sands were swiftly running out for 6th Army.

[3] Schröter, pp. 74–75.
[4] Ibid., p. 75.

In the north, Russian forces, approaching the Don on a wide front, went for a new bridge at Berezovski near Kalach and took it in a predawn coup de main.

In the south, though enemy mine fields slowed the way, Volski's 4th Mechanized Corps seized Buzinovka and moved up toward Sovietski near the confluence of the Don and the Karpovka.

In short, the jaws of the trap were closing when Paulus and Schmidt, obeying the Fuehrer's orders, flew into Stalingrad. At six o'clock that night Paulus reported from a new command post near Gumrak airport:

ARMY ENCIRCLED. DESPITE HEROIC RESISTANCE WHOLE OF TSARITSA VALLEY, RAILWAY FROM SOVIETSKI TO KALACH, THE DON BRIDGE AT KALACH, HIGH GROUND ON WEST BANK AS FAR AS GOLUBINSKAYA [Golubinski], OLSINSKI AND KRAINI INCLUSIVE NOW IN RUSSIAN HANDS.

FURTHER, ENEMY FORCES ARE ADVANCING FROM THE SOUTHEAST THROUGH BUZINOVKA NORTHWARDS AND ALSO IN GREAT STRENGTH FROM THE WEST.

SITUATION AT SUROVIKINO AND CHIR UNKNOWN.

INTENSE PATROL ACTIVITY ON THE STALINGRAD AND NORTHERN FRONTS. ATTACKS ON IV ARMY CORPS REPULSED AND ALSO ON 76TH INFANTRY DIVISION. 76TH INFANTRY DIVISION REPORTS SMALL LOCAL PENETRATIONS.

ARMY HOPES TO BE ABLE TO CONSTRUCT A WESTERN FRONT EAST OF THE DON ALONG THE GOLUBAYA LINE. SOUTHERN FRONT EAST OF THE DON STILL OPEN. WHETHER INTENSIVE WEAKENING OF THE NORTHERN FLANK WILL PERMIT CONSTRUCTION OF THIN LINE RUNNING KARPOVKA-MARINOVKA-GOLUBINKA APPEARS PROBLEMATICAL.

THE DON NOW FROZEN AND CAN BE CROSSED.

FUEL SUPPLIES ALMOST EXHAUSTED. TANKS AND HEAVY WEAPONS WILL THEN BE IMMOBILIZED. AMMUNITION SITUATION ACUTE. FUEL SUPPLIES AVAILABLE FOR A FURTHER SIX DAYS.

THE ARMY INTENDS TO HOLD THE AREA STILL IN ITS POSSESSION BETWEEN STALINGRAD AND THE DON AND HAS TAKEN ALL STEPS TO IMPLEMENT THIS DECISION.

THIS IS, HOWEVER, CONDITIONAL ON CLOSING THE SOUTHERN FRONT AND ON RECEIVING AMPLE AIRBORNE SUPPLIES.

REQUEST FREEDOM OF DECISION IN THE EVENT OF FAILURE TO CONSTRUCT SOUTHERN DEFENSIVE POSITION. THE SITUATION COULD THEN COMPEL THE ABANDONMENT OF STALINGRAD AND THE NORTHERN FRONT, AND AN ATTACK IN MAXIMUM STRENGTH AGAINST ENEMY ON SOUTHERN FRONT BETWEEN THE DON AND THE VOLGA WITH OBJECTIVE THE RE-ESTABLISHMENT OF CONTACT WITH FOURTH PANZER ARMY. PROSPECTS OF A SUCCESSFUL ATTACK WESTWARDS ARE UNPROMISING IN VIEW OF ENEMY STRENGTH AND TERRAIN DIFFICULTIES THAT SECTOR.[5]

One senses the desperate earnestness of a doomed field commander whose only hope if he has one is that the Fuehrer will change his mind.

*

It was all over on Monday, the twenty-third. At 12:20 P.M. the 36th Brigade of Volski's mechanized corps pulled up along the south bank of the Karpovka in and on both sides of Sovietski, and

[5] Ibid., p. 91.

at 4:00 the 45th Brigade of the 4th Tank Corps, coming down from the north, reached the opposite bank.[6]

Paulus was caught—how tightly was not yet certain but Weichs at Army Group B's command post in Starobelsk was sufficiently alarmed to send the following teletype to the high command at 6:45 P.M. that day:

DESPITE THE EXCEPTIONAL GRAVITY OF THE DECISION TO BE TAKEN, WITH THE FAR-REACHING CONSEQUENCES OF WHICH I AM WELL AWARE, I MUST REPORT THAT I REGARD IT AS NECESSARY TO ACCEPT GENERAL PAULUS'S PROPOSAL FOR THE WITHDRAWAL OF SIXTH ARMY. MY REASONS ARE AS FOLLOWS:

1. THE SUPPLYING OF THE TWENTY DIVISIONS THAT CONSTITUTE THIS ARMY IS NOT FEASIBLE BY AIR WITH THE AIR TRANSPORT AVAILABLE, AND IN FAVORABLE WEATHER CONDITIONS IT WILL ONLY BE POSSIBLE TO SUPPLY THE ENCIRCLED FORCES BY AIR WITH ONE-TENTH OF THEIR ESSENTIAL DAILY REQUIREMENTS.

2. SINCE THE PROBABLE FUTURE DEVELOPMENTS DO NOT OFFER ANY CERTAINTY OF RAPID PENETRATION OF THE ENCIRCLING ENEMY FORCES FROM THE OUTSIDE, THE ATTACK TO RELIEVE SIXTH ARMY CANNOT, IN VIEW OF THE TIME REQUIRED TO ASSEMBLE THE RELIEVING FORCE, BE MOUNTED BEFORE THE 10TH OF DECEMBER. THE ARMY GENERAL STAFF HAS BEEN INFORMED OF THE DETAILED TIMETABLE FOR THE ASSEMBLY OF THE UNITS IN QUESTION. THE RAPID DETERIORATION OF SIXTH ARMY'S SITUATION AS REGARDS SUPPLIES INDICATES THAT THESE MUST BE EXHAUSTED WITHIN A FEW

---

[6] Sovietski no longer exists, its inhabitants having been transferred during the construction of the Volga-Don Canal after the war.

DAYS. AMMUNITION WILL SOON BE EXPENDED, SINCE THE ENCIRCLED FORCE IS BEING ATTACKED FROM ALL SIDES.

HOWEVER, I BELIEVE THAT A BREAKTHROUGH BY SIXTH ARMY IN A SOUTHWESTERLY DIRECTION WILL RESULT IN FAVORABLE DEVELOPMENTS TO THE SITUATION AS A WHOLE.

WITH THE TOTAL DISSOLUTION OF THE THIRD ROMANIAN ARMY, SIXTH ARMY IS NOW THE ONLY FIGHTING FORMATION CAPABLE OF INFLICTING DAMAGE ON THE ENEMY. THE PROPOSED DIRECTION OF ATTACK, OPENING TOWARD THE SOUTHWEST AND THEN BEING FOLLOWED BY THE NORTHERN WING ADVANCING ALONG THE RAILWAY FROM CHIR TO MOROZOVSKAYA, WILL RESULT IN A RELAXATION OF THE EXISTING TENSION IN THE SVETNOYE-KOTELNIKOVO AREA. FINALLY, THE REMAINING COMBAT STRENGTH OF SIXTH ARMY WILL PROVIDE AN ESSENTIAL REINFORCEMENT FOR THE NEW DEFENSIVE FRONT THAT MUST NOW BE BUILT AND FOR THE PREPARATION OF OUR COUNTERATTACK.

I AM WELL AWARE THAT THIS PROPOSED OPERATION WILL ENTAIL HEAVY LOSSES, PARTICULARLY IN ARMS AND EQUIPMENT, BUT THESE WILL BE FAR LESS THAN THOSE THAT MUST ENSUE IF THE SITUATION IS LEFT TO DEVELOP, AS IT MUST DO, IN EXISTING CONDITIONS, WITH THE INEVITABLE STARVING OUT OF THE ENCIRCLED ARMY AS THE CERTAIN RESULT.[7]

So far as is known, Weichs received no direct reply to his wire, which must be regarded as a remarkably accurate appraisal early

[7] Ibid., p. 92.

on and a courageous attempt to sway his dictator's stubborn mind, for, as he foresaw, the Luftwaffe could not supply the trapped force and there was no chance of a rescue operation before December 10.

Whether 6th Army, which now included part of 4th Panzer, could blast its way out was another matter, but to the group commander the alternative—to stand and fight—meant certain destruction.

4

By November 23 when he returned to his command post in East Prussia, Adolf Hitler had no choice left but of errors and no rational hope of avoiding disaster except in the mistakes of his enemies and in chance. Such, wrote Ségur, is the "peculiarity of false positions." To be sure, he might have sued for peace in the east or west or both, but short of that no promising course of action lay before him, neither retreat, as some generals recommended, nor combat, which was his instinctive response. In the event, he swiftly organized a relief force to free Paulus and slowly reinforced his Tunisian troops by denuding Sicily and Italy. Soon three panzer divisions from afar were moving into and on Kotelnikovo for a thrust toward the Stalingrad pocket seventy-five miles to the northeast. They were the 6th from distant France, the 17th from Orel southwest of Moscow, and the 23rd from the Caucasus. Meanwhile the Russians went for Paulus with 480,000 men in the apparent belief he had 85,000 to 90,000 when in fact there were 260,000 to 296,000 in the ring.[1] They struck on the twenty-fourth

[1] The Russians have never explained this intelligence error which is the only major blunder of any kind I am aware of that has not been blamed on someone—on someone else by Stalin before his death in 1953—on Stalin at a

and made some progress that first day, a Tuesday, and the next day and the day after that, but nothing like what the Kremlin expected, a situation that called for intervention by the Supreme. On Friday the twenty-seventh he got hold of Vasilievsky, who was at Vatutin's headquarters on the middle Don:

Stalin to Mikhailov[2]

ENEMY TROOPS SURROUNDED AT STALINGRAD MUST BE LIQUIDATED IN ORDER TO FREE THREE ARMIES FOR OUR OBJECTIVE.[3]

He said there must be co-ordination between Rokossovsky and Eremenko while Vatutin prepared to move on Italian and Hungarian forces on the middle and upper Don.

IT IS NECESSARY FOR MIKHAILOV TO ESTABLISH COMMAND POST WITH TEN TO FIFTEEN MEN NEAR LIAPICHEV[4] OR WEST OF THAT POINT AND, SQUEEZING TIGHTER AND TIGHTER, DIRECT LIQUIDATION OF ENEMY'S STALINGRAD GROUP. THIS IS VERY IMPORTANT ASSIGNMENT. MORE IMPORTANT THAN OPERATION SATURN.[5] MIKHAILOV MUST CONCENTRATE ON THIS ONE ASSIGNMENT.

Vasilievsky thought Liapichev was the wrong place but he knew how to handle Stalin:

Mikhailov to Stalin

CAN QUICKLY ORGANIZE MANAGEMENT OF BOTH FRONTS FROM DONTSOV'S COMMAND POST

---

later date by men who survived him. The mistake is acknowledged by Russian historians but bears investigation by students of the shaky art of military intelligence for it persisted to the end of the battle in early February. Rokossovsky in his memoirs suggests that Stavka, thinking that each headquarters provided an estimate for all forces in the ring, failed to add reports received from the Don and Stalingrad fronts. If it had added them, however, it would still have seriously underestimated German troop strength.

[2] Vasilievsky's code name.
[3] Rostov on the Don to cut off German forces in the Caucasus.
[4] Liapichev is on the rail line west of Stalingrad and south of Kalach.
[5] A planned offensive from the middle Don to the southwest.

WHERE COMMUNICATIONS AVAILABLE AND CAN BE THERE TOMORROW.[6] REQUEST YOUR DEFINITIVE ORDER SO CAN PROCEED TO ITS EXECUTION IMMEDIATELY.

Stalin to Mikhailov

ALL RIGHT. PROCEED TO DONTSOV'S COMMAND POST. COLLECT WORKERS YOU NEED AND ORGANIZE COORDINATION OF DONTSOV'S AND IVANOV'S ACTIONS.[7] LET VORONOV WORK WITH VATUTIN IN PREPARATION OPERATION SATURN.[8]

As the BODO conversation continued, the Supreme became more precise:

NOW, FOR COMRADE MIKHAILOV. TAKE AN ORDER:

1. IN PRESENT SITUATION YOUR JOB IS TO COORDINATE ACTIONS OF DONTSOV AND IVANOV IN LIQUIDATION OF ENCIRCLED ENEMY GROUP. I ASK YOU TO DO THIS ONE JOB ONLY AND NOT TO BE DIVERTED BY ANY OTHER TASK.

2. ALL AVIATION OF DON AND STALINGRAD FRONTS, TOGETHER WITH NOVIKOV[9] AS WELL AS PE-2 BOMBER CORPS DESTINED FOR DON FRONT, WILL BE AT YOUR DISPOSAL. AIR MISSION: TO RAID ENCIRCLED ENEMY GROUP AND GIVE IT NO REST.

3. CAN SEND YOUR RESERVES ONE TANK CORPS TO BE USED AT YOUR DISCRETION TO STRENGTHEN DONTSOV AND IVANOV. IF YOU

---

[6] Dontsov was Rokossovsky's code name as commander of the Don front.

[7] Ivanov was Eremenko's code name as head of the Stalingrad front.

[8] Voronov was Chief of Artillery of the Red Army then at the headquarters of the southwest front.

[9] Commander of the Red Air Force.

NEED MORE RESERVES, LET ME KNOW TOMORROW.

4. YOU MUST HAVE DIRECT AND CONTINUOUS COMMUNICATIONS WITH STAVKA AND REGULARLY INFORM IT OF ALL DEVELOPMENTS IN DONTSOV'S AND IVANOV'S SECTORS.

5. REPORT TOMORROW WHETHER 62ND ARMY SHOULD BE TRANSFERRED TO DON FRONT COMMAND.[10] REPORT TOMORROW WHERE TO SEND TANK CORPS. HAVE YOU ANY QUESTIONS? IS EVERYTHING UNDERSTOOD?

Mikhailov to Stalin

EVERYTHING IS UNDERSTOOD AND WILL BE DONE.

Stalin then summoned Vatutin to the line:

COMRADE FEDOROV, TAKE AN ORDER:

1. YOU NOW HAVE TWO ASSIGNMENTS. FIRST ASSIGNMENT—TO DIRECT OPERATIONS OF ROMANENKO[11] AND LELYUSHENKO[12] FROM NIZHNYE CHIRSKAYA AND NIZHNYE KRIVSKAYA. THE OTHER—TO GET READY FOR OPERATION SATURN.

2. COMRADE VORONOV IS AT FEDOROV'S DISPOSAL FOR PREPARATION OPERATION SATURN, ALSO TO HELP LELYUSHENKO.

3. IN ADDITION TO 1ST COMBINED AIR CORPS WHICH REMAINS AT FEDOROV'S DISPOSAL YOU WILL RECEIVE IN FEW DAYS ONE OTHER COMBINED AIR CORPS WITH ONE DIVISION OF FIGHTER PLANES AND ONE DIVISION OF ATTACK

---

[10] From the Stalingrad front.
[11] Commander of the 5th Tank Army.
[12] Commander of the 1st Guards Army.

PLANES. FALALAYEV[13] WILL HANDLE FEDOROV'S AIR GROUP THAT WILL BE SENT TO YOU IN MATTER OF DAYS.[14]

On this Friday while Stalin was working on the liquidation of the Stalingrad pocket, Gen. T. T. Shapkin's 4th Cavalry Corps of two cavalry and two rifle divisions moved off to the southwest along the rail line from Stalingrad to Kotelnikovo in a modest effort to plug a hole in the outer ring of encirclement.[15] It pushed back several crippled divisions of a newly formed 4th Romanian Army and on the night of November 30 broke into the town.

There it ran into a hornet's nest in the form of 6th Panzer Division, which was just pulling in from France.[16]

[13] F. Ya. Falalayev, an air force general attached to Stavka.

[14] The source for this exchange is Samsonov, pp. 436–37.

[15] At this time the strong inner ring around Paulus was 45 to 50 miles wide from east to west and 20 to 25 deep from north to south. The outer ring that was intended to block a rescue effort extended for 280 miles from the middle Don to the lower Volga but 165 of them were unmanned.

[16] I later asked Malinovsky why cavalry against tanks or why cavalry at all in an enemy-held town. "If we had had more trucks, we would have used less cavalry," he said.

5

The unexpected appearance of 6th Panzer in the Kotelnikovo direction hit Stalin at a time when he was wrestling with a political problem that had been in the making for six months. He had foreseen it of course—allowed it to develop when it suited his purpose—been willing to live without a landing in France in 1942 if to get it he had to reveal to his western allies his true strength on the eastern front. But now that his power stood exposed, now that 6th Army was trapped in the Stalingrad area, now that American and British forces were in distant North Africa, not Europe, how would they react? Would Churchill and Roosevelt think he had deceived them? Would they decide in consequence to let him go on fighting the war in his own way? Or could he placate them by some disarming move and thereby get what he still most eagerly sought—an invasion of France in 1943 which Churchill had "promised" in mid-August? Stalin had cause for concern—more cause than he suspected—as the published correspondence the President and Prime Minister exchanged in this period discloses. It shows that even before they understood what was happening on the Russian front they were formulating a new strategy based on operations in the Mediterranean and that they looked to France before 1944 only in the event of German collapse. It indicates that if they considered any other policy, such as what to do in the light of the Russian counteroffensive, they did so in messages and telephone conversations that have not been revealed to this day.[1] This brings us to a new and more striking phase of the relations between East and West that would influence the future conduct of the war and its bitter and long-lasting aftermath.

The reader will recall that on October 3, when Stalingrad was just about won, Stalin told Roosevelt and Churchill the military situation was getting "worse." He will also remember that Stalin's failure to respond to their replies caused them at the end of the month to wonder what was going on. The President unveiled his thinking in the matter on November 11:

Roosevelt to Churchill[2]

". . . This brings up the additional steps that should be taken when and if the south shore of the Mediterranean is cleared and under our control. It is hoped that you with your Chiefs of Staff in London and I with the Combined Staff here may make a survey of the possibilities, including a forward movement directed against Sardinia, Sicily, Italy, Greece, and other Balkan areas and including the possibility of obtaining Turkish support for an attack through the Black Sea against Germany's flank."

They understood each other—then or soon after—as is shown by a wire from the Prime Minister to the President on November 24, the day after the encirclement of 6th Army, and the President's reply the next day. Significantly, in the published correspondence the President never mentioned the Russian counteroffensive and Churchill referred to it only once in a limited context:

Churchill to Roosevelt[3]

". . . It may well be that, try as we will, our strength will not reach the necessary levels in 1943 [to invade France]. But if so it becomes all the more important to make sure we do not miss 1944.

[1] In his calls to the White House which are not yet included in the public record Churchill used the code name John Martin. (Sherwood, p. 840.)
[2] *Roosevelt and Churchill*, pp. 278–79. This book on "their secret wartime correspondence" reprints only 600 of the 1,700 messages they exchanged.
[3] Ibid., p. 285.

"Even in 1943 a chance may come. Should Stalin's offensive reach Rostov, which is his aim, a first-class disaster may overtake the German southern armies.[4] Our Mediterranean operations following on Torch may drive Italy out of the war. Widespread demoralization may set in among the Germans, and we must be ready to profit by any opportunity which offers."

What "Mediterranean operations following on Torch"? The Mediterranean strategy was not agreed to officially until the Casablanca conference in January where Marshall opposed it. Yet Churchill wrote as if there were an understanding between them, and Roosevelt answered promptly along the same lines:

Roosevelt to Churchill[5]

"In reply to your 211 [message number]. We of course have no intention of abandoning Roundup.[6] No one can possibly know now whether we may have the opportunity to strike across the Channel in 1943 and if the opportunity comes we must obviously grasp it. However the determination as to the size of the force we should have in Bolero[7] in 1943 is a matter which should require our joint strategic consideration. It is my present thought that we should build up, as rapidly as active operations permit, a growing striking force in the U.K. to be used quickly in event of German collapse or a very large force *later* [italics added] if Germany remains intact and assumes a defensive position."

One wonders just what the President thought at this time, not whether he felt entitled to an explanation from Stalin—there is no evidence of that—but whether he fully understood what was happening in the east, for on the same day he held a wide-ranging military conference with Adm. William D. Leahy, his personal Chief of Staff, Marshall, King, Arnold, and Hopkins, during which, according to the record, Stalingrad was not mentioned. Indeed, when Roosevelt asked Marshall what lines of action were open to the Axis powers, Marshall replied he considered that "in order of probability" they were as follows: "first, occupation of Spain; sec-

---

[4] This is the only reference to the Russian counteroffensive in the published correspondence.
[5] *Roosevelt and Churchill*, p. 286.
[6] Code name for the invasion of France. No time fixed.
[7] Code name for the build-up for the invasion of France.

ond, a continued drive through the Caucasus; and third, an attempt against the British Isles."[8]

A continued drive through the Caucasus? An attempt against the British Isles? After the encirclement of 6th Army? Did Washington realize a turning point had come in the war on the Russian front? Probably not, which would explain why in the published correspondence there is only one reference to Stalingrad and no discussion in the light of Stalingrad of a strategy based on the invasion of France in 1943.

Under the circumstances as he saw them, the President thought it would be a good idea, he told Churchill, to have a "military strategical conference" with the Russians in a month or six weeks or "as soon as we have knocked the Germans out of Tunisia, and have secured the danger against any real threat from Spain."[9]

But Churchill, who had a political problem of his own—his "promise" to Stalin about 1943—was not so sure. He doubted "very much" whether a purely military conference would be of "much value."

"I think I can tell you in advance," he wrote the President the next day, "what the Soviet view will be. They will say to us both, 'How many German divisions will you be engaging in the summer of 1943? How many have you engaged in 1942?' They will certainly demand a strong Second Front in 1943 by the heavy invasion of the Continent either from the west or from the south or both. This sort of argument, of which I had plenty in Moscow, requires to be met either by principals or by naval and shipping authorities who would certainly have to be present. It would be very difficult to spare all of our chiefs for so long a time."[10]

He suggested instead a summit meeting with Stalin, an idea Roosevelt found so appealing that on December 2 he wired an invitation to Moscow suggesting the three of them get together on or about January 15.

There was no chance of that. Stalin had Stalingrad to finish and no intention of entering into any conversations that would give his western allies an opportunity to back away from France in 1943. Besides, he had already handled his political problem to his own

[8] Sherwood, pp. 658–59.
[9] *Roosevelt and Churchill*, pp. 286–87.
[10] Churchill, *The Hinge of Fate*, pp. 662–63.

satisfaction—taken advantage of the fact they had asked him no questions about his counteroffensive, neither how come he was suddenly so strong nor how he viewed the immediate outlook. His solution took the form of an "amiable and even cordial" reply to Churchill who on November 24 had suggested a tripartite military staff conference—with emphasis on hopes of persuading Turkey to enter the war. This was Stalin's opportunity, and he seized it to break "his long and apparently ominous silence."

He congratulated Churchill on the developments in Egypt and in the Torch area. He shared Churchill's view on the importance of developing personal relations. He was grateful for measures taken to resume convoys to Murmansk. He was in full agreement with Churchill and Roosevelt about Turkey and the arrangement of a Moscow conference on future military plans. This was the carrot—now for a little dissimulation and the stick. He had been successful so far, he said, partly because of weather conditions—fog and snow—that had interfered with the operations of the Luftwaffe. And he hoped accordingly there was no change of mind "in regard to your promise given in Moscow to establish a Second Front in Europe in 1943."[11]

His explanation or alibi went unchallenged. He got away with it, and his reminder evidently bothered Churchill for on December 3 Brooke wrote in his diary of a Chiefs of Staff meeting in London at which the Prime Minister was "again swinging back towards a Western Front in 1943." Brooke later recalled:

"At that afternoon meeting, after saying the [British] Army would have to fight the German Army in 1943, he said: 'You must not think you can get off with your Sardines [referring to Sicily and Sardinia] in 1943; no—we must establish a Western Front, and what is more, we promised Stalin we should do so when in Moscow.' To which I replied: 'No, *we* did not promise.' He stopped and stared at me for a few seconds, during which I think he remembered that, if any promise was made, it was on that last evening when he went to say good-bye to Stalin and when I was not there. He said no more and according to the diary gave me the impression that he was inclined to return to the Mediterranean strategy."[12]

[11] Sherwood, pp. 659–60.
[12] Bryant, pp. 579–80. Excluding Stalin's reminders, which Churchill and Roosevelt did not contest, this is the second piece of solid evidence there

A summit meeting? Stalin answered on December 6. No, he would not be free on or about January 15. He again needled Churchill in the copy of his reply that went to London: "I am awaiting your reply to the paragraph of my preceding letter dealing with the establishment of a Second Front in Western Europe in the spring of 1943."

Roosevelt tried again on the eighth. He had never met Stalin. What about getting together on or about March 1?[13]

Before Stalin declined for a second time, thereby avoiding a conference that might have put the three allies on the same track, the Germans hit him from the Kotelnikovo direction.

---

actually was a Churchill "promise" in the matter, the first being his minute to the Chiefs of Staff on November 18 cited in the footnote on p. 211. It is not clear whether the "promise" was given with Roosevelt's prior approval or when and how he learned of it.

[13] It was characteristic of Stalin that the initiative for every summit conference that was proposed or held during the war came from Roosevelt or Churchill. Prior to Potsdam he accepted four times: with Churchill in August 1942, with Roosevelt and Churchill at Teheran in late 1943, with Churchill in October 1944, and with Roosevelt and Churchill at Yalta in February 1945.

6

Hitler's early decision to hold 6th Army in the Stalingrad pocket and liberate it with a makeshift force may have been his worst possible option when he imposed it but it soon became the only one—short of surrender—as the army's low stocks of food, fuel, and ammunition dwindled sharply. There was a time in the last week of November when he might have pulled Army Group A out of the Caucasus and gone for Paulus with everything he could put together, although it would have been very, very difficult. There was also a time—it is not likely but a possibility—when Paulus might have fought his way out with heavy loss of life. By early December, however, no course of action lay open other than the one the Fuehrer had chosen. It was too late to assemble a strong force, and Paulus was almost immobile. In the circumstances, the Germans mounted an effort that for spectacular futility is reminiscent of the Charge of the Light Brigade in 1854—with this difference, that instead of the 673 British cavalrymen who rode into the valley of death at Balaclava they had three panzer divisions (which were new to the area) and supporting units (which were dazed from recent combat). It was a strange piece of business. Whether anyone at the High Command seriously thought 75,000 men and

500 tanks could break through to Stalingrad seventy-five miles to the northeast or whether this was a sacrificial operation that one conception of military honor seems to demand may never be known. It is certain, however, they never had a chance. Everything was against them—time, weather, the terrain, manpower, firepower, long lines of communication and supply. There were guns to the right of them, guns to the left of them, and, as always since late July, more Russians out ahead than the generals realized or would acknowledge.

Preparations were mighty on both sides of the line. On the German side, General Field Marshal von Manstein was brought down from the Leningrad front to conduct the operation. Manstein was a good general as generals go, but in this period he had an inhibiting desire to replace Hitler through Hitler's favor as commander of all forces on the Russian front. Hoth's 4th Panzer Army headquarters was charged with handling the infantry and cavalry that were largely Romanian and the command staff of 57th Panzer Corps that was pulled in from the Caucasus to control the armor—6th Panzer Division from France, the 17th from Orel near Moscow, and the 23rd from the Caucasus. Soon there was a plan. Fifty-seventh Panzer Corps with the Romanians protecting its flanks would move out of the Kotelnikovo area along both sides of the rail line. When it reached the Mishkova River, it would be joined for a lunge to the pocket by 48th Panzer Corps that held a thin bridgehead at the Don crossings. At a suitable moment 6th Army, without giving up what little territory it held, would come out to meet them. There were, however, obvious difficulties. Fifty-seventh Corps would start without 17th Panzer because it was delayed en route. Forty-eighth Corps with 11th Panzer was weak as a cat, and Paulus was not getting by air lift anything like the supplies he needed to carry out his part of the plan. There was another difficulty. The weather was rotten—rain, snow, rain again—thaw, freeze, thaw again. D day was fixed for December 8, then the tenth, finally the twelfth.

Meanwhile, the Russians, thinking they could destroy Paulus before the German attempt, tried to eat their cake and have it. They strengthened their outer line of encirclement at the expense of the inner line, then ordered reinforcements to the inner line from far away. On December 1 they began moving men of the

51st Army from the inner ring toward Kotelnikovo. The 51st had 34,000 men, 77 tanks, and 419 guns and mortars. On the third they activated Malinovsky's 1st Reserve Army as the 2nd Guards and ordered it in a wide sweep from the distant upper Don to the inner ring.[1] And on the ninth, getting wind of activity near the Don crossings where 48th Corps was gathering, they organized a new 5th Shock Army to meet a threat from that direction. The 5th was hastily put together but it had 71,000 men, 252 tanks, and 804 guns and mortars—strong enough with the 51st, thought Stavka, to block the Germans until Paulus was crushed.[2] As late as the eleventh, Stalin (Vasiliev) told Vasilievsky (Mikhailov) to go ahead with a new plan for destroying 6th Army:

TO MIKHAILOV. PERSONAL ONLY.

1. CARRY OUT OPERATION KOLTSO [RING] IN TWO STAGES.

2. FIRST STAGE—ENTRY INTO BASARGINO AND VOROPONOVO AREAS AND LIQUIDATION OF ENEMY'S WESTERN AND SOUTHERN GROUPS.[3]

3. SECOND STAGE—GENERAL ASSAULT WITH ALL ARMIES OF BOTH FRONTS TO LIQUIDATE GREAT BULK OF ENEMY FORCES WEST AND NORTHWEST OF STALINGRAD.[4]

4. LAUNCH FIRST STAGE OF OPERATION NOT LATER THAN DATE FIXED DURING TELEPHONE CONVERSATION BETWEEN VASILIEV AND MIKHAILOV.

5. FINISH FIRST STAGE OF OPERATION NOT LATER THAN DECEMBER 23RD.

VASILIEV[5]

[1] The 1st Reserve Army was a mechanized force originally intended to take part in a drive on Rostov to cut off Army Group A in the Caucasus.
[2] The 5th's command staff came from the 10th, the last of the original reserve field armies, its units from new reserves and active armies.
[3] Basargino and Voroponovo were on the southern face of the pocket.
[4] By both fronts he meant the Don and Stalingrad fronts.
[5] Samsonov, p. 440.

But General Hoth, who under Manstein's control was in command of *Wintergewitter* (Operation Winter Gale), struck first. Not waiting for 17th Panzer to arrive from Tormosin, he took off on the twelfth with 6th Panzer to the left of the rail line and 23rd Panzer to the right. The suffering in 6th Army was becoming unbearable; further delay could be fatal.

Stalin hesitated. Could he crush 6th Army and then deal with the relief force, or would it have to be the relief force and then the encircled army?

Saturday, December 12

No decision. Formations of the 51st Army tried to stem the tide.

Sunday, December 13

Still no decision. Hoth shoved back the 51st and crossed the Aksai River.

Monday, December 14

With 5th Shock Army Eremenko liquidated 48th Panzer Corps' bridgehead at the Don crossings, but alarmed by Hoth's penetration of his left he called for reinforcements. Specifically he asked Stalin for the 2nd Guards Army that was unloading from trains in the north and moving down to join Rokossovsky's assault on the ring.

Stalin called Vasilievsky, who was at Rokossovsky's command post. What about it? he asked. Rokossovsky took the phone.

The 2nd Guards? No, said Rokossovsky. Eremenko could have the 21st Army, a weaker force, but he, Rokossovsky, needed the Guards. With the Guards he could finish the 6th quickly, then the relief force could be overcome and all armies move on Rostov to cut off the Germans in the Caucasus.

Stalin spoke to Vasilievsky again. What did he think? Vasilievsky sided with Eremenko.

All right, said Stalin. Orders would be cut sending the Guards to the south. But, objected Rokossovsky, 6th Army could not be crushed without it. In that case, said Stalin, let it go for now.

Tuesday, December 15

Hoth's drive stalled.

Wednesday, December 16

Seventeenth Panzer Division, long delayed, began to take its place in the German line.

Thursday, December 17

It snowed during the night and rained during the day—bad tank weather for Hoth, who resumed his advance west of the rail line with 17th Panzer on his left, 6th Panzer in the center, and the 23rd to his right. Despite the mud and Russian resistance, 6th Panzer reached the Mishkova.

But Hoth was in trouble. Forty-eighth Panzer Corps could not come out to join him, and although he had moved forty miles since Saturday and had only thirty-five to go, casualties were severe and irreplaceable, the nights long and freezing.

On this day not one transport plane got through to 6th Army, which was thought to have scarcely enough fuel to move some tank and motorized units eighteen miles out of the pocket.

Friday, December 18

Sixth Panzer won a bridgehead on the north side of the Mishkova.

Malinovsky activated his command post beyond the bridgehead. Because his powerful 2nd Guards Army was strung out behind him—the men marching night and day—Stavka gave him the 4th Mechanized Corps, the 87th Division, and the remnants of Shapkin's cavalry corps.

Saturday, December 19

The Guards were pulling in, first the 98th Division of the 1st Corps, then the 3rd Guards of the 13th Corps. K. V. Sviridov's 2nd Mechanized Corps was right behind them.

What did the Germans know about them? Nothing whatsoever. They were not mentioned in an estimate of the situation which Manstein passed on to Zeitzler this day or in a long, equivocal "order" he sent to Paulus which seemed to say (a) that Paulus was to come out to meet Hoth "as soon as possible" but without giving up the pocket (Operation Winter Gale as approved by Hitler) and (b) that the developing situation might make it necessary for Paulus to pull out entirely but that he should do so only upon receipt of an "express order" (Operation Thunderclap, which was not yet—and never to be—approved).[6] In short, Manstein wanted Paulus, with the little intelligence available to him, to fight his way through Russian forces of undetermined strength over a distance for which he did not have the fuel and at precisely a time when because of the arrival of the Guards the Manstein-Hoth drive was about stopped in its tracks. Later on, after the war, Manstein would show he tried to persuade Hitler to approve Thunderclap and say Paulus should have launched it with or without permission, but no one to this day has been able to explain how Thunderclap or Winter Gale could have been carried out.

Sunday, December 20

Hoth, whose men were exhausted now from lack of sleep, gained a few more miles, but to Zeitzler in East Prussia Manstein reported "radio traffic of a new 2nd Army of three corps in the area northwest of Stalingrad." The Guards were not northwest of Stalingrad; they were southwest of it and directly before Hoth's panzers.

Monday, December 21

More Guards units arrived. Their numbers were overwhelming.

Tuesday, December 22

Hoth had only twenty-two to twenty-five miles to go. If he gained another ten or twelve, Paulus might have a chance to meet him.

But the turning point had come. The Russian 6th Mechanized Corps reached the field of battle. Rotmistrov's 7th Tank Corps was shifted from 5th Shock to further strengthen the Guards.

Hoth could not advance. He could not stay where he was. He must pull back.

Wednesday, December 23

Sixth Panzer was moved to the west side of the Don to meet a threat to the distant German left.

Thursday, December 24

The day before Christmas, and the Russians launched a general

[6] Carell, p. 656.

offensive against Hoth with the 2nd Guards, 5th Shock, and 51st Armies.

Friday, December 25

Christmas Day, and Hoth was in full retreat. The Russians pushed on until four days later they took Kotelnikovo, Hoth's point of departure.

*

I was in Kotelnikovo a few days after its capture. In the center of town there was a small park, a block square, that had been turned into a German cemetery.

On one side of the square there were neat graves outlined in brick, at the head of each a wooden cross on which were burned the name of a soldier, his date of birth, his date of death, his rank and serial number. The days of death were all in October and early November.

On another side of the square mounds of freshly turned earth covered hastily prepared graves. There were no lines of brick around them and the crosses were rudely fashioned. The days of death were late November and early December.

And then there was a gaping hole in which a soldier was being buried as the Russians entered the town. There were no bricks. There was no cross. No dirt covered his body. I saw him lying there. His feet were bare. His clothing had been removed except for a suit of woolen underwear that was sprinkled with snow that had fallen that morning.

There are many paths of glory. One of them stopped in Kotelnikovo at the end of a hopeless effort to rescue 6th Army.

7

The last act in the drama of Stalingrad, the obliteration of the great 6th Army, is a story of incomprehensible suffering that is made all the more appalling by the stunning fact it will never be known how many men died in the course of it or later on of wounds or exposure or exhaustion or typhus or God knows what. While Roosevelt and Churchill were meeting in Casablanca and approving a Mediterranean strategy that would delay the invasion of France until 1944, the 6th disintegrated under orders from Adolf Hitler to gain time for the withdrawal of 1st Panzer and 17th Armies from the Caucasus. This was the January explanation, and by then it was valid enough. In late November and December, however, they might have been pulled out in time to allow 6th Army to lay down its arms. But this was not the way of the Nazis on the Russian front. To them the Russians were *untermensch*, an outlook for which they paid a price. To speak only of the last casualties of 6th Army:

Encircled in November[1]

German source : 318,000
Russian source : 330,000

[1] These figures apparently include some 34,000 who were "lost" during the encirclement operation. It should also be pointed out that in recent years

Flown out to safety

German source	:	29,000
Russian source	:	42,000

Killed in action[1]

German source	:	166,000
Russian source	:	197,000

Taken prisoner

German source	:	123,000
Russian source	:	91,000

Of Russian casualties in the final days we know nothing except that they were very heavy and that any estimate of their numbers is no more than a wild guess.

But figures are meaningless. They cannot suggest what it was like, for it was not like anything. It was like many things—fear to one man, cold to another, hunger, thirst, unendurable pain, like living in a ditch with a freezing friend or intentionally walking upright into a burst of machine-gun fire, like evaporating hope, paralyzing despair, and the collapse of the only world one has ever known.

We cannot understand, and as the years roll by, Stalingrad fades into obscurity like Belleau Wood and the Argonne, Anzio and the Ardennes, Inchon and the Tet offensive.

Only the consequences linger on.

*

On January 10 after an ultimatum that Paulus rejected, the Russians opened their final assault with a barrage from 7,000 guns and mortars and 15,000 rocket chutes. On the fifteenth they broke into their old center defense or "K" line. On the twentieth Paulus

---

new and conflicting numbers have surfaced in West Germany. Lt. Col. Manfred Kehrig wrote in his Stalingrad study, which was published in 1974, that 72,885 were killed, 24,497 flown out, and 201,191 taken prisoner. Walter Goerlitz wrote in *Die Welt* on February 26, 1977, that, according to his sources, there were 110,500 killed, 42,000 flown out, and 107,500 taken prisoner.

moved his command post from Gumrak airport to the Univermag department store in Stalingrad city after sending this wireless message to Weichs of Army Group B and the High Command in East Prussia:

> COMBAT CAPABILITY OF TROOPS IS SINKING FAST IN VIEW OF CATASTROPHIC SITUATION WITH REGARD TO FOOD, FUEL AND AMMUNITION. HAVE 16,000 WOUNDED WHO RECEIVING NO CARE WHATSOEVER. WITH EXCEPTION OF THOSE ON VOLGA FRONT, TROOPS HAVE NOT SUITABLE POSITIONS, BILLETS OR FIREWOOD. THERE ARE SIGNS MORALE IS SINKING. ONCE AGAIN I REQUEST FREEDOM OF ACTION IN ORDER TO CONTINUE RESIST AS LONG AS POSSIBLE OR CEASE MILITARY ACTIVITY IF CANNOT BE CONTINUED, WOUNDED CANNOT BE CARED FOR AND TOTAL DEMORALIZATION AVOIDED.

But 1st Panzer and 17th Armies were now pulling out of the Caucasus under heavy pressure. Back from East Prussia came the answer of the High Command. It was short, unequivocal, brutal:

> CAPITULATION IS OUT OF THE QUESTION. ARMIES ARE FULFILLING THEIR HISTORIC OBLIGATION IN ORDER BY THEIR STAUNCH RESISTANCE TO MAXIMUM TO FACILITATE CREATION OF NEW FRONT AT ROSTOV AND WITHDRAWAL OF CAUCASIAN ARMY GROUP.[2]

Rostov fell to the Russians on February 14, but 1st Panzer and 17th Armies ultimately got out by retreating to the Crimea.

By January 26, 6th Army was reduced to two separate groups inside the city, and it was time to stiffen the will of its commander —encourage him to fight on. On the thirtieth in a grandiose gesture Hitler elevated him to the rank of general field marshal. General field marshals don't surrender. Paulus did two days later, and that

---

[2] Samsonov, p. 506. The quotations are attributed to the personal files of Paulus. They were first published in the *Voenno-istoricheski Zhurnal*, 1960, 2nd issue, p. 90.

night political warfare teams at Russian headquarters developed film showing him in captivity. The prints were pinned or pasted to surrender leaflets and dropped with first light on Tuesday, February 2, on the last pocket of resistance.

Sixth Army died that day. The guns went silent. As Clausewitz had written more than a hundred years before:

> Russia, by the campaign of 1812, has taught us, first, that an Empire of great dimensions is not to be conquered . . . , secondly, that the probability of final success does not in all cases diminish in the same measure as battles, capitals and provinces are lost . . . but that a nation is often strongest in the heart of its country if the enemy's offensive power has exhausted itself and with what enormous force the defensive springs over to the offensive.

The man who captured Paulus was Fedor Ilchenko, a twenty-one-year-old lieutenant from Uman near Kiev in the Ukraine. I talked to him a few days later. Ilchenko:

"The Germans kept on shooting, so at seven o'clock we opened artillery and mortar fire. After fifteen minutes of this, General Roske sent out his adjutant and an interpreter. He said his big chief wanted to talk to the Russian big chief. I said: 'I am the big chief here. Take me to your man.'

"We started toward the door [of the Univermag department store] but some Germans in the courtyard yelled out that the entrance was mined. They showed us another way in.

"I had fifteen men with me, including two officers. We got into the cellar and saw it was jammed with soldiers trying to escape from our mortars. We almost had to fight our way through the crowd.

"An officer showed us the room but he said only one man could go in at a time. I wanted the fifteen men to come with me. I thought: After all, there are Germans in there. And I did not like the idea of going in alone. So I insisted and they let two men go with me. Inside I saw Roske and General Schmidt [Paulus's Chief of Staff]. I said: 'Where is Paulus?' And they said they were negotiating in his name."

Several hours later Paulus was taken to 64th Army headquarters at Beketovka immediately south of the city, then in the afternoon to Rokossovsky's command post some miles to the north.

I saw Paulus on Thursday, February 4. He came out of a peasant's hut followed by Schmidt and Adam, the adjutant of the army. Paulus was six feet four, Schmidt short and stocky, Adam of medium height with a boyish face. They stood there in silence in the snow before the doorway, Paulus wearing a hat of gray rabbit fur and a long gray overcoat without medals, decorations, or service ribbons. His insignia were those of a colonel general, the rank to which he was promoted at the end of November.

Before coming out, Paulus sent word he would not answer questions, and in reply to all but two he acted as if he heard nothing. He did not even shake his head, and the only movement I noticed was caused by his nervous affliction. From time to time his right eye, his right cheek, and, I thought, the right side of his nose twitched convulsively. The two questions and his answers:

"Your first name?" Strange as it may seem, none of us knew it.

"Friedrich."

"Your age?"

"Fifty-two."

That was all.

*

Four days later the Square of Fallen Heroes was crawling with Russians. Here was a man with a bucket of water, there a woman carrying a heavy bundle. A boy threw a snowball at a passing tank. A labor gang swept snow and rubble from a side street. Stiff bodies of the frozen dead lay in snowdrifts along the sidewalk. They looked pitifully small, like wax figures, as if they had never been alive. Not a building was intact.

On the south side of the square stood the ruins of the Red Army Building with great holes torn in its scorched walls. All about were broken submachine guns, smashed rifles, grimy identification cards, German maps of Russia, brief cases, creased and soiled letters from home, blood-soaked rags, chips of brick, wrecked cars, pieces of metal. In the courtyard were bodies, legs, arms, and torsos partially covered with snow. In the basement were some three hundred wounded Germans, most of them too weak to move or be moved. They lay crowded together on the floor or sat leaning against the walls. They did not cry. They stared at the cellar stairs. It was very cold.

Occasionally, a soldier, his uniform in tatters, a scarf wrapped about his head, climbed painfully up the stairs on frostbitten feet to get water from a pail on the landing.

*

Outside of Stalingrad that night the temperature dropped to 39° below zero Fahrenheit and a piercing wind blew from the northeast. Along a snowy highway a ribbon of light stabbed the darkness. Headlights weaved and bobbed. There were many bonfires. A Guards division was moving to the west and another battle.

A team of panting horses, tugging at the traces, came by pulling an antitank gun. The crew walked. When the gun slipped to one side and got stuck in a drift, a soldier grabbed the spokes of the carriage and shoved while another pushed on the barrel that trailed behind.

Trucks rolled by with steam blowing from their radiators. A driver got out and used whatever was at hand—gasoline, smashed rifle stocks, other bits of wood—to light a fire. His companion took a tire from a wrecked German car and threw it on the flames where it burned with a great heat. Then the driver put some coals into a bucket and slid the bucket under the engine.

Submachine gunners gathered about. Some warmed their hands by thrusting them into the flames for a second or two. They were cold and tired and they spoke little to each other. Along came a field gun. When a straining horse tripped and fell, two men stepped toward him, two others toward the gun.

"*Raz! Dva! Vzvali!*"

One! Two! Heave!

And so through the freezing night the division pushed on to the west while a few miles behind it a seemingly interminable line of prisoners of war stumbled painfully, hopelessly, to the east and captivity over the rough Volga ice.

Stalingrad was behind them all. It belonged to history.

EPILOGUE

After Stalingrad the uneasy relationship between East and West took a sharp turn for the worse from which it never fully recovered. In February, Churchill and Roosevelt, fresh from their summit meeting at Casablanca, indicated they would invade France in August after they had cleared North Africa of the enemy and seized Sicily. "If the operation is delayed by weather or other reasons," Churchill wired Stalin, "it will be prepared with stronger forces for September."[1] In June they said it could not be August or September. "Under the present plans," wrote Roosevelt, "there should be a sufficiently large concentration of men and matériel in the British Isles in the spring of 1944 to permit a full-scale invasion at that time."[2] Stalin exploded in angry messages that suggested he would neither forgive nor forget—except of course his own role in the allied confusion that had prevented and would prevent to the end the development of a common strategy for the defeat of Nazi Germany. There followed Teheran in late 1943, Yalta in early 1945, the break at Potsdam that summer, cold war at the dawn of the nuclear age, then détente, the SALT I agreement, the

[1] *Roosevelt and Churchill*, pp. 315–16.
[2] *Stalin's Correspondence*, Vol. 2, No. 90.

SALT II talks, but continuing uneasiness and high-level controversy about the capabilities and intentions of the other side.

In the text I have sought to show how this came about, where it began, what Stalin knew, what he did not know, what Churchill and Roosevelt knew, what they did not know, how three totally different men, each reacting to the situation as he understood it, sowed seeds of suspicion that flowered to mutual fear and distrust in the hour of victory. But this is only a beginning, for a significant part of the history of that period still lies buried in Soviet, British, and American archives, as effectively hidden from public knowledge as if it had been destroyed along with so much of the record of the Wehrmacht in 1945.

Why did Stalin play his cards so close to his chest when it would appear (to us) that his best chance of getting what he most anxiously sought was to lay them on the table? Only the Kremlin knows. Having done so, could he believe the United States and Great Britain tried to "bleed" Russia "white"? Could Khrushchev who came after him? Or Brezhnev who followed Khrushchev? Perhaps. A regime that has lost 20 million military and civilian dead can "know" a lot about those years without "understanding."

Was it unclear to Roosevelt and Churchill that Stalingrad marked a turning point in the war on the eastern front? That it might be advisable to adjust western policy to that turning point? In the published reports of the Casablanca proceedings and in the memoirs of those who were present there is no evidence the matter was discussed. Did they have any idea there might be a race for Berlin, Prague, and Vienna and that the side which won would have a lot to say about the new map of Europe? Or, feeling they had been duped by Stalin, did they fear in consequence that if they invaded France in 1943, before they were fully ready, he might stop at his own frontier leaving them to fight alone? Only the archives know, and the archives are mute.

But hindsight is an able instructor, and although the lessons of those days may now be evident to the reader, I cannot refrain from listing a few of them here as they appear to me. One is that in dealing with the Russians there is little to be gained and much to be lost by timid joviality or pretentious good nature. The Russians do not like it; it makes them uneasy. A second is a corollary of the first. It is that there is much to be gained and little to be lost by courteous candor and hardheaded interrogation. And a third is that the Russians do not know us any better than we know them.

There are a fourth and a fifth. The fourth is that military intelligence, however sound in theory, is weak in practice. It is supposed to operate from the ground up—from the roots to the trunk—from the field to higher and higher authority. Yet time and again throughout the war Stalin, Churchill, Roosevelt, Hitler, and their closest advisers imposed their intelligence thinking on those beneath them. (There were occasions when intelligence chiefs were not even advised of decisions taken or agreements reached.[3]) At the outbreak of the war on the Russian front the British Chiefs of Staff considered the Germans capable of reaching Moscow in six weeks; the War Department in Washington thought two months. In the face of such estimates only a brave or foolhardy officer is willing to jeopardize his career by insisting upon information to the contrary. It happens in our day.

The fifth and final lesson is one I hope will not be forgotten. It is that for thirty years now we—both the Russians and ourselves—have been dealing with consequences rather than causes—with what occurred at Potsdam and after instead of what brought it about. This is understandable. The consequences are real enough:

[3] One such instance involves a personal anecdote. In the summer of 1945 I was in the army in Berlin on the staff of Allen W. Dulles, then head of the German Mission of the Office of Strategic Services (OSS). One day during the Potsdam conference, hearing the Russians were pressing for the transfer to Poland of German territory east of the Oder-Neisse line and knowing that German inhabitants were being expelled from the area, Dulles drove out to Potsdam to tell President Truman that if he accepted the line temporarily pending the conclusion of a peace conference, that acceptance would turn out to be irrevocable. I accompanied him on what turned out to be a futile excursion, for what Dulles did not know was that at Teheran Roosevelt had told Stalin he "would like to see the eastern border of Poland moved further to the west and [its] western border moved even to the Oder River" (*Roosevelt and Churchill*, p. 396). Nor was Dulles aware that a month after Teheran Churchill told the Polish government-in-exile (and Stalin) that "in the west they [the Poles] would be free and aided to occupy Germany up to the line of the Oder" (ibid., p. 421). Unable to see Truman, Dulles passed on what he knew and thought to Harriman, by this time ambassador to the Soviet Union, and Robert P. Patterson, the Secretary of War, neither one of whom mentioned, if he was aware of, these prior commitments or understandings. They gave Dulles the impression they were interested in what he had to say, and Dulles returned to Berlin in the belief he had performed a useful service.

mutual fear, the crushing burden of nuclear and conventional arms, uncertainty about the nature or extent of the threat, the possibility we may someday blow each other off the face of the earth. But so are the causes, and the only way to get at them, to understand them, to deal effectively with the consequences, is, I think, through publication, full disclosure, a joint effort in which the record of those fateful years is laid bare, something like an International Historical Year (IHY) during which Russian, British, American, and other scholars would expose the origins of the mess we are in. Such a project may cause some embarrassment, but I have no doubt there is enough to go around and the process may well reveal that neither side has as much to fear as it thinks.

BIBLIOGRAPHY

RUSSIAN

Biryukov, Nikolai I. *Na Ognennikh Rubezhakh*. Volgograd: Nizhnye-Volzhskoye Knizhnoye Izdatelstvo, 1972.

Chuikov, Vasili I. *Nachalo Puti*. Volgograd: Nizhnye-Volzhskoye Knizhnoye Izdatelstvo, 1967.

Chuyanov, Aleksei S. *Stalingradskii Dnyevnik 1941–1943*. Volgograd: Nizhnye-Volzhskoye Knizhnoye Izdatelstvo, 1968.

Eremenko, Andrei I. *Stalingrad*. Moscow: Military Publishing House of the Ministry of Defense of the U.S.S.R., 1961.

Grechko, Andrei A. *Battle for the Caucasus*. Translated from the Russian *Bitva za Kavkaz* by David Fidlon. Moscow: Progress Publishing House, 1971.

Kalinin, Stepan A. *Razmishlaya o Minuvshyem*. Moscow: Military Publishing House of the Ministry of Defense of the U.S.S.R., 1963.

Kazakov, Mikhail I. *Nad Kartoi Bylykh Srazhenii*. Moscow: Military Publishing House of the Ministry of Defense of the U.S.S.R., 1965.

Meretskov, Kirill A. *Serving the People.* Translated from the Russian *Na Sluzhbu Narodu* by David Fidlon. Moscow: Progress Publishing House, 1971.

Moskalenko, Kirill S. *Na Yugo-Zapadnom Napravlenii; Vospominanya Komandarma.* Moscow: "NAUKA," 1969.

Oshchepkov, Pavel T. *Pa Dorogam Boivoi Slavi.* Volgograd: Nizhnye-Volzhskoye Knizhnoye Izdatelstvo, 1971.

Rodimtsev, Aleksandr I. *Na Poslednyem Rubezhe.* Volgograd: Nizhnye-Volzhskoye Knizhnoye Izdatelstvo, 1964.

Rokossovsky, Konstantin K. *Soldatski Dolg.* Moscow: Military Publishing House of the Ministry of Defense of the U.S.S.R., 1972.

Rotmistrov, Pavel A. *Vremya i Tanki.* Moscow: Military Publishing House of the Ministry of Defense of the U.S.S.R., 1972.

Samsonov, Aleksandr M. *Stalingradskaya Bitva.* Moscow: "NAUKA," 1968.

Shtemenko, Sergei M. *Generalni Shtab v Godi Voini.* Moscow: Military Publishing House of the Ministry of Defense of the U.S.S.R., 1968.

Vodolagin, M. A. *U Sten Stalingrada.* Moscow: Gospolitizdat, 1958.

Voyetekhov, Boris. *The Last Days of Sevastopol.* Translated from the Russian by Ralph Parker and V. M. Genne. New York: Alfred A. Knopf, 1943.

Zhukov, Georgi K. *Vospominaniya i Razmishleniya.* Moscow: The Novosti Press Agency, 1969.

Zhukov, Yuri. *Lyudi 40-kh Godov. Zapiski Voennogo Korrespondenta.* Moscow: Izdatelstvo Sovietskaya Rossiya, 1969.

GERMAN

Adam, Wilhelm. *Der Schwere Entschluss.* Berlin: Verlag der Nation, 1965. Or *Trudnoye Resheniye,* the Russian translation for its running Russian commentary. Moscow: Progress Publishing House, 1967.

Carell, Paul. *Hitler Moves East 1941–1943*. Translated from the German *Unternehmen Barbarossa* by Ewald Osers. Boston: Little, Brown & Company, 1965.

Clausewitz, Carl von. *On War*. London: Kegan Paul, Trench, Truebner & Co., Ltd., 1918.

Doerr, Hans. *Der Feldzug nach Stalingrad*. Darmstadt: E. S. Mittler & Sohn, 1955.

Gehlen, Reinhard. *The Service. The Memoirs of General Reinhard Gehlen*. Translated by David Irving. New York: The World Publishing Company, 1972.

Goebbels, Dr. Paul Joseph. *The Goebbels Diaries 1942–1943*. Translated by Louis P. Lochner. Garden City, N.Y.: Doubleday & Company, Inc., 1948.

Goerlitz, Walter. *Paulus and Stalingrad; a life of Field Marshal Friedrich Paulus*. Translated from the German by R. H. Stevens. London: Methuen, 1964.

Greiner, Helmut. *Die Oberste Wehrmachtführung 1939–43*. Wiesbaden: Limes Verlag, 1951.

Halder, Franz. *The Personal Diary of Generaloberst Franz Halder, Chief of the Army General Staff*. Historical Section, the United States Army.

Also, *Generaloberst Halder. Kriegstagebuch*. Edited by Hans-Adolf Jacobsen. Stuttgart: W. Kohlhammer Verlag, 1964.

Hitler, Adolf. *My Struggle*. Translated from the German *Mein Kampf*. London: Hurst & Blackett, Ltd., 1938.

Kehrig, Manfred. *Stalingrad. Analyse und Dokumentation einer Schlacht*. Stuttgart: Deutsche Verlags-Anstalt, 1974.

Keitel, Wilhelm. *The Memoirs of Field-Marshal Keitel*. New York: Stein & Day, 1966.

Manstein, Erich von. *Lost Victories*. London: Methuen, 1958.

Schröter, Hans. *Stalingrad*. Translated from the German *Stalingrad . . . bis zur Letzen Patrone* by Constantine Fitzgibbon. New York: E. P. Dutton & Co., Inc., 1958.

Speer, Albert. *Inside the Third Reich*. Translated from the German by Richard and Clara Winston. New York: The Macmillan Company, 1970.

Vagts, Alfred. *A History of Militarism. Romance and Realities of a Profession.* New York: W. W. Norton & Co., Inc., 1937.

Warlimont, Walter. *Inside Hitler's Headquarters.* New York: Frederick A. Praeger, 1964.

OTHER

Bryant, Arthur. *The Turn of the Tide.* Garden City, N.Y.: Doubleday & Company, Inc., 1957.

Burns, James MacGregor. *Roosevelt: The Lion and the Fox.* New York: Harcourt, Brace & Co., Inc., 1956.

Churchill, Winston S. *The Hinge of Fate.* One of six volumes. Boston: Houghton Mifflin Company, 1948.

Craig, William. *Enemy at the Gates: The Battle for Stalingrad.* New York: Reader's Digest Press, 1973.

Eisenhower, Dwight D. *Crusade in Europe.* Garden City, N.Y.: Doubleday & Company, Inc., 1948.

Erickson, John. *The Road to Stalingrad: Stalin's War with Germany.* London: George Weidenfeld & Nicolson, 1975.

Feis, Herbert. *Churchill, Roosevelt, Stalin. The War They Waged and the Peace They Sought.* Princeton, N.J.: Princeton University Press, 1957.

Harriman, W. Averell, and Abel, Elie. *Special Envoy to Churchill and Stalin 1941–1946.* New York: Random House, 1975.

Jordan, Philip. *Russian Glory.* London: The Cresset Press, 1942.

Kerr, Walter. *The Russian Army: Its Men, Its Leaders and Its Battles.* New York: Alfred A. Knopf, 1944.

Leahy, William D. *I Was There.* New York: McGraw-Hill Book Co., 1950.

Liddell Hart, B. H. *Strategy.* New York: Frederick A. Praeger, 1968.

Mackintosh, Malcolm. *Juggernaut: A History of the Soviet Armed Forces.* New York: The Macmillan Company, 1967.

Payne, Robert. *The Life and Death of Lenin.* New York: Simon & Schuster, 1964.

Seaton, Col. Albert. *The Russo-German War 1941–45.* New York: Frederick A. Praeger, 1970.

Sherwood, Robert E. *Roosevelt and Hopkins: An Intimate History.* New York: Grosset & Dunlap, 1950.

Shirer, William L. *The Rise and Fall of the Third Reich: A History of Nazi Germany.* New York: Simon & Schuster, 1960.

Standley, William H., and Ageton, Arthur A. *Admiral Ambassador to Russia.* Chicago: Henry Regnery Company, 1955.

Trevor-Roper, H. R. *Hitler's War Directives.* London: Sidgwick & Jackson, 1964.

Ulam, Adam B. *Stalin: The Man and His Era.* New York: The Viking Press, 1973.

Werth, Alexander. *Russia at War 1941–1945.* New York: E. P. Dutton & Co., Inc., 1964.

Willkie, Wendell L. *One World.* New York: Simon & Schuster, 1943.

COLLECTIVE WORKS

Bitva za Stalingrad. Fifty-three chapters by fifth-three Soviet commanders and political workers. Volgograd: Nizhnye-Volzhskoye Knizhnoye Izdatelstvo, 1972.

Hitler Directs His War. The Secret Records of His Daily Military Conferences. Annotated by Felix Gilbert. New York: Oxford University Press, 1950.

Kriegstagebuch des Oberkommandos der Wehrmacht (Wehrmachtführungsstab). Vol. II (2 sections) 1 January 1942–31 December 1942. (This is a collection of those parts of the war diary that survived destruction.) Frankfurt am Main: Verlag für Wehrwesen, 1963.

Roosevelt and Churchill. Their Secret Wartime Correspondence. Edited by Francis L. Loewenheim, Harold D. Langley, and

Manfred Jonas. New York: The Saturday Review Press/ E. P. Dutton & Co., Inc., 1975.

Stalin and His Generals. Soviet Military Memoirs of World War II. Edited by Seweryn Bialer. New York: Western Publishing Company, 1969.

Stalin's Correspondence (with Roosevelt and Churchill). The Ministry of Foreign Affairs of the U.S.S.R. Capricorn Books Edition. Printed in the United States of America, 1965.

Vspomni, Tovarishch. Twenty chapters on twenty Russians who fought at Stalingrad. Volgograd: Nizhnye-Volzhskoye Knizhnoye Izdatelstvo, 1972.

APPENDIX I

1. Soviet divisions assigned to Stalingrad commanders on or before July 16, 1942:

(a) From the Strategic Reserve

Division	Commander	Army
33rd Guards	Col. Afanasiev	62nd
147th Rifle	Gen. Volkhin	62nd
181st Rifle	Gen. Novikov	62nd
184th Rifle	Col. Koïda	62nd
192nd Rifle	Col. Zakharchenko	62nd
196th Rifle	Brig. Comm. Averin	62nd
14th Guards	Gen. Griaznov	63rd
1st Rifle	Gen. Semenov	63rd
127th Rifle	Col. Zaitsev	63rd
153rd Rifle	Col. Nikitin	63rd
197th Rifle	Col. Zaporozhchenko	63rd
203rd Rifle	Col. Kashlayev	63rd
29th Rifle	Col. Kolobutin	64th
112th Rifle	Col. Sologub	64th

Division	Commander	Army
214th Rifle	Gen. Biryukov	64th
229th Rifle	Col. Sazhin	64th
18th Rifle	Col. Seregin	reserve
131st Rifle	Col. Dzhakhua	reserve
244th Rifle	Col. Afanasiev	reserve

(b) From Shattered Front-line Armies

Division	Commander	Army
63rd Rifle	Col. Kozin	21st
76th Rifle	Col. Penkovski	21st
124th Rifle	Gen. Belov	21st
9th Guards	Gen. Beloborodov	38th
226th Rifle	Col. Usenko	38th
277th Rifle	Col. Chernov	38th
278th Rifle	Col. Monakhov	38th
293rd Rifle	Gen. Lagutin	38th
300th Rifle	Col. Afonin	38th
304th Rifle	Col. Khazov	38th
343rd Rifle	Col. Chuvashev	38th
138th Rifle	Col. Lyudnikov	51st
157th Rifle	Col. Kuropatenko	51st
302nd Rifle	Col. Zubkov	51st
15th Guards	Lt. Col. Ovsienko	57th
38th Rifle	Col. Safiulin	57th

2. Soviet divisions assigned to Stalingrad commanders after July 16, 1942, and before General Halder's dismissal as Chief of the German General Staff on September 24, 1942:

Date	Division	Commander
July 26	5th Guards Cavalry	Col. Chepurkin
July 26	6th Guards Cavalry	Col. Belogorski

July 26	32nd Cavalry	Col. Moskalenko
July 26	422nd Rifle	Col. Morozov
July 27	204th Rifle	Col. Skvortsov
July 27	321st Rifle	Lt. Col. Valyugin
July 28	126th Rifle	Col. Sorokin
July 28	205th Rifle	Col. Makarenko
July 28	399th Rifle	Col. Travnikov
July 30	208th Rifle	Col. Voskoboinikov
July 31	87th Rifle	Col. Kazartsev
August 1	91st Rifle	Gen. Kalinin
August 1	115th Cavalry	Col. Skorokhod
August 4	98th Rifle	Gen. Barinov
August 5	96th Rifle	Col. Zherebin
August 10	35th Guards	Gen. Glazkov
August 11	36th Guards	Col. Denisenko
August 12	39th Guards	Gen. Guriev
August 12	40th Guards	Gen. Pastrevich
August 15	38th Guards	Col. Onufriev
August 15	41st Guards	Col. Ivanov
August 16	37th Guards	Gen. Zholudev
August 18	4th Guards	Gen. Lilenkov
August 18	27th Guards	Col. Glebov
August 18	23rd Rifle	Col. Vakhrameyev
August 20	315th Rifle	Gen. Knyazev
August 22	84th Rifle	Gen. Fomenko
August 25	64th Rifle	Col. Ignatov
August 26	221st Rifle	Col. Bunyashin
August 26	308th Rifle	Col. Gurtiev
August 28	24th Rifle	Col. Prokhorov
August 28	116th Rifle	Col. Makarov
August 28	298th Rifle	Gen. Vasiliev
August 30	49th Rifle	Gen. Dodonov
August 30	99th Rifle	Gen. Vladimirov
August 30	120th Rifle	Gen. Ryakin
August 30	299th Rifle	Col. Baklanov
August 30	316th Rifle	Col. Zubarev
September 1	173rd Rifle	Col. Khokhlov
September 1	207th Rifle	Col. Guzenko

Date	Division	Commander
September 9	13th Guards	Gen. Rodimtsev
September 10	34th Guards	Gen. Gubarevich
September 10	248th Rifle	Col. Alexeyev
September 16	169th Rifle	Gen. Rogachevski
September 17	193rd Rifle	Gen. Smekhotvorov
September 17	284th Rifle	Col. Batiuk
September 18	95th Rifle	Col. Gorishny
September 18	258th Rifle	Col. Khaustovich
September 18	260th Rifle	Col. Miroshnichenko
September 18	273rd Rifle	Lt. Col. Valyugin

3. Soviet divisions assigned to Stalingrad commanders after Halder's dismissal as Chief of the German General Staff on September 24, 1942:

Date	Division	Commander
September 25	233rd Rifle	Gen. Barinov
September 29	47th Guards	Gen. Fokanov
October 2	333rd Rifle	Gen. Matveyev
October 7	62nd Rifle	Col. Frolov
October 11	277th Rifle	Col. Chernov
October 11	300th Rifle	Col. Afonin
October 11	61st Cavalry	Col. Stavenkov
October 11	81st Cavalry	Col. Baumshtein
October 14	212th Rifle	Col. Anisimov
October 15	45th Rifle	Col. Sokolov
October 17	293rd Rifle*	Gen. Lagutin*
October 18	252nd Rifle	Col. Shekhtman
October 22	346th Rifle	Col. Tolstov
October 29	119th Rifle	Col. Kulagin
October 29	159th Rifle	Col. Anashkin
November 2	21st Cavalry	Gen. Yakunin
November 2	55th Cavalry	Col. Chalenko

* Lagutin's 293rd Rifle Division was a front-line formation that was pulled out of combat in August and September.

November 2	112th Cavalry	Gen. Shaimuratov
November 20	266th Rifle	Gen. Vetoshnikov
November 21	44th Guards	Gen. Kuprianov
November 21	195th Rifle	Col. Karuna
December 15	3rd Guards	Gen. Tsalikov
December 15	24th Guards	Gen. Koshevoi
December 15	49th Guards	Gen. Podshivailov
December 15	387th Rifle	Col. Makariev
December 16	160th Rifle	Col. Seryugin
December 16	172nd Rifle	Col. Sorokin
December 16	267th Rifle	Col. Kudryashov
December 16	350th Rifle	Gen. Gritsenko

APPENDIX II

Up through September 1942 the Russians had eleven armies in the Caucasus in which there were fifty rifle divisions, thirteen cavalry divisions, thirty-six rifle brigades, nine marine brigades, four infantry regiments, two marine regiments, and supporting tank, artillery, tank destroyer, and other forces.

THE RIFLE DIVISIONS

2nd and 32nd Guards, 9th (mountain), 20th (mountain), 21st (motorized), 30th (a special division from Irkutsk in Siberia), 31st, 61st, 77th, 83rd (mountain), 89th, 91st, 116th, 138th, 151st, 157th, 176th, 197th, 203rd, 216th, 223rd, 236th, 242nd (mountain), 271st, 275th, 276th, 295th, 302nd, 317th, 318th, 319th, 328th, 337th, 339th, 347th, 349th, 351st, 353rd, 383rd, 389th, 392nd, 394th, 395th, 402nd, 408th, 414th, 416th, 417th, 11th NKVD, and the Makhachkala NKVD.

THE CAVALRY DIVISIONS

9th, 10th, 11th, and 12th Guards, 11th, 12th, 13th, 15th, 30th, 63rd, 110th, 115th, and 116th.

INDEX

Abramov, Konstantin K., 67
Adam, Col. Wilhelm, 19
Afanasiev, Col. G. A., 172
Algeria, 207
Andryusenko, Col. K. M., 171
Anisimov, Gen. N. P., 131
Antonyuk, Maxim, 32
Armavir, 99
Arnold, Lt. Gen. H. H., 73, 228
Aseyev, Capt. V. A., 176
Astrakhan, 77, 78n, 81

Babko, Lt., 126
Bagramian, Gen. Ivan, 14, 40, 77
Baku, 12, 106, 108, 110
Bataan, 11
Batiuk, Col. Nikolai F., 178, 182–83, 186, 188
Batov, Pavel I., 175n, 196, 210
Batrakov, Col. M. S., 172
Belgium, 23
Benghazi, 11
Beria, Lavrenti P., 110
   Stalin and, 141

Biryukov, Nikolai I., 123, 128, 175n
Blumentritt, Guenther, 147n
Bock, Gen. Field Marshal Fedor von, 39
Bodin, P. I., 77, 110–11
Boineburg-Lengsfeld, Gen. von, 42
Bokov, F. E., 110
Bolero Operation, 35, 228
Bolvinov, Lt. Col. V. A., 171
Bormann, Martin, 178
Borodin, 124–25
Brezhnev, Leonid, 190n, 246
Brooke, Sir Alan, 4n, 91, 104–10, 230
Broud, Gen. Ya. I., 67
Bubnov, Maj. Nikolai V., 172
Budenny, Marshal Semeon M., 7, 99–100
Burilov, Col., 67
Burma, 11
Burmakov, Col. Ivan D., 171

Cadogan, Sir Alexander, 104–5
Casablanca Conference, 228, 239, 245, 246
Cassidy, Henry, 194
Caucasus, the, 16–24, 48, 76, 81, 90–91, 99–111, 148, 166, 178–79, 190, 194–96, 229, 235, 241
　food supplies, 24
　Hitler, 20–22, 48, 112, 137, 145, 190
　natural gas, 24
　oil, 16–17, 24, 34, 88, 100, 199
　Stalin, 91, 99–100, 106, 109–10, 196, 235
　struggle for approaches to, 62–93
Central Intelligence Agency, 17
Central Museum of the Armed Forces, 29
Cherviakov, Lt. E. P., 174–75
Chervlennaya River, 148
Chibisov, Nikandr, 32, 59
　Lizukov and, 60–61
Chistiakov, Ivan M., 196, 210, 212
Chuikov, Marshal Vasili, 29n, 32, 44, 67–68, 75, 87, 167–72, 176, 187–88, 197, 202–3, 208
　Eremenko and, 160, 212n
　Gordov and, 79, 82
　Kirlov and, 171
　Stalin and, 82
Churchill, Sir Winston, x, 4n, 28, 30, 98, 247
　code name of, 227n
　Harriman and, 101–9
　invasion of North Africa, 73–74, 81, 91, 97, 102–4, 109, 194–95, 211n
　Molotov and, 25–27, 30, 36, 57, 101, 104n
　plans to invade Norway, 73
　plans to invade western Europe, 11–15, 35–36, 66, 73–74, 77, 80–82, 97, 102–6, 185–86, 211n, 226–31, 239, 245–46
　Roosevelt and, 35–36, 66, 73–74, 80–82, 91, 101–2, 109, 166, 194–96, 211n, 226–31, 239, 245–46
　Stalin and, 11–15, 25–27, 57, 76–77, 80–82, 90–91, 165n, 166, 194–96, 211n, 226–31
　Churchill's visit to Moscow, 100–9
　Willkie and, 186
Chuyanov, Aleksei S., 125, 128, 133, 153, 189
　Stalin and, 77–80
Clark-Kerr, Sir Archibald, 4, 103
Clausewitz, Gen. Karl von, 63, 64, 242
Clausewitz Operation, 63–64
Crimea, the, 38, 42, 46, 54, 158, 159
　disaster in, 14

Danilov, A. I., 196
Denmark, 23
Dill, Field Marshal Sir John G., 81, 102n
Don River, 58–61, 64–76, 80, 81, 84, 89, 112–24, 138, 139, 145, 174, 199, 216
　description of, 71
Dubiansky, Col. V. P., 124, 169, 172
Dulles, Allen W., 247n
Duncan, Capt. John, 4

Edelweis Operation, 81
Egypt, 42, 90, 91, 104, 195, 203, 230
8th Air Corps (German), 128, 145n
8th Army (British), 90, 91
8th Army (Italian), 113, 145, 179, 197, 212
8th Cavalry Corps, 52, 118
8th Reserve Army, 61, 84, 119, 123, 130, 132, 138–40

18th Independent Tank Corps, 56, 76*n*
Eisenhower, Gen. Dwight D., 27, 35, 59, 73, 204
Engels, Friedrich, 8
Eremenko, Andrei, 79, 93, 98, 122–25, 132, 149–51, 187–89, 198, 201
  Chuikov and, 160, 212*n*
  code name of, 189, 223*n*
  mobilization orders, 135–36
  Rokossovsky and, 222–24, 235
  Stalin and, 107–8, 128–29, 138, 141, 142, 165*n*
  Vasilievsky and, 189, 235

Falalayev, F. Ya., 225
Fedorenko, Yakov N., 54, 55
Finland, 17
1st Guards Army, 91, 92, 98, 100, 107, 118, 139, 142, 151–53, 163, 179, 189, 197
1st Panzer Army, 64, 190, 240, 241
1st Reserve Army, 29, 61, 66, 67, 70, 199, 204
1st Tank Corps, 52, 53, 54, 60, 84, 93, 118, 151
4th Panzer Army, 53, 57–59, 64, 80, 112, 113, 119, 139, 143–50, 154, 198, 201, 212, 214, 220, 233
4th Reserve Army, 61, 66
4th Tank Corps, 53, 54, 56, 84, 107, 120, 190, 196, 198, 212–18
5th Reserve Army, 29, 56, 58, 61, 62, 70
5th Shock Army, 234–38
5th Tank Army, 32, 52, 56–61, 64, 66, 76*n*, 87, 119, 196–98, 207, 210, 212
14th Panzer Corps, 121, 122, 125, 138, 142, 144, 148, 149, 152, 168, 172, 173
40th Army, 52–56, 76*n*, 82, 116
42nd Regiment, 174–77, 180, 182, 188
48th Panzer Corps, 233–36
51st Army, 196, 198, 207, 213, 234, 235, 238
57th Army, 90, 93, 118, 198, 207, 214
France, ix–x, 23, 117
  allied invasion plans, 11–15, 34–36, 57, 66, 73–74, 77, 80–82, 97, 102–6, 185–86, 194, 211*n*, 226–31, 239, 245–46
  unoccupied, German seizure of, 204, 207
Frankfurter Zeitung, 20
Franz, Lieut. Col., 42
Frederick the Great, 34
Front Artillery Group (FAG), 187
Frunze, Mikhail, 29

Galanin, Gen. I. V., 196
Garibaldi, Col. Gen. Italo, 113
Gehlen, Lt. Col. Reinhard, 17–20, 23, 28, 29*n*, 30, 44*n*, 87–89, 100*n*, 117, 118, 205–7
  Halder and, 114, 146
  Hitler and, 54*n*
George VI, King, 109
Gerasimenko, V. F., 77, 78
  Stalin and, 78*n*
Germany
  Afrika Korps, 11
  arrogance of, 22–24, 42–43
  Foreign Armies East, 17, 19, 23, 44*n*
  invasion of U.S.S.R., ix–x, 4, 13–14
  miscalculations of strength of U.S.S.R., 16–24, 27–34, 85*n*–86*n*, 87–89, 114
  need for food, 24
  need for oil, 16–17, 23, 34, 199

reorganization of armor (1942), 53n
seizure of unoccupied France, 204, 207
Siegfried-Blau-Braunschweig operation, 22–24
summer offensive (1942), 51–93
  first phase of, 51–61
  Operation Clausewitz, 63–64
  second phase of, 62–93
  See also Caucasus, the; names of armies, persons, and places; Stalingrad, Battle of
Gettysburg, Battle of, 85
Gibraltar, 204, 205
Glazkov, Gen. Vasili A., 123–25, 128, 169
Goebbels, Paul Joseph, 20–21
Goering, Hermann, 24, 145
Goerlitz, Walter, 240n
Golikov, Gen. Filipp I., 44, 52–60, 98, 188, 196
  background of, 43
  Stalin and, 54–55, 62–63
Golubinski, 212, 214
Gordov, V. N., 59, 79–80, 98, 139, 150–51, 188
  Chuikov and, 79, 82
  Rokossovsky and, 79–80
  Stalin and, 79, 82–83, 142
  Vasilievsky and, 84
  Zhukov and, 80, 143
Gorishny, Col. Vasili A., 178, 181, 183, 186, 188, 202
Gorki Park of Culture and Rest, 5
Gorokhov, Col. Sergei F., 171, 202
Gorshechnoye, 56
Great Britain, 46–47, 118, 199
  aid to U.S.S.R., 11, 185
  invasion of North Africa, ix, 73–74, 81, 91, 97, 102–4, 109, 194–95, 204, 211n

plans to invade Norway, 73
plans to invade western Europe, 11–15, 35–36, 66, 73–74, 77, 80–82, 97, 102–6, 185–86, 211n, 226–31, 239, 245–46
scarcity of information available to, 4, 11
Grechko, Marshal Andrei A., 57, 111
Greece, 227
Greiner, Helmut, 113–15, 117, 145–46, 200
Grossman, Vasili, 170
Guriev, Stepan S., 189
Gurov, Kuzma A., 188
Gurtiev, L. N., 189, 202
Gymnast Operation, 73

Halder, Gen. Franz, 17–24, 27, 28, 37n, 39, 48, 61n, 64, 86n, 100n, 144–48
  background of, 47
  Gehlen and, 114, 146
  Hitler and, 112–18, 154, 161–62, 177, 183
  Keitel and, 146–47
  miscalculations of strength of U.S.S.R., 87–89
Harriman, W. Averell, 98, 247n
  Churchill and, 101–9
  Roosevelt and, 101–2
Hauffe, Gen., 115
Heron Operation, 81
Hilgruber, Andreas, 19n
Himmler, Heinrich, 113
History of the Second World War (Liddell Hart), 29
Hitler, Adolf, 25, 27, 39, 64, 74, 84, 90, 167, 203, 205, 233, 247
  arrogance of, 22–24, 42–43
  Battle of Stalingrad, 97, 112–14, 118–19, 137, 144–47, 153–54, 161–62, 173, 177–78, 190, 199–201, 213–16, 221, 232, 236–37

266

the Caucasus, 20–22, 48, 112, 137, 145, 190
confidence of, 42–43, 48
Directive No. 45, 81
Gehlen and, 54n
Halder and, 112–18, 154, 161–62, 177, 183
Jodl and, 112, 161, 178, 207, 213, 215
Keitel and, 112, 153, 161–62, 178, 207, 213, 215
miscalculations about strength of U.S.S.R., 16–24, 31, 85n–86n, 89, 114
Operational Order No. 1, 200–1
the Reichel papers, 42–43
Siegfried-Blau-Braunschweig Operation, 22–24
takes command of OKH and OKW, 154
Zeitzler and, 177, 183
Hopkins, Harry, 11, 35, 77
Roosevelt and, 11, 73–74, 228
Hoth, Hermann, 53–60, 64, 89–90, 93, 118, 139, 143–49, 152, 161, 214–15, 233–38
Hube, Gen. Hans, 128, 149

Ibarruri, Dolores ("La Pasionaria"), 124, 125n
Ibarruri, Capt. Ruben R., 124, 125n
Ilchenko, Fedor, 242
Inside Hitler's Headquarters (Warlimont), 85n–86n
International Historical Year (IHY), 248
Iran, 48, 108
Italy, 227, 228
Ivanov, Col. S. P., 171

Jany, Gen. Gustav von, 113
Japan, 73–74
Jodl, Alfred, 113
Hitler and, 112, 161, 178, 207, 213, 215

Jupiter Operation, 73

Kalach, 198, 199, 207, 212, 216
Kalinin, Gen. Stepan A., 30n, 129–31
background of, 129
Kalinin Front, 45, 46, 57
Kamishin, 130–31, 143
Kastornoye, 54, 56, 57
Katukov, Mikhail, 54, 60
Kehrig, Lt. Col. Manfred, 240n
Keitel, Wilhelm, 115
Halder and, 146–47
Hitler and, 112, 153, 161–62, 178, 207, 213, 215
Kharitonov, Fedor, 32
Khopko, Maj. S. N., 171
Khrushchev, Nikita, 14, 40, 77, 78, 189, 246
Kielmannsegg, Maj. Count, 87–88, 117
King, Adm. Ernest J., 36, 77
Roosevelt and, 73–74, 102, 228
Kinzel, Col. Eberhard, 18–20
Kirichenko, Nikolai F., 189
Kissinger, Henry, 12n
Kleist, Gen. Ewald von, 190
Kluge, Gen. Field Marshal Guenther von, 21, 45
Knyazev, Gen. M. S., 171
Koïda, Col. S. T., 83
Kolomiets, T. K., 196
Kolpakchi, Gen. Vladimir, 32, 45, 68–74, 80, 84, 90, 151, 175n
Stalin and, 82–83
Koniev, Gen. I. S., 46
Kostuchenko, K. A., 126–27
Kotelnikovo, 233, 234, 238
Kotluban, 123–25
Kovalenko, K. A., 124
Kozlov, Gen. Dmitri T., 14, 32, 139, 152, 153, 196
Krichmanov, Lt. Col. V. D., 171, 172
Kriegk, Dr. Otto, 21
Kriegstagebuch, 16, 113

267

Krilov, Gen. Nikolai, 151, 156, 159, 168, 185
   Chuikov and, 171
Kruchenkin, V. D., 196
Kursk region, 47, 52–53
Kursk-Voronezh rail line, 53, 54
Kutuzov, Mikhail, 8
Kuznetsov, Vasili, 32

Lageberichte, 16, 113–14
Lagevortrage, 113–15
Leahy, Adm. William D., 228
Lelyushenko, Gen. Dmitri D., 185
Lenin, Nikolai, 5, 8
Leningrad, 3, 16, 201
Liddell Hart, B. H., 29
Lisbon, 21*n*
List, Gen. Field Marshal Wilhelm, 117, 145, 154, 177
Litvinov, Maxim, 13
Lizukov, Gen. Aleksandr, 32, 59, 60–61
   Chibisov and, 60–61
   Stalin and, 60–61
Lopatin, Anton, 90, 151
Lyudnikov, Ivan, 202, 208

Maikop, 99
Maisky, Ivan, 28
Malaya, 11
Malaya Ivanovka, 143
Malenkov, Georgi M., 110, 179
   Stalin and, 129, 138, 163–65
Malinin, Gen. M. S., 189
Malinovsky, Gen. Rodion, 32, 64, 76*n*, 84, 89–90, 131, 139, 175*n*, 179, 196, 199, 225*n*, 234, 236
   background of, 43
Mamayev, Kurgan, 156–57, 159, 167, 172–76, 181, 186, 188, 201–3
Manstein, Gen. Erich von, 14, 233–37
   Paulus and, 236–37
   Zeitzler and, 236
Marshall, Gen. George C., 11, 35, 36, 77, 81

Roosevelt and, 11, 73–74, 102, 228–29
Marx, Karl, 8
Maslennikov, Gen. Ivan, 110
Mechetka River, 172, 208
Mekhlis, Lev, 14
Meretskov, Gen. Kirill, 37, 46
Michela, Col. Joseph A., 4
Mikoyan, Anastas I., 110
Mokraya Mechetka, 127
Molotov, Vyacheslav M., 7, 13–14, 81, 103, 105, 107, 110
   Churchill and, 25–27, 30, 36, 57, 101, 104*n*
   Roosevelt and, 12–14, 25–27, 33–36, 57
   Stalin and, 12–14, 25–27, 141
Montgomery, Sir Bernard Law, 195, 207
Morell, Theodor, 115
Morocco, 207
Moscow, 16, 22, 44, 52, 64
   population exodus, 5
   rumors in, 6
   secretiveness in, 3, 64–66
   wartime atmosphere, 4–7
Moscow, Battle of, 11, 29
Moscow-Rostov railroad, 54
Moscow-Stalingrad railroad, 92, 179
Moskalenko, Kirill, 32, 59, 75, 79, 93, 98, 139, 150–53
   Stalin and, 142, 152
   Zhukov and, 142, 143

Nachalo Puti (Chuikov), 29*n*
Napoleon I, 158–59
Neithardt von Gneisenau, Count August, 63
Netherlands, the, 23
New York *Herald Tribune,* x, 211
Nicolson, Harold, 28
9th Reserve Army, 61, 76*n*, 84, 119, 138–40
95th Division, 180, 182, 183, 186, 188, 202

Nixon, Richard M., 12*n*
Nizhnye Chirskaya, 214
Nizhnye Olshanets, 51–52, 56
North Africa, 11, 46–47, 203, 204
  invasion of, ix, 73–74, 81, 91, 97, 102–4, 109, 194–95, 204, 211*n*
Norway, 23
  plans for invasion of, 73

Oberkommando der Heeres (OKH), 16–20, 24, 28, 74, 86*n*, 89, 112, 113, 118, 146, 199
  Hitler takes command of, 154
Oberkommando der Wehrmacht (OKW), 16–20, 24, 74, 85*n*, 86*n*, 89, 112, 113, 116, 117, 144, 173, 199, 200, 213
  Hitler takes command of, 154
Oil, 108
  the Caucasus, 16–17, 24, 34, 88, 100, 199
  Germany's need for, 16–17, 23, 34, 199
112th Army, 100, 107, 176–77, 189, 202*n*
Onyanov, Gen. Leonid V., 44
Orel-Moscow highway, 52
Orel region, 44, 47, 52
Oskol River, 59

Panikhin, Maj. Dmitri I., 186–87
Parsegov, M. A., 52–56
Patterson, Robert P., 247*n*
Patton, Gen. George S., Jr., 44*n*
Patton Papers, The, 44*n*
Paulus, Gen. Friedrich, 19, 39, 59, 71–72, 75, 82, 89, 114–22, 140, 144–53, 161, 162, 172, 176, 182, 201, 202, 212–18, 221, 232, 240–43
  appearance of, 71
  Manstein and, 236–37
Pavelkin, M. I., 54

Pearl Harbor, 11
Pesochkin, Col. M. A., 172
Philippines, the, 11
Plotnikov, Col., 120*n*
Poland, 12, 23, 247*n*
Popov, Markian, 32, 214
Poskrebyshev, Col. Aleksandr N., 7
Potsdam Conference, x, 245, 247
PQ 17 (convoy), 77, 81
PQ 18 (convoy), 76–77, 81

Railways, secret, 69–70
Rangoon, 11
Reichel, Maj. Joachim, 39, 56
Reichel papers, 39–44
Richthofen, Gen. Freiherr Wolfgang von, 145, 173, 177
Rise and Fall of the Third Reich, The (Shirer), 88–89
Rodimtsev, Gen. Aleksandr I., 174–75, 182, 208, 209
Rodina, 158
Rokossovsky, Gen. Konstantin, 37, 177*n*, 188–89, 198, 204, 205, 210, 222*n*, 235, 242
  code name of, 189, 223*n*
  Eremenko and, 222–24, 235
  Gordov and, 79–80
Romanenko, Prokofi, 32, 197, 210, 212
Rommel, Gen. Erwin, 11, 104, 195, 207
Roosevelt, Franklin D., x, 30, 77, 165–66, 247
  Churchill and, 35–36, 66, 73–74, 80–82, 91, 101–2, 109, 166, 194–96, 211*n*, 226–31, 239, 245–46
  Harriman and, 101–2
  Hopkins and, 11, 73–74, 228
  invasion of North Africa, 73–74, 81, 97, 102, 194–95
  King and, 73–74, 102, 228
  Marshall and, 11, 73–74, 102, 228–29

269

Molotov and, 12–14, 25–27, 33–36, 57
personal diplomacy of, 12*n*
plans to invade western Europe, 11–15, 34–36, 66, 73–74, 77, 80–82, 97, 102, 186, 226–31, 239, 245–46
Stalin and, 11–15, 25–27, 80–81, 102, 194–96, 226–31
Standley and, 12*n*, 57*n*, 186*n*
Willkie and, 184, 186
Roske, Gen., 16, 80, 84, 89, 112, 117, 198–99, 222*n*, 228, 235, 241, 242
Rostov, 54, 89, 112, 117, 198–99, 222*n*, 228, 235, 241
Rotmistrov, Pavel A., 60, 237
Roundup Operation, 73, 102*n*, 211, 228
Ruoff, Gen., 190
Russia at War 1941–1945 (Werth), 184*n*
Ryabishev, D. I., 59

SALT I agreement, 245
SALT II talks, 246
Samsonov, Aleksandr M., 29*n*
on reserve armies, 45
Saratov, 30*n*, 103, 131
Sarayev, Col. A. A., 128, 171, 172
Sardinia, 227, 230
Sarkisian, Capt., 126
Scherff, Col. Walter, 114
Schmidt, Gen. Arthur, 214, 216, 242, 243
Schröter, Hans, 87*n*
2nd Guards Army, 196, 234–38
2nd Hungarian Army, 113, 212
2nd Reserve Army, 61, 84, 91, 92
Ségur, Louis Philippe de, 158, 221
Semenov, Yevgeni Ivanovich, 212
Serafimovich, 204, 205, 207

Sevastopol, 3, 14, 37, 42, 46, 54
7th Reserve Army, 29, 64, 66, 68, 70
17th Army, 64, 190, 240, 241
17th Panzer Division, 221, 233, 236
17th Tank Corps, 53, 54
Shapkin, Gen. T. T., 225
Shaposhnikov, Marshal Boris M., 4*n*, 7
Shchadenko, Gen. E. A., 131
Sheean, Vincent, 28*n*
Sherwood, Robert E., 34, 102, 138*n*
Shestakov, Gen. V. F., 131
Shirer, William L., 88–89
Shtemenko, Gen. S. M., 8*n*, 15*n*, 110, 142*n*
Shumilov, Gen. Mikhail S., 90, 93, 175*n*, 197
Sicily, 227, 230, 245
Sidorin, Col. T. M., 67
Siegfried-Blau-Braunschweig Operation, 22–24
Singapore, 11
6th Army (German), 19, 39, 55, 56, 59, 64, 71, 74, 76, 80, 82, 98, 112–20, 125, 128, 137, 142–54, 161, 168, 170, 197, 198, 201, 211*n*, 212–15, 219, 220, 229, 232–39, 242
6th Army (U.S.S.R.), 62, 66, 87
6th Panzer Corps, 221, 225–26, 233, 236, 237
6th Reserve Army, 29, 56, 58, 61, 62
16th Panzer Division, 83, 128, 149
16th Tank Corps, 52, 53, 54, 60
60th Army, 62, 87
62nd Army, 68–70, 72, 74–76, 80–84, 87, 89, 98, 100, 107, 109, 118–23, 128, 138, 148–52, 156, 160, 167, 171–73, 183, 197, 198, 207, 212

63rd Army, 62, 70, 87
64th Army, 68, 70, 75, 76, 82, 87, 90, 93, 118, 138, 148, 160, 173, 197, 198, 202, 207
65th Army, 196, 198, 207, 210
66th Army, 132, 139–42, 152, 153, 163, 179, 196, 198, 202
Sledgehammer Operation, 66, 73–74, 81, 102, 105
Smekhotvorov, Fedor I., 178, 183, 188, 202
SMERSH (counterespionage organization), 63
Smuts, Gen. Jan Christiaan, 109
Sologub, Col. Ivan, 100, 177*n*, 202*n*
Sorokin, Gen. V. Ye., 169*n*
Spain, 228, 229
Spanish Civil War, 124, 175
Stalin, Joseph, 34, 44, 52–54, 85, 247
   Battle of Stalingrad, 97, 119, 122, 128–29, 138–42, 148*n*, 151–53, 161–65, 169*n*, 179, 186, 194, 198–99, 215, 222–27, 235
   Beria and, 141
   the Caucasus, 91, 99–100, 106, 109–10, 196, 235
   Chuikov and, 82
   Churchill and, 11–15, 25–27, 57, 76–77, 80–82, 90–91, 165*n*, 166, 194–96, 211*n*, 226–31
     Churchill's visit to Moscow, 100–9
   Chuyanov and, 77–80
   code name of, 189
   Eremenko and, 107–8, 128–29, 138, 141, 142, 165*n*
   Gerasimenko and, 78*n*
   German summer offensive (1942)
     first phase of, 53–54, 57, 59, 61
     second phase of, 62–63, 66, 75, 78, 81–83
   Golikov and, 54–55, 62–63
   Gordov and, 79, 82–83, 142
   Kolpakchi and, 82–83
   Lizukov and, 60–61
   Malenkov and, 129, 138, 163–65
   Molotov and, 12–14, 25–27, 141
   Moskalenko and, 142, 152
   offices held by, 6
   Order No. 227, 80
   personality of, 6
   plans to invade western Europe, 12–15, 57, 66, 77, 80–82, 97, 102–6, 186, 194, 226–31, 245–46
   as a political professional, 42–43
   Poskrebyshev and, 7
   power of, 5–9
   Roosevelt and, 11–15, 25–27, 80–81, 102, 194–96, 226–31
   secretiveness of, 4*n*, 11, 108–9
   Standley and, 57
   as Supreme High Commander, 4, 6–9
   suspicious nature of, 10–11, 77
   tensions created by, 8–9
   Timoshenko and, 39–41, 59, 77–80
   on treason (treachery), 80
   Vasilievsky and, 9, 122, 138, 141, 152, 163, 165, 179, 198, 222–24, 234, 235
   Vatutin and, 63, 224–25
   Voroshilov and, 141
   Willkie and, 184–86, 194
   working schedule, 6
   Zhukov and, 142, 152–53, 161–65, 198, 205
Stalingrad, 68–70, 76, 78, 92, 179
   administrative districts of, 135*n*
   change of the name of, 47*n*
   description of, 47–48

made major target, 81
military museum at, 169*n*
rumors in, 155–56
struggle for approaches to, 81–93
vastness of the front, 85
Stalingrad, Battle of, 47*n*, 97–244
  air raids, 132–33, 168
  barricades, building of, 134, 169
  beginning of, 64–70
  casualties, 135, 239–40
  citizen participation, 155–60, 169, 170, 180
  end of, 239–44
  food shortages, 170
  Gumrak airport, 70, 154, 216
  Hitler, 97, 112–14, 118–19, 137, 144–47, 153–54, 161–62, 173, 177–78, 190, 199–201, 213–16, 221, 232, 236–37
  house-to-house fighting, 183
  mobilization orders, 135–36
  reasons for, 22–24, 64
  the Reichel papers, 39–44
  Stalin, 97, 119, 122, 128–29, 138–42, 148*n*, 151–53, 161–65, 169*n*, 179, 186, 194, 198–99, 215, 222–27, 235
  state of siege declared, 133
  Stavka, 122, 139, 141–42, 151, 179
  use of reserve armies, 29–34, 48, 116, 162, 179, 196
  See also names of persons and places
Stalingradskaya Bitva (Samsonov), 29*n*, 45
Standley, Adm. William H., 4, 27, 103
  Roosevelt and, 12*n*, 57*n*, 186*n*
  Stalin and, 57
  Willkie and, 186*n*
Stavka, 4, 6–9, 14, 27, 30, 39, 59, 75, 90, 98–100

Battle of Stalingrad, 122, 139, 141–42, 151, 179
reserve armies, 44–46, 52, 53, 64–70, 118, 119, 130, 137–38, 179
Stavropol, 99
Stepanov, Comrade, 132
Stimson, Henry L., 35, 73
Strategy, 29
Stumme, Gen. George, 42
Sukhaya Mechetka, 127
Sun Tsu, 10, 11
Supreme Headquarters Allied Expeditionary Forces (SHAEF), 44*n*
Suvorov, Aleksandr, 8
Sviridov, K. V., 236

Taranovich, Gen. V. Ye., 187
Tbilisi (Tiflis), 110–11
Tedder, Sir Arthur William, 105
Teheran Conference, x, 231*n*, 245, 247*n*
3rd Army, 52, 66
3rd Reserve Army, 29, 56, 58, 61, 62
3rd Romanian Army, 179, 183, 190, 197, 212, 219
3rd Tank Army, 61, 84, 119
10th Reserve Army, 61, 84, 119
13th Army, 52–55
13th Guards Division, 174, 175, 179, 186, 208
38th Army, 59, 64, 66, 75, 76*n*, 151
39th Regiment, 175, 176, 179, 202
Thomas, Gen. Georg, 116
Thunderclap Operation, 237
Timoshenko, Marshal Semeon K., 7, 14, 38, 39, 45, 46, 51–53, 55, 56, 59, 64, 70, 74–75, 76*n*, 78, 88, 110
  background of, 43
  Stalin and, 39–41, 59, 77–80
Tobruk, 11, 46–47
Tolbukhin, Fedor I., 214

272

Torch Operation, 102n, 104–6, 194, 211, 228
Trotsky, Leon, 29
Trufanov, N. I., 196, 214
Truman, Harry S, 247n
Tsaritsa River, 159–60, 172, 179–80
Tsimla River, 75
Tunisia, 207, 229
Turkey, 108, 230
21st Army, 59, 66, 76n, 196–98, 207, 210, 235
22nd Panzer Division, 114, 115, 173
23rd Panzer Division, 56, 221, 233, 235, 236
24th Army, 139, 140, 142, 153, 163, 179, 189, 196, 198
24th Panzer Division, 54, 168
24th Tank Corps, 53, 54, 56
26th Tank Corps, 212, 214
28th Army, 59, 64, 66, 76n, 198
29th Army, 18, 19
284th Division, 182–83, 186, 208
Tyulenev, Gen. I. V., 110–11

Union of Soviet Socialist Republics
  aid to
    Great Britain, 11, 185
    U.S., 11, 57, 185
  casualties in World War II, x
  invasion of, ix–x, 4, 13–14
  members of Supreme High Command, 6–7
  miscalculations about strength of, 16–24, 27–34, 85n–86n, 87–89, 114
  the Politburo, 6, 7, 8, 110
  reorganization of armor (1942), 53n–54n
  reserve armies, 27–34, 44–46, 48, 52, 62–70, 82–84, 85, 87–88, 116, 118, 119, 130, 137–38, 162, 179, 196
    first major use of, 56–61
    maps, 31, 58, 64
    second major use of, 64–66
    secret railways, 69–70
    size of, 18
  State Defense Committee, 6, 7, 9, 110, 111
  war with Finland (1939–40), 17
  See also Caucasus, the; names of armies, persons, and places; Stalingrad, Battle of
United States of America, 4, 17, 118, 199
  aid to U.S.S.R., 11, 57, 185
  invasion of North Africa, ix, 73–74, 81, 97, 102–4, 194–95, 204
  military establishment, size of (1939), 33
  Pearl Harbor, 11
  plans to invade western Europe, 11–15, 34–36, 57, 66, 73–74, 77, 80–82, 97, 102, 185–86, 226–31, 239, 245–46
  scarcity of information available to, 4, 11
  See also names of persons
Uranus Operation, 207–9

Varrenikov, Ivan, 196
Vasilchenko, Col. K. F., 110
Vasilievsky, Aleksandr M., 4, 39–40, 52, 60, 100, 110, 122, 210, 211
  background of, 47
  code name of, 189, 222n
  Eremenko and, 189, 235
  Gordov and, 84
  the Reichel papers, 43–44
  Stalin and, 9, 122, 138, 141, 152, 163, 165, 179, 198, 222–24, 234, 235
  Zhukov and, 143
Vatutin, Gen. Nikolai F., 63, 197, 204, 210, 222

Stalin and, 63, 224–25
Velvet Operation, 111*n*
Verevkin, Col. F. A., 172
Verkhnye Buzinovka, 83
Vertyachi, 120, 123
Vietnam War, 12*n*
Vladivostok, 13
Vlasov, Gen. Andrei, 37, 42, 61
Volga River, 47–48, 58, 69–70, 77, 81, 86–90, 115, 120, 123, 127–32, 150, 156, 172, 180–82, 187–88, 199, 208, 214
  pontoon bridge over, 131–32
Volgograd, *see* Stalingrad
Vologda, 45
Volski, Gen. Vasili T., 214, 216, 217
Voronezh, 45, 52–54, 57–66, 89, 199
Voronov, Gen. Nikolai N., 175*n*, 205
Voroshilov, Marshal Klimenti E., 7, 8, 12, 103
  Stalin and, 141

Wainwright, Gen. Jonathan, 11
Warlimont, Gen. Walter, 85*n*–86*n*, 113, 115, 145, 146, 153–54, 178
Waterloo, Battle of, 85
Wavell, Sir Archibald P., 104–5
Weichs, Baron Maximilian von, 148–49, 161, 162, 212–13, 218–20, 241
Werth, Alexander, 184*n*
Wietersheim, Gustav von, 121, 144, 153

Willkie, Wendell L.
  Churchill and, 186
  Roosevelt and, 184, 186
  Stalin and, 184–86, 194
  Standley and, 186*n*
Winter, Gen. August, 113
Winter Gale Operation, 235–37

Yalta Conference, x, 231*n*, 245
Yefremov, 44, 59, 60
Yermolkin, Col. I. E., 171, 177*n*

Zadorozhni, K. A., 125
Zakharchenko, Col. A. S., 83
Zakharov, Gen. G. F., 189, 196
Zeitzler, Kurt, 147*n*, 200, 205, 213, 237
  Hitler and, 177, 183
  Manstein and, 236
Zemliansk, 60
Zhadov, A. S., 196
Zheltov, A. S., 189
Zholudev, Viktor G., 190, 202
Zhukov, Gen. Georgi K., 7, 29*n*, 32*n*, 35, 37, 44, 51, 78*n*, 119*n*, 150–51, 179, 189, 204–5
  background of, 43
  code name of, 189
  Gordov and, 80, 143
  limitations on authority of, 142
  Moskalenko and, 142, 143
  on reserve armies, 45–46
  Stalin and, 142, 152–53, 161–65, 198, 205
  Vasilievsky and, 143
Zhuravlev, Col. K. A., 83